ALSO by
Maurice Samuel

LITTLE DID I KNOW

THE SECOND CRUCIFIXION

THE PROFESSOR AND THE FOSSIL

CERTAIN PEOPLE OF THE BOOK

LEVEL SUNLIGHT

THE DEVIL THAT FAILED

THE GENTLEMAN AND THE JEW

PRINCE OF THE GHETTO

WEB OF LUCIFER

THE WORLD OF SHOLOM ALEICHEM

These are BORZOI BOOKS, *published in New York
by* ALFRED A. KNOPF

BLOOD ACCUSATION

BLOOD ACCUSATION

<hr>

THE STRANGE HISTORY OF
THE BEILISS CASE

<hr>

by MAURICE SAMUEL

NEW YORK : ALFRED · A · KNOPF : 1966

THIS IS A BORZOI BOOK
PUBLISHED BY ALFRED A. KNOPF, INC.

FIRST EDITION

To Edith

ACKNOWLEDGMENTS
AND ADVICE

A COMPLETE LIST of all who have been helpful to me in the writing of this book would defeat the purpose of an acknowledgment. I limit myself to those whose assistance involved considerable time and effort. These are:

Professor Elias Tartak, of the New School for Social Research, whose encyclopaedic knowledge of Russian literature spared me a great deal of undirected background reading, and who discussed with me at great length the human aspects of the case;

Mrs. Helene H. Fineman, assistant editor of the Franklin Papers, at Yale, who devoted two years of her spare time to helping me scrutinize the European press;

Mme. Eugenia Tolmachoff, formerly of the Bestuzhev Women's University of St. Petersburg, and Mr. Roy Milton, head of the foreign language department of the Franklin School, New York, who helped with research and translation;

Isaac Chomski, M.D., who went over the voluminous medical material with me in Russian and English and made it intelligible to a layman;

Dr. Alexis Goldenweiser, graduate of the law faculty of the University of Kiev (1912) and member of the Kiev bar till 1921; he was on the scene at the time of the trial and was intimately associated with leading figures in the Jewish community of Kiev, including the Beiliss Defense Committee; Dr. Jacob J. Frumkin, graduate of the University of St. Petersburg (1903), member of the St. Petersburg bar till its dissolution by the Soviet government, who was active in Jewish social organizations and from 1902 to 1917 a member of the Advisory Committee to the Jewish Members of the Duma; Dr. Jacob Robinson, graduate of the Russian Law School, Warsaw (1914), and special counsel to Justice Jackson on Jewish aspects at the trials held by the International Military Tribunal in Nuremberg; Dr. Samuel Kucherov, graduate of the law faculty of the University of Kiev (1912), Ph.D. from Columbia University, and from 1949 to 1963 expert on Soviet affairs and law to the Library of Congress.

I wish to acknowledge a special debt to my daughter, Mrs. Chester Rapkin; her managerial skill was of crucial help in the organization of the research.

Finally I would like to add that I could not have completed this task without the generous encouragement of Justice Arthur J. Goldberg.

I must point out that although it would have been impossible for me to produce this work without the faithful advice and help of the Russian experts listed above, I have differed with them at various points on the interpretation of events; nor are they responsible for the errors that may have crept into the narrative. I can only hope that in the aggregate these do not affect the basic accuracy of the account.

I should further like it understood that in presenting the history of the case I have used no fictional devices and invented no conversations; and I have tried to make clear where the interpretation of events is mine and where it is that of others.

I have had to choose between two systems of notes. The first deforms the bottom of the page with lines in different type; this looks very scholarly and is as convenient as it is repulsive. The second transfers the notes to the back of the book. Every note at the back is introduced by a page number and the first few words of the statement in the text to which it refers. In the text itself there are asterisks that indicate a pertinent note is to be found at the back. Only a small—but very important—number of my readers will be interested in the notes; I am sorry to inconvenience them for the benefit of the majority.

Dates in the Russian part of the narrative are Old Style (i.e., Julian calendar). Thirteen days must be added to make them correspond to the Gregorian calendar now in universal use.

CONTENTS

CONTENTS   xii

DRAMATIS PERSONAE

THE READER will find it useful to repeat the longer Russian names till they become familiar sounds. To simplify, I omit the patronymics and often the given names, too, in the narrative. Where they are known, they appear in the list below or in the index.

The following are most of the characters connected directly with the Beiliss case. I have italicized, here and in the index, the accented syllable when the name is unfamiliar. (Italicized *i* is pronounced as in machine.)

Beiliss, Mendel: accused of the ritual murder of the boy Yushchinsky.

Be*let*sky, Stepan: director of the Department of Police in the Ministry of the Interior.

*Bol*dyrev, Feodor: presiding judge at Beiliss trial.

*Bran*dorf: state prosecutor, Kiev Superior Court.

Bra*zul*-Brush*kov*sky: journalist.

Chap*lin*sky: state prosecutor, Appellate Court, Kiev.

Cheber*yak*, Vera: center of a criminal gang in Kiev; wife of

Vasily Cheberyak, postal service employee.

Cheberyak, Lyudmilla: their daughter.

Cheberyak, Valya (Valentina): their daughter.

Cheberyak, Zhenya (Eugene): their son; friend of Yushchinsky.

Fenenko: investigating magistrate for important cases, Kiev.

Golubev, Vladimir: student, Kiev University; leader of local monarchist, Rightist, anti-Semitic groups.

Gruzenberg, Oscar O.: attorney, titular head of Beiliss defense team.

Ivanov, Pavel: lieutenant colonel of Kiev gendarmery.

Karabchevsky, N. P.: attorney, member of Beiliss defense team.

Karayev, Amzor: a young revolutionary associated with Makhalin (see below).

Karpinsky, Dr. A. I.: city coroner, Kiev.

Kosorotov: professor of forensic medicine, St. Petersburg; medical expert for the prosecution.

Kozachenko: convict and stool pigeon.

Krasovsky, Nikolai: detective.

Latyshev, Ivan: member of the Cheberyak gang, and more particularly of the "Troika."

Lyadov, A. V.: director of a department in the Ministry of Justice.

Makhalin, Sergei: a young revolutionary, associated with Karayev (see above).

Maklakov, V. A.: attorney, Liberal deputy in the Duma; member of Beiliss defense team.

Margolin, Arnold: Beiliss's first attorney.

Mashkevich: investigating magistrate, St. Petersburg; sent to replace Investigating Magistrate Fenenko on Beiliss case.

Miffle: a young Frenchman, Vera Cheberyak's lover.

Mishchuk: chief of Kiev secret police; first investigator of Yushchinsky murder.

Nizhinsky, Nataliya: Yushchinsky's aunt.

Nizhinsky, Olympiada: Yushchinsky's grandmother.

Obolonsky: professor of forensic medicine, Kiev University.

Polishchuk: agent of the secret police.

Pranaitis, Father Justin: Roman Catholic priest; religious expert for the prosecution.

Prikhodko, Alexandra: Yushchinsky's mother.

Prikhodko, Luka: Yushchinsky's stepfather.

Rudzinsky, Boris: member of Cheberyak gang, and more particularly of the "Troika."

Shakhovsky, Kazimir: a lamplighter.

Shakhovskaya, Yuliana: his wife.

Shcheglovitov, I. G.: minister of Justice.

Shmakov: attorney, extreme anti-Semite; prosecuting counsel in Beiliss trial.

Shneyerson: a hay and straw dealer.

Shredel, Colonel A.: head of Kiev gendarmery.

Shulgin, V. V.: editor-in-chief of Rightist daily in Kiev; deputy in the Duma.

Sikorsky, I. A.: professor emeritus of psychiatry, Kiev University; expert for the prosecution.

Singayevsky, Pyotr: member of Cheberyak gang, and more particularly of the "Troika"; Vera Cheberyak's half-brother.

("Troika," the: name I have given to the three gangsters Latyshev, Rudzinsky, Singayevsky).

Tufanov: anatomist, Kiev University.

Vipper: state prosecutor in Beiliss trial.

Yushchinsky, Andrei (Andrew, Andryusha): pupil at the St. Sophia Parochial Preparatory School, Kiev.

Zamyslovsky, S. G.: attorney, Rightist deputy in the Duma; prosecuting counsel in Beiliss case.

Zarudny, A. S.: attorney, member of Beiliss defense team.

BLOOD ACCUSATION

INTRODUCTION

1

W HEN I BEGAN in the fall of 1962 to read up on the all but forgotten Beiliss case, so famous in its day, it was not with the thought of writing a book on it. The subject was tempting, but I had other, long-cherished plans and not many years for their execution. I read only to revisit that far-off time and to occupy some in-between weeks. The weeks stretched into months, the research widened and deepened; the perspective of five decades brought out new and contemporaneous meanings in old memories; the inquiry became an obsession, and the result is herewith submitted.

I was a student at an English university, occupied chiefly with extracurricular activities for the improvement of the human condition, when Mendel Beiliss, an employee in a Kiev (Russia) brick factory, was brought to trial in September 1913 on the charge of having murdered a Christian boy in order to use his blood for ritual purposes prescribed by the Jewish religion. I recall vividly, I live through again the incredulity followed by indignation that the case aroused and, finally, the sense of an insolent challenge flung in the face of twentieth-century enlightenment. Above all I remember the anxiety with which the outcome of the trial was awaited; and because the reawakened feeling of participation is so strong, I have permitted a personal note to enter here and there into this historical record.

2

The Blood Accusation, as it is called, the accusation that the Jewish religion calls for the periodic ritualistic consumption of the blood of a Christian, was born in the Middle Ages at about the time of the First Crusade; it was a revival, with certain changes, of the accusation leveled at the early Christians by the Romans. Young William of Norwich (d. 1144) was the first victim to be claimed by the legend; after him, like a pestilence that had lain dormant for a thousand years, it kept on reappearing here and there across the centuries. It was denounced by four popes* as a sinful slander; not one pope, even among those whose attitude toward the Jews was the harshest, ever endorsed it. Nevertheless the Blood Accusation persisted down into modern times, and nearly every recurrence was attended by the threat or perpetration of massacre and pillage.

The nineteenth century was particularly rich in such episodes, the most famous among them being those of Damascus (1860), Saratov, Russia (1857), and Tisza-Eszlar, Hungary (1882). In the twentieth century, before the Beiliss case, there occurred, among others, the case of Blondes, a Jewish barber of Vilna; but this, the best known till Beiliss, attracted little attention outside Russia. In every instance, however, no matter what degree of notoriety it achieved, the action had been carried through by provincial authorities. What shocked and frightened us in the Beiliss case was its sponsorship by a national government. True, this was Russia, the land of absolutism and reaction; but Russia was in, if not wholly of, the twentieth century. She had her ambassadors and consuls in every civilized country; she had her alliances and trade agreements. She must, we thought, have some

"decent respect to the opinions of mankind." Her official anti-
Semitism was disgraceful enough; and there were the pogroms,
for which the government disclaimed responsibility, however
unconvincingly. But this! This endorsement in high places of a
bugaboo, a blood-stained superstition which had to be defended
by Russia's representatives at the Western courts! What did it
mean?

We also knew that Russia was not all darkness and autocracy. She had given us Dostoevsky and Turgenev, Gorky and
Mendeleyev and Lobachevsky, and above all Tolstoy, one of the
grandest moral figures of the ages. In spite of a stupid censorship
the press was predominantly liberal, and the Russian judiciary
system was—in theory, at least—one of the best in Europe. Nor
did we think the Russian masses a horde of savages. Illiterate
they might be, but not brutish, and if superstitious, not viciously
so. In our Manchester community there were thousands of
Russian Jews, many of them refugees from the pogroms of the
1880's and of 1903–1906; they spoke of the Russian people without rancor, often with affection. The pogroms were the work of
the hooligan groups known as the Black Hundreds and of a
complacent and sometimes cooperative government. The workers
and the peasants—the latter forming the vast majority of the
population—were by nature good-humored and kindly. Their lot
was one of toil and hunger; many of them were improvident and
given to drinking, but suffering had not dehumanized them. We
saw them waiting, with slowly dwindling patience, for the revolution, and we waited hopefully with them.

In our political vocabulary "Russia" and "revolution" were
twin words, and though we blindly sympathized with all revolutionaries, Tolstoy was the highest symbol of our hopes. To the
present generation he is the literary genius; to the last generation
but one—my generation—he was that, too, and also something
weightier and more meaningful. What we felt about him was
finely expressed by one of his younger contemporaries: "His
name was a kind of magic, unifying word, equally understandable throughout the length and breadth of the world." Tolstoy-

ism was a faith and a way of life, a fount of spiritual rebirth and
of new social forms. *He* was the essential Russia and her promise,
and such was his moral stature that on him alone among the
enemies of the system the government had never laid a hand.
He died a year before the Beiliss case was launched, and I
remember someone saying: "They wouldn't have dared to do this
if Tolstoy were alive." It was naïvely said, but it brings back the
reverence and the awe attached to the name, and our faith in
the soundness of the Russian masses.

3

Our memories naturally turned back to the Dreyfus case,* the
closing phases of which haunted my childhood (I was eleven
years old when Dreyfus was finally rehabilitated in 1906). There
were great differences amidst the similarities between the two
cases. To begin with, the fellow officers who framed Captain
Alfred Dreyfus as a German spy had no intention of launching
a great anti-Semitic episode; indeed, their interest lay in keeping
the affair as quiet as possible. It was the maniacally anti-Semitic
Edouard Drumont, editor of *La Libre Parole* and author of the
enormously successful *La France juive*, who leaked the Dreyfus
case to the public and set off the agitation that kept France in
a turmoil for more than a decade. As against this, the Beiliss case
was manufactured by Russian governmental authorities expressly
to inflame the populace against the Jews.

There was a second important difference. Drumont was one
of the leading representatives of what may be called modern
hallucinatory anti-Semitism,* which sees in the Jewish people a
vast and close-knit international force about to complete its
conquest of Christian civilization. Everything is in its hands—
press, finance, war, revolution. According to Drumont's book
(which sold over two hundred thousand copies), France had
already fallen, as the title indicates. The rest of the world would
follow shortly unless drastic action were taken. The Jews, co-
ordinated by a central body and everywhere traitors to the lands
that harbor them, relentlessly pursue the same objective, the

ruin of an ancient enemy. That they are rapacious, pitiless, cunning, and power-mad—also repellent as human beings— goes without saying; but by implication they are supremely able and practical, icy calculators and farsighted planners. All of this the manufacturers of the Beiliss case endorsed, but to this list of Jewish characteristics something was added belonging to another age, something altogether incongruous for such a setting, namely, an addiction to cannibalism with an exclusive preference for Christian blood. This touch of the mentally deranged (*Chacun à son goût*, remarked Heine of the Damascus Jews charged with drinking the blood of an elderly monk) turned the magnificently sinister into the feeble-mindedly grotesque. What was the Russian government driving at?

We could only conclude that it was trying to synthesize two types of anti-Semitism, the modern secularist and the medieval demonological, making a simultaneous play for the "sophisti- cated" urbanite and the superstitious peasant.

However, the Dreyfus case and the Beiliss case had the same fundamental purpose—to arrest and turn back the forces of progress; and time showed that in each instance the particular case was but an episode or an instrument in the larger historical struggle. In France anti-Dreyfusism* had been related to the rejection of the 1789 revolution and it was accompanied by a romantic nostalgia for the illusory simplicities and sweetnesses of the *ancien régime*; but Pétainism and collaborationism in World War II were an expression of the same rejection and echoed the language of the Dreyfus case. In Russia the Beiliss case was mounted by men who hoped by means of it to strengthen the autocracy and to crush the liberal spirit that was reviving after the defeat of the 1905 revolution. The same men were later responsible for the spread of *The Protocols of the Elders of Zion*,* that extraordinary anti-Semitic forgery which outsold, in pamphlet and book form, in magazine and newspaper reprints, in the original and in scores of translations, all other modern anti-Semitic works combined.

The Dreyfus and Beiliss cases shocked us each in its own particular way, but the biggest difference between them sprang from the difference in tradition between France and Russia, especially in regard to their treatment of the Jews. Russia was the very symbol of Jewish oppression, while France had led in the movement for Jewish emancipation. Who would have dreamed that a virulent anti-Semitism could convulse so large a proportion of the French people? And yet there had been no pogroms in modern France, and we did not believe there ever would be. There had been riots during the progress of the Dreyfus case, in metropolitan France and in the colonies, but no pogroms, that is, riots connived at, encouraged, or instigated by the government. My family and I were immigrants to France in 1900, in the very thick of the Dreyfus case; my sister and I went to school in a Paris slum and shared with our Christian fellow pupils the free lunches provided for the children of the poor; we were not molested or insulted; we came and went with a feeling of complete safety. And later, in England, while the Dreyfus case was pending and after it was closed, I never heard from my elders the kind of remarks about France they were wont to make about Rumania, the country of our origin, or about Russia. When Dreyfus was vindicated, the rejoicing among Jews was mingled with the sentiment: "It was bound to be so in France." *La France, quand-même!*

4

Looking back across half a century my generation wonders why the Beiliss case has fallen into near oblivion. Every educated person has heard of the Dreyfus case, and many have at least a notion of what it was about. Of a dozen educated persons below the age of fifty perhaps one or two will respond to the name Beiliss, and then with: "Some sort of trial, wasn't it?" The Dreyfus case has been kept alive by books and movies; only one full-length book* has been written on the Beiliss case, and that too is quite forgotten. Nor was it widely read when it appeared in America in 1935.

Yet many of us deeply believe that as a battlefield in the war

between progress and reaction, the Beiliss case has a claim on
our attention equal with that of the Dreyfus case. It was not
simply a detached episode of a bizarre and terrifying character
without relevance to the problems of that time and ours. It
belongs to the continuing struggle, and, as with the Dreyfus case,
its implications, far from being confined to the Jewish question,
overflow widely into the general field. Why, then, has it practically vanished from sight, while the Dreyfus case is part of the
common stock of knowledge?

There are several reasons. It was the historical good luck of
the Dreyfus case that it was easy to write about. With its intrigues, its complicated forgeries, and its theatrical diplomatic
background it made a good detective story. The Beiliss case is
not a detective story, in spite of the many detectives, professional
and amateur, who move through it. Its fascination as a story
derives from its background and from the range of the personali-
ties involved; and whereas the Dreyfus case has the prestige of
remembered and respected names—Clemenceau, Zola, Anatole
France—those connected with the Beiliss case were with one
exception unknown outside of Russia and today are unremem-
bered even there.

It was also the historical misfortune of the Beiliss case to be
followed closely by World War I, which swallowed it up and
robbed it of its chance to settle into the public memory. Today
it is on the point of joining the larger part of history, that which
has happened but is not known to have happened.

The greatest handicap of the Beiliss case is, however, its improbability, and by this I mean not only the inanity of the
attempt to prove the Blood Accusation but also the entire struc-
ture of the conspiracy. A bare recital of the facts, however
strongly documented, would leave the reader incredulous. He
must be introduced along the way into a world in which impossible incidents, some pure Gilbert and Sullivan, others pure
Dostoevsky, become natural and in which a self-satirizing legal
and political performance tries to pass itself off as a grave affair
of state. To make the picture convincing and yet to keep a

straight face is, despite the bloodiness of the theme, beyond
normal capacity, and this too explains why historians have shied
away from the subject.

5

The contrast between our outlook on the world today and that
of fifty odd years ago can only be conveyed in personal terms.
I was young, and the century even younger; and we had a high
opinion of ourselves.

> We did then*
> Divinely stand, not knowing yet against us
> Sentence had passed,

and we gave no ear to "the world's knives* bickering in their
sheathes." Whatever the designs and indecencies of the Beiliss
case, we saw it as the last convulsion of an ancient tyranny,
never dreaming that it was a hint of unimaginable tyrannies yet
to come.

My own interest in the Jewish people was at that time peripheral and negative, and the Jewish aspect of the case was
overborne for me by the universal struggle for freedom and
justice. Russia, vast, unhappy, mysterious, with its entrenched
and embattled autocracy confronted by a people hungry for
bread, land, and liberty, was a far more important element in
the general picture. In any case, anti-Semitism was a diversionary
invention; to take it seriously was to fall into the trap set by the
common enemy. Ignored, it would never again play a role in
historical events. Besides, discussions of anti-Semitism, always
so plaintive and parochial, bored and wearied me, not only because there was nothing interesting to be said about it but also
because, like slavery and the divine right of kings, it was no
longer a genuine issue.

The Jewish problem belonged, in that view, to the past; the
living issue was the all-human one. The last battle was on for
the destruction of tyranny, autocracy, and oppression in all their

forms, and in reality this battle was already won. Only the rulers of Russia and of a few other benighted countries did not yet realize it. We, the Liberals and Socialists of those days, chanted exultantly the credo of the great John Morley, formulated a generation earlier: "The right of thinking freely and acting independently, of using our minds without excessive awe of authority, and shaping our lives without unquestioning obedience to custom, is now a finally accepted principle in some sense or other by every school of thought which has the smallest chance of commanding a future."*

Now well on in years, the century and I soberly assess the record. Our "finally accepted principle" is still fighting for its life. Our complacency of fifty years ago proved almost fatal; and if the principle still has a chance of commanding the future, it is because we are no longer complacent. We know that the war of the schools of thought is far from decided, and we no longer think that the liberal idea will triumph naturally and of itself. We are healthily aware that its enemies to the right and to the left are powerful in numbers and fertile in the disguises with which they throw us into confusion. Only in one area is the old complacency returning: because of the general revulsion from the hideous crimes the Nazis committed against the Jews, the belief is now prevalent that at last, and this time unmistakably, anti-Semitism is on the way out, that before long it will be, as an issue, not only forgotten, but unintelligible. And it is true that today only a primitive and derided minority permits itself an open avowal of anti-Semitism; but that this minority represents the whole or even the greatest part of the anti-Semitic phenomenon in the world is a widespread assumption that may have unhappy consequences.

PART ONE

THE SETTING UP

OF THE CASE

C H A P T E R   1

HOW IT BEGAN

1

BETWEEN SIX AND SEVEN O'CLOCK on the morning of Saturday, March 12, 1911, the thirteen-year-old boy Andrei (usually called by the diminutive Andryusha) Yushchinsky left his small, two-room home in Slobodka, a suburb of Kiev on the left bank of the Dnieper, ostensibly for school. The parents were at work, the younger children still slept. He wore his overcoat and regulation school cap and carried his textbooks and notebooks bound in a leather strap. The day was raw and there were traces of snow on the ground.

Andryusha did not turn up at school. He had chosen for once —literally for once—to play truant and visit a friend in Lukyanovka, an outlying district of Kiev on the other side of the river. Two school children saw him before he crossed the bridge; he was not reported as having been seen along whatever route he followed thereafter, whether through the heart of the city or along the right bank and up the suburban slopes. The number of persons who saw him that morning in Lukyanovka was in dispute at the trial two and a half years later, but among them were, as admitted by both sides, two lamplighters (husband and wife) and Andryusha's friend Zhenya Cheberyak. What happened to Andryusha that morning was to become a matter of world concern.

He was found, a ghastly sight, eight days later (Sunday, March 20) in one of the Lukyanovka caves about equidistant from Zhenya Cheberyak's home and the brickworks where the Jew Mendel Beiliss was employed and lived with his family. The body, half dressed, had forty-seven wounds, major and minor, about the head, neck, and torso, and all had been made with a stabbing instrument; it had lost the greater part of its blood. The shirt and drawers and the sock on one foot were caked with dried blood. Nearby lay Andryusha's cap, jacket, and belt and the other sock, similarly caked. In the jacket pocket was found a blood-stained rag, part of a pillowcase; on analysis the rag showed traces of semen. The notebooks, rolled into a cylinder, lay on a ledge above the head of the partly recumbent corpse, and since Andryusha's name was written in each of them, it was inferred that the murderers (it was always assumed that there was more than one) had been either unbelievably careless or else unconcerned with concealing the identity of the victim. The missing clothing—overcoat and trousers—and the textbooks were never found.

The body was removed to the morgue, and an autopsy was performed by City Coroner Karpinsky on Tuesday, March 22. His report was handed in on March 24 and appeared in the newspapers the following morning. A second autopsy was performed by Professor Obolonsky and Anatomist Tufanov, both of Kiev University, on March 26, the body then being in an advanced state of decay. Professor Obolonsky and Anatomist Tufanov did not issue their report *officially* until April 25, thirty days later. The significance of this delay will be duly discussed.

Andryusha was buried on Sunday, March 27, with a substitute *vertex cranii* (cranium top), his own having been removed at the first autopsy together with part of the viscera, including the heart, and preserved for further examination and as material evidence. He was dressed for burial in a new black suit, a patent leather sash of a greenish color, a blue calico shirt, and new cotton socks tied with a blue ribbon. On his breast was a cross of cypress wood, tied round his neck with a blue ribbon, and in his right trouser pocket were ten one-kopek coins.

Mimeographed leaflets were distributed along the funeral route and at the graveside. They read:

ORTHODOX CHRISTIANS!

The Yids have tortured Andryusha Yushchinsky to death! Every year, before their Passover, they torture to death several dozens of Christian children in order to get their blood to mix with their *matzos*. They do this in commemoration of our Saviour, whom they tortured to death on the cross. The official doctors found that before the Yids tortured Yushchinsky they stripped him naked and tied him up, stabbing him in the principal veins so as to get as much blood as possible. They pierced him in fifty places. Russians! If your children are dear to you, beat up the Yids! Beat them up until there is not a single Yid left in Russia. Have pity on your children! Avenge the unhappy martyr! It is time! It is time!*

2

The youthfulness of the victim and the beastliness of the crime created a stir in Kiev with repercussions throughout the country; but there was no popular response to the Blood Accusation, and there were no pogroms. The Jews did not take alarm, or, better said, their continuous feeling of insecurity remained at its customary level. The distribution of leaflets calling for pogroms or spreading the Blood Accusation, especially at the Easter season, coinciding approximately with the Passover, was routine with the extreme Rightist groups. A child might be missing* for a few hours, a Christian servant girl might have quarreled with her Jewish employers, the body of a murdered Christian might have been found in a mixed neighborhood, and at once there would be meetings in dark places, mutterings and shouts of "Yid blood-drinkers!" and the distribution of inflammatory leaflets. The agitation died down when the child was found, the servant girl closely questioned, or the murderer arrested. There was no reason to think that this incident would end differently.

At the time of the Yushchinsky murder, pogroms were not being countenanced by the administration; therefore they did not occur. The last wave, sustained from 1903 to 1906, had attracted too much attention abroad and had disgusted the majority of public-minded Russians, including the majority of anti-Semites. What most anti-Semites wanted was an unobtrusive, unspectacular, but effective policy of repression. As one of their organs put it: "The Yids must be placed under such conditions that they will gradually die out. This is one of the tasks of the government and of the best men in the country."*

That the pattern of the last five years was in fact not followed in this instance was due to a number of circumstances connecting the Kiev and the national administrations with the extreme reactionary organizations. It must be understood, however, that the word "administration" is used throughout this narrative in two senses. First and most frequently, it refers to a group of high officials in St. Petersburg and Kiev who controlled the judiciary and the police and were therefore the "effective" administration: anti-Semites, extreme nationalists and reactionaries, power seekers who saw themselves as the wave of the future, they were determined to put an end to Jewish demands for equality and to deal a decisive blow to all liberal tendencies associated with such demands. In the other sense "administration" refers to officialdom as a whole, which was not a party to the conspiracy and members of which, in the judiciary and the police departments, fought it. The context will, I hope, make clear at each point in what sense the word is being used.

There were in Kiev, as in most cities, branches of the Union of the Russian People and of the Association of the Archangel Michael; there was also a local organization, the Double-Headed Eagle. All were monarchist, fiercely reactionary and anti-Semitic. Count Witte—the foremost Russian statesman of the early twentieth century, who might have saved Russia if Nicholas II, the last of the Romanov rulers, had not been what he was—thus describes the membership of the Union of the Russian People, and the description applies with unessential changes to the sister organizations: "The embodiment of nihilistic patriotism, feeding on lies, deceit, slander, savage and cowardly despera- tion. . . . Mostly dark-minded, the leaders are unhanged vil- lains." He adds: "And the poor, misguided Emperor dreams of restoring Russian grandeur with the aid of this party."

3

Nikolai Pavlovich, the man who distributed the leaflets at Andryusha's funeral, was arrested for disorderly conduct. He was a member of the Union of the Russian People and of the Double-Headed Eagle, and he appears in the story only because the reaction to his arrest and to the raiding of the offices of the Double-Headed Eagle was the opening gun of the campaign that was to develop into the Beiliss case.

A student at Kiev University, Vladimir Golubev, fired the shot. He too was a member of both the Union of the Russian People and the Double-Headed Eagle, but, unlike Pavlovich, a leader. He was nineteen years of age, slim, handsome, unbalanced, a hysterical believer in the Blood Accusation and a protégé of the prominent anti-Semite and demagogic Duma (Parliament) Deputy Zamyslovsky, who was to be one of the prosecuting attorneys at the trial. This relationship is important, for Deputy Zamyslovsky was a *persona grata* at the Ministry of Justice in St. Petersburg, and the Minister of Justice, Shcheglovitov, had the ear of the Czar. Through his high connections at the capital and through the support of his two organizations as well as their bully-boys the Black Hundreds, student Golubev exercised considerable influence in the Kiev administration despite his youth. Golubev may be regarded as the initiator of the Beiliss case; he was not, however, the creator of the circumstances that made the Beiliss case possible.

The arrest of Pavlovich was immediately protested by

Golubev, who called a meeting of the council of the Union of the Russian People and appealed to St. Petersburg. At first it looked like, and indeed was, a tempest in a teapot; it was not expected that the national administration would suddenly intervene in a trivial and commonplace local incident. But that was what happened, and the peremptory nature of the intervention may be judged by the celerity with which the Kiev administration responded. On April 15, the day when the council of the Union of the Russian People met, Pavlovich was released. The Kiev gendarmery* (the security or political police, a subordinate branch of which was the *okhrana*) and the Office of the Prosecuting Attorneys advised the Department of Police and the Ministry of Justice in St. Petersburg that action against Pavlovich and his organizations had been suspended.

It was still no great matter. Student Golubev had shown the Kiev administration who was who; his organizations continued their Blood Accusation agitation; but a trial for ritual murder was as yet only the fantasy of a handful of crackpots.

4

Detective Mishchuk, head of the Kiev secret police (criminal and nonpolitical; not to be confused with the gendarmery and *okhrana*), had at once made the Yushchinsky murder his personal assignment. The Blood Accusation leaflets had not yet been distributed, and even when they were, he cannot have taken them as a presage of trouble for himself, of official obstruction and sabotage. He might have had an inkling, however, from a conversation he had with Chaplinsky, prosecutor of the Kiev Appellate Court, one of the most powerful local officials, some days before the unexpected release of Pavlovich. Asking whether the charges against Pavlovich and the Double-Headed Eagle would be pressed, Mishchuk received a warning by way of answer: "If one comes in conflict with the Black Hundreds, one never gets rid of complications. It is better to be on good terms with them, and I advise you to bear this in mind."*

Chaplinsky was known as a careerist *pur sang* and a time-server; to the extent that he could afford a principle, he was anti-Semitic, and he was ardently so when principle coincided with prospects of promotion. Cleverer than Mishchuk, he was waiting to see how far the national administration was willing to indulge Golubev. The order from St. Petersburg was for him the first signal that the local Blood Accusation propaganda, still continuing after Pavlovich's arrest, was awakening sympathetic interest on higher levels of power. That was on April 15. On April 17 the St. Petersburg reactionary daily *Russkoye znamya** demanded that "the Jewish ritual murderers of Yushchinsky" be found, and a day later a group of extreme Rightist Duma deputies resolved to enter an interpellation criticizing the government for its laxity in going after the "guilty Jewish parties" in the Kiev "ritual murder." This succession of signals alerted Chaplinsky to important developments big with promise for himself. It was what the Germans are fond of calling a *Konjunktur*—anti-Semitism and self-interest were "in phase." Chaplinsky was to become the leading local figure of the conspiracy in Kiev, in obsequious cooperation with Minister of Justice Shcheglovitov, the central figure at national headquarters.

Heedless of warnings and perhaps blind to signals, Detective Mishchuk went about his work with all honesty. His chief suspects were Andryusha's family, to outward appearance quiet and respectable people, and Vera Cheberyak, the mother of Andryusha's friend and a woman with an evil reputation. There was a rumor that Andryusha was the beneficiary of a trust fund that would revert to his parents on his death. The friendship between Andryusha and Zhenya Cheberyak seemed to speak badly for Andryusha's parents. It was very odd that on the only occasion he had ever played truant, he should have gone to visit his friend, and that the morning of his murder. It was possible that he had been sent.

Mishchuk's first act was to arrest Andryusha's parents and a number of his relatives, including his grandmother. They were kept under arrest and brutally used for two weeks. The mother, five months gone in pregnancy, was interrogated for long stretches at all hours; her pleas to attend the funeral of her son, even under escort, were denied. The other relatives were similarly treated.

Nothing came of it. The parents had perfect alibis, the other relatives furnished no clues, the trust fund turned out to be idle gossip.

Mishchuk was also for arresting Vera Cheberyak. Her apartment had long been known as the hangout of thieves and gangsters, and she herself as a fence, but she had managed, with one exception, to be noted later,* to keep out of trouble with the police until two days before Andryusha's murder. On that date, March 10, 1911, her apartment was raided for stolen goods. Whether the raid was the result of a tip-off or whether it took place on general grounds was never made clear. It may well have been the latter, for during February and the early part of March there had been an epidemic of thefts and burglaries in Kiev, and the police had been prodded into unusual activity. No stolen goods were found at that time in the Cheberyak apartment, and Mishchuk saw no connection between the murder and a police raid two days earlier. As it happened, a connection did exist, but it took an abler man than Mishchuk to establish it.

The reason Mishchuk did not arrest Cheberyak is simple. He was prevented by Chaplinsky, who, together with student Golubev, was watching him with increasing uneasiness and forbade the arrest with a second warning: "Why do you harass an innocent woman?"* The best Mishchuk could do was to have Cheberyak brought in for interrogation by the investigating magistrate.

Golubev and Chaplinsky had somewhat different grounds for their uneasiness. Golubev wanted the search concentrated exclusively on Jews; what Chaplinsky wanted was more complicated. He was not yet wholly committed to the conspiracy; he did not know how far St. Petersburg was prepared to go. Minister of Justice Shcheglovitov obviously meant well, but the chances of getting a Jew convicted on a charge of ritual murder were not good. Previous attempts had failed, though that was before the Shcheglovitov era; if the government was ready to cooperate, and above all if the Czar showed sympathetic interest, it would be different. In that case the first task before Chaplinsky and his confederates would be to find the murderers and to shield them, at least for the time being. Then if St. Petersburg suddenly called a halt to the conspiracy, Kiev would produce the murderers and no harm done. If, on the other hand, St. Petersburg waited too long and compromised itself, Kiev could show that it had acted on orders.

Mishchuk's professional zeal, which infuriated Golubev, would have been heartily approved by Chaplinsky if he could have counted on drawing Mishchuk into the conspiracy. But Mishchuk did not cooperate; he immediately and unmistakably showed that he would have none of it, that he was going to do a straight job. What happened to Mishchuk is a perfect introduction to the techniques used by the administration in setting up the Beiliss case.

5

All that the investigating magistrate got from Vera Cheberyak was a statement of opinion. She had not seen Andryusha on the day of the murder, but she had been in the large crowd that attended his funeral, and: "I was told that Andryusha was most probably murdered by the Jews. When the coffin was lowered into the grave, some leaflets were thrown up into the air. . . . I saw that these were proclamations which stated that the Jews had killed Andryusha. I think now myself that probably the Jews did kill Andryusha, because nobody else desired his death. I cannot, however, present any evidence supporting my opinion."*

The boy Zhenya was also brought in for questioning. He stated that Andryusha had come to see him one morning about two weeks before the body was found. Since Andryusha's visits to Lukyanovka were infrequent, this was taken to mean the morning of March 12. According to Zhenya, Andryusha, without entering the house, had invited him to come out, and he had refused; then Andryusha had gone off alone. Cheberyak, Zhenya's mother, had not been at home at the time.

It was to be shown later that Zhenya was lying; he had in fact come out and joined Andryusha; and his mother was in the house. But at this stage Mishchuk, whether or not he suspected Zhenya and Cheberyak of lying, based his theory of the crime on other considerations.

Shortly after the discovery of Andryusha's body, several anonymous letters were received by his mother, by the police, and by others, all declaring that Andryusha was the victim of a Jewish ritual murder. The letters may or may not have pointed to a concerted campaign; as clues all but two were worthless. And these two were remarkable for a peculiar reason.

One, addressed to Andryusha's mother, was postmarked in the early hours of March 24, and must have been mailed the previous day. It gave with close approximation the number of wounds which the first autopsy had counted on the body. The report, we must recall, was completed on March 24 and was published in the newspapers on March 25. The other letter was delivered to City Coroner Karpinsky on the morning of the twenty-second, while he was on his way to perform the autopsy, and it also gave with close approximation the number of wounds he later counted on the body.

The possibility that someone saw the body and counted the wounds between the time it was deposited in the cave and the performance of the official autopsy must be ruled out. The examination would have had to be made by a medical man and with the proper lighting and equipment, for many of the wounds were tiny, scarcely more than pricks with a stabbing instrument. Such facilities could not have been introduced into the cave or the morgue. It is also impossible that a thorough and therefore protracted examination could have been carried out in the anatomical theater without Dr. Karpinsky learning of it. The conclusion was inescapable that the two letters had been written or inspired by a person or persons privy to the murder. From the condition of the body Mishchuk concluded that an attempt had been made to simulate a ritual murder.

Here, as at several other points, I must anticipate the trial of Mendel Beiliss, which took place two and a half years later. The administration and the prosecution (they must be seen here as two branches of the conspiracy) contended that this was an authentic and not a simulated ritual murder. The defense, for tactical reasons that will be given in the proper place, avoided the inference that a simulation of ritual murder had been attempted. The defense and the administration, each for its own reasons, therefore passed without comment over the two strange letters, though they were brought to the attention of the court and their contents described.

Mishchuk's report, which he refused to suppress, was that the murder had been committed by a gang of criminals, that the place where it had been committed was the apartment of Vera Cheberyak, and that its motive was to provoke a pogrom with its usual accompaniment of mass looting. The evidence that made him fix on the Cheberyak apartment is not given in any of the records I have been able to consult, nor is this surprising in view of the haste with which Mishchuk was removed from the scene. On general grounds he was influenced by the characters of Vera Cheberyak and of the men who frequented the place; and on specific grounds by the blood-clotted, semen-stained section of pillowslip found in the dead boy's coat pocket.

At the trial a long and bitter wrangle developed round the section of pillowslip. It was asserted by two witnesses for the defense that soon after the murder, one of the slips of the four pillows in the Cheberyak living room was observed to be missing. They further asserted that the pattern embroidered on the fragment was identical with the pattern on the other slips. The prosecution of course denied it. The consensus of the foreign reporters and of those Russian reporters who were not anti-Semitic was on the side of the defense. It is a reasonable assumption that Mishchuk, who in his "harassment" of Vera

Cheberyak had searched her apartment, also agreed with the defense.

6

By mid-April, less than a month after the murder, the clamor raised in Kiev about a ritual murder had been taken up by the extreme Rightist press. A spate of venomous articles poured out over the country, linking subversive liberalism with any suggestions for the mitigation of Jewish disabilities. "May Russia be saved from Jewish equality even more than from fire, sword, and open invasion by enemies," wrote one paper. "Our slobbering liberals seem not to understand what kind of species the Jews are with whom they are dealing. The gist of the Jewish question is contained not in their religion, though the latter is eternally hostile to Christianity. . . . Here is something one cannot fail to see, namely, their most dangerous anthropological and sociological traits, their rapacity and parasitic instincts. They are so dreadful because they are an exclusively criminal species which brings death to any wholesome society."*

At the end of April the interpellation of the Rightist deputies was entered in the Duma: "Are the Minister of Justice and the Minister of the Interior aware that there exists in Russia a criminal sect of Jews who use Christian blood in their religious ceremonies, and that members of the sect tortured to death the boy Andrei Yushchinsky in March 1911? If the Ministers are aware of this fact, what measures are they taking to suppress this sect and to bring to justice the murderers of this boy?"*

The reader will note the cautious phrase "a criminal sect of Jews." This was the official way of putting it. Unofficially it was always "the Jewish people" in its entirety or the Jewish religion as such; and even officially the protestations of the Jews that they knew nothing of the existence of such a sect were interpreted as evidence of complicity.

Meanwhile no Jew had been arrested or interrogated in connection with the murder. Months were to pass before Mendel Beiliss was fastened on. There was as yet no "Beiliss case," only

a Yushchinsky case. The frustration of the extreme Rightists
vented itself on the government, the police, and of course the
Jews.

The frustration was the more intense because neither the
Duma as a whole nor the populace was responding satisfactorily
to the clamor. The interpellation in the Duma moved the
Conservatives, Liberals, and Leftists to angry remonstrance at
the dishonor it brought upon Russia, the only modern country
with a national representative assembly that would let itself be
used for such a shameless exhibition of obscurantism and incite-
ment to murder. To this a Rightist deputy shouted the reply:
"On the day when you Liberals convince the Russian people
that a Jew cannot be brought to justice for murdering a Christian child, your Jews will not be saved by judges or police or
governors or ministers, because on that day there will be
pogroms. . . . They'll kill the Jews to the last man, and make
an end of them."

George Kennan (uncle of the former United States ambassador to the Soviet Union, George F. Kennan) thus describes the
scene in the Duma and the general mood of the country: "The
Caucasian Deputy Gegechkory, a Social Democrat, amid yells
of defiance from the Right benches, denounced the 'Real Russians' as 'a band of robbers and murderers.' . . . The interpellation was finally defeated by a vote of 108 to 93. . . . The powerful
influence of the liberal press kept the people sane and quiet,
in spite of the incitements to violence in *Zemshchina* and *The
Russian Standard* of St. Petersburg and *The Double-Headed
Eagle* of Kiev and in countless proclamations, appeals and
inflammatory leaflets which were scattered broadcast by Rightist
deputies and the anti-Semitic societies."

7

Student Golubov would not wait until a Jew had actually been
accused of the Yushchinsky murder before proposing punitive
action against the Jewish community. On April 17 Golubev
submitted a petition to the governor of Kiev to expel three

thousand Jews from Kiev, the names to be supplied by the organization. The governor refused. At the same time Golubev was probing the authorities on the matter of a pogrom: were they still opposed, or would they revert to the old permissive or even cooperative attitude?

The Kiev and St. Petersburg administrations were beginning to feel that Golubev was rushing things. His ideas were excellent, his energy was commendable, but he lacked a sense of timing. Occasionally he could be embarrassing; he was in and out of the offices of the investigating magistrates and the prosecutors almost daily. He was indispensable to the plot, but it was necessary to curb his youthful enthusiasm.

Early in May Minister of Justice Shcheglovitov sent Lyadov, the director of a department in the Ministry, to Kiev, with instructions to look into the state of affairs and to take Golubev in hand. By this time an immensely important change had taken place in the status of the conspiracy. The interest of the "Supreme Power"* had been engaged. We know this because as far back as April 18 Shcheglovitov himself had submitted to the Emperor a report on the Yushchinsky murder. We know from developments that followed shortly that the imperial interest was sympathetic. It was now necessary to coordinate the plans of the local and national administrations.

The following curious conversation took place in Kiev between Lyadov, of the Ministry of Justice, and the nineteen-year-old Golubev:*

LYADOV: I do not think the organization of a pogrom would serve your interests.

GOLUBEV: Why?

LYADOV: Because the governor-general has told me of the expected visit of the Czar for the unveiling of the monument to Alexander II. If some of your collaborators should start a pogrom, you would no more see this celebration than you can see your ears, whereas you and your union would probably appreciate very much the opportunity of having the Czar with you.

GOLUBEV: This thought did not occur to me. I promise you there will be no pogrom.

This matter settled, Lyadov turned the conversation to the Yushchinsky case, and Golubev brought up the subject of the contumacious Mishchuk. The man was impossible; he not only refused to follow instructions, he openly expressed the most subversive views on the Blood Accusation, which he derided as a rank superstition. He had to go. To this Lyadov agreed.

But it was not enough to take Mishchuk off the case and transfer him to another city where he could not interfere. He had to be taught a lesson which all members of the police department would take to heart.

A smalltime criminal, Kushnir by name, was suddenly attached to Mishchuk as special assistant. What instructions he received and from whom we do not know; what he did came to light in due course and created a scandal of its own— one of the innumerable satellite scandals orbiting round the central scandal of the Beiliss case. On a hill in Lukyanovka, the district where the body was found, he planted a bundle containing some charred fabric, a pair of suspenders, and various other objects. Then with much mysterious circumstance he handed over to Mishchuk an anonymous letter he said he had received which gave the approximate location of the bundle and named certain well-known gangsters, frequenters of the Cheberyak apartment, as the murderers. In the bundle, according to the letter, would be found the remains of Andryusha's missing articles of clothing—overcoat, trousers, and suspenders—and the remnants of his schoolbooks.

Mishchuk had the area painstakingly searched. The bundle was dug up, and sure enough there were some half-burned clothes, a pair of suspenders, and some charred paper. Mishchuk at once presented the letter and the bundle to the investigating magistrate, declaring the case solved.

It must be admitted that Mishchuk, an experienced officer not unacquainted with the standards and methods of some of his colleagues and not unaware of the hostility which surrounded him, showed a surprising lack of vigilance. But he was exasperated by Golubev's insolence, he was smarting under the rebuff from St. Petersburg, and he was competing for the five-hundred-ruble award offered for the discovery of the murderers.

It turned out that the suspenders were those of an adult—and Andryusha had never worn suspenders; the scraps of fabric did not come from the overcoat and trousers Andryusha had worn, and the charred paper was unidentifiable. Mishchuk was arrested and charged with obstructing justice and forging material evidence. He was sentenced to three months imprisonment with loss of civil rights, and he was prevented from appearing at the Beiliss trial.

But things did not go off entirely as planned. There was some difficulty in getting the sentence confirmed, especially after Kushnir* confessed publicly to having framed Mishchuk; and though the administration was successful in its main purpose, it was a bungled job. There was angry comment in liberal circles, and if the administration was contemptuous of these opinions, it was certainly not inclined to supply them with ammunition against itself. Yet this is what it did over and over again throughout its conduct of the case, sometimes unnecessarily, out of stupidity, arrogance, viciousness and vengefulness, sometimes unavoidably by reason of the trashy subhuman material that alone was prepared to do its bidding. As if in an artistically conceived prelude, it sounded both lines at the outset in the hounding of Mishchuk and the employment of Kushnir.

◇◇◇◇◇◇◇◇◇◇◇◇◇◇◇◇

CHAPTER   2

◇◇◇◇◇◇◇◇◇◇◇◇◇◇◇◇

THE DARK PLACE

1

WHILE GOLUBEV AND CHAPLINSKY are considering a replacement for Mishchuk, and while the anti-Semitic organizations and periodicals keep up their agitation for the discovery of "the Jewish ritual murderers of Yushchinsky," we may take a closer look at some of the small folk who were to achieve brief world fame during the trial two and a half years later. For these pictures I have drawn on the stenographic report of the trial (the trial itself will be given substantial treatment in due course), on newspaper descriptions, and on memoirs. I have also interviewed contemporaries of the trial then resident or present in Kiev, some of them spectators of the trial.

The Lukyanovka district lies on the heights at the western end of the ancient and sacred city of Kiev and looks down on the Dnieper River. Kiev is built on several levels, and Lukyanovka, with its own hills and valleys, was in those days half-open country. Of the built-up sections part was slum, part lower middle-class, part industrial. A small section consisted of the summer homes of well-to-do Kievans, for the area was naturally pleasant, visited by fresh winds in the spring and summer. It was a favorite place for picnickers, and children liked to play in its clayey ravines and numerous caves; so did the gangsters of Kiev in grimmer games, shooting it out with the police in pitched battles suggestive of American Westerns. The slums of Lukyanovka had an ugly name: "a dark place" they were called, meaning delinquency as well as ignorance and illiteracy. But in every district of that kind the decent and helpless poor must predominate; it could not otherwise serve as a hide-out for criminals. We shall meet both the criminals and the decent poor in this account.

Vera Cheberyak lived in Lukyanovka with her husband and three children. She was usually referred to in the vicinity as Cheberyachka, a sardonic form of "the Cheberyak woman," and sometimes more suggestively as Siberyachka, "the Siberia woman." Her husband was a telegraph operator, that is, a *chinovnik,* or government official, for which reason his wife was also known, especially in criminal circles, as Verka the *chinovnitsa* (the feminine form of *chinovnik*). The husband's role in the story is small and sordid, and it was thrust upon him by his domineering wife. He once told a neighbor that he would like to break loose from this woman and lead a simple life, but breaking loose from Cheberyachka was not an easy thing. Her landlord had been trying to do it for years and succeeded only when the police finally came to his assistance.

Vera Cheberyak's age is not in the records. At the trial one witness put it in the early thirties, another called her middle-aged. Her penchant was for young men within or just out of their teens. She was a smallish, brawling woman, free with her hands. She slapped her downstairs neighbor, the woman who attended the government liquor store; she slapped her servant; she slapped a young woman on the street for trespassing, as she thought, on one of her love affairs. And she did not stop at slapping. In a fit of jealousy she blinded her French lover, Miffle, aged nineteen, by throwing sulfuric acid in his face, but

such was her hold over him that at her trial he pleaded for her
and obtained a favorable verdict from the jury. Their relationship continued, and she helped him occasionally with small sums
of money; she would also send food over to his lodgings, which
were in the same yard as her apartment. Nor did the relationship
end when he, jealous in turn of another youngster of the same
stripe, seized her and beat her up so savagely that she went
about for weeks with a bandaged head.

At the Beiliss trial every witness testified that her apartment
was the headquarters of a large gang of criminals. There was a
constant coming and going of men and women; the men often
arrived in the uniforms of students or officials of various kinds
and left in plain clothes, and vice versa. It was remarked that
no grass grew in front of the Cheberyak door on the yard, and
drunks were often found lying there. And yet, as already noted,
her only known brush with the police, until her apartment was
raided two days before the murder, was over the blinding of
her young lover.

Cheberyak was, by general consent, the outstanding figure at
the trial of Mendel Beiliss; and hers is the name that occurs
most frequently as a witness or as the subject of testimony.
Scores of witnesses were interrogated about her, and one looks
in vain for a word in her favor. The best I could find is a neighbor's defense of her against the imputation of keeping a whore-
house; she was, he said, only "a flighty woman," and he explained that it was her mother who was a procuress. Whatever
kind of house it was that Cheberyak kept, the detectives who
examined the walls of her living room for traces of blood found
them bespattered with traces of semen.

We shall see that Cheberyak and her family, coached by her,
were among the principal witnesses against Beiliss, though the
administration and the prosecution knew that there was no
case against Beiliss and were morally certain that Cheberyak
had been a party to the murder. During the course of the trial
one of the prosecutors, wriggling in this difficult situation, was
prepared to consider the likelihood of Cheberyak's guilt if it

could be shown that she was Beiliss's accomplice. But no such link could be established. This same prosecutor kept a diary that was discovered among his effects after the February Revolution in 1917, and an entry made on the day when Cheberyak's testimony had been pulverized by the defense reads: "She has enmeshed herself in her own lies, the lying bitch [*sterva*] and this is the hinge of the whole affair." An agent of the national administration,* sent down to make confidential reports on the trial, wrote in connection with the death of Cheberyak's two older children, which had occurred in the fall of 1911, soon after Beiliss's arrest: "It is possible that the mother herself poisoned them, a matter which competent persons consider more than likely."

Witnesses and correspondents were in unanimous agreement that Cheberyak was no ordinary thievish drab. She had received some training as a midwife or medical aide, though she never practiced professionally; she played the piano passably. Above all, she had "personality." "A woman of striking character," writes the great Vladimir Korolenko, an observer at the trial. *The New York Times* correspondent: "Cheberyak continues to be the most striking figure at the trial. She sits with sphinx-like expression in front of the witness stand and is never at a loss for an answer when she is confronted with those who give testimony against her." A Jewish journalist: "She is clever, crafty, understands how to lead people by the nose and how to command the underworld. Say what you like, when one observes how she carries it off, how full of ideas she is, a certain respect rises in you. She is without a doubt a genius of a woman, a very rare criminal type."*

This was a little overdone, no doubt. More sober is the description by Arnold Margolin, Beiliss's first attorney, who saw Cheberyak in the office of the investigating magistrate shortly after she had been beaten up by Miffle: "A small, thin, restless figure. The upper portion of her head and one eye were bandaged. It was sufficient, however, to see only one eye to gain an idea that she was a dangerous woman. She was casting hateful,

feverish glances in every direction, scrutinizing everybody
suspiciously."

Vera Cheberyak had married early, and her husband, shy,
amorous, and timid, was pitied by witnesses, correspondents—
and the prosecution. He knew of the carryings-on in his home,
though he was often on night work. He was fascinated by her
and wanted to get away from her. All in all we seem to have in
Vera Cheberyak a woman born out of her time and setting. In the
Italy of Cesare Borgia and Caterina Sforza she might have found
an adequate field for her varied talents; in the Kiev of half a
century ago she was fated to operate in mean circumstances and
with mean accomplices.

This helps to explain the ups and downs in her mediocre
fortunes. When she was in the money—never really much—she
was extravagant and dressed her two little girls "like princesses";
but there were times when she had to ask for handouts of a few
rubles, and then the children, including the boy Zhenya,
Andryusha's friend, were miserably neglected. Cabined, cribbed,
confined in her operations, she had to content herself, at her
most prosperous, with the meager yields of snatches, goods
robberies, and chance holdups. Now and again she had to do a
little shoplifting of her own.

Her criminal connections were numerous, but we are concerned with no more than three of them, the men implicated in
the murder. They were her half-brother, Pyotr Singayevsky, a
lummox with a retarded mind who happened to be a first-rate
picklock; Ivan Latyshev, a nervous and unstable thief regarded
by his confederates as a coward; and Boris Rudzinsky, to whom
violence was second nature. The last two had criminal records
long before the Beiliss trial. Singayevsky, like his half-sister,
had managed to stay out of trouble. For convenience, I shall
refer to the three men as the "Troika."

At the trial the prosecution made a striking distinction between Cherberyak and her accomplices. It was as reluctant as
the witnesses to put in a good word for her, and on occasion
went out of its way to emphasize its low opinion of her. The

Troika, on the other hand, was treated, in a grotesque sob-sister plea, with a consideration bordering on tenderness. Singayevsky and Rudzinsky appeared at the trial as witnesses, but Latyshev was dead. During an interrogation on the Yushchinsky murder he had made a dash for freedom, had tried to clamber down an outside wall, had fallen several stories to the ground and broken his neck. The jury must have marveled—the newspapers certainly did—to hear the three men described as decent people who, to be sure, committed robberies from time to time, but otherwise were excellent, soft-hearted fellows.

The distinction was part of the strategy of the prosecution. In any case, by the time of the trial so much had been revealed about Cheberyak's manner of life, she had become so notorious, that the most inspired courtroom sophistry could do nothing for her. It was the better strategy to concede and thus sterilize in advance the defense's attack on her trustworthiness: the prosecution's case was so impregnable that Cheberyak's lies could not damage it.

One bright, brief episode in the history of the gang was the Kiev pogrom of 1905.* The loot brought in from the foray was too much for Cheberyak's market; she had to burn in the stove bundles of silk she dared not keep. Those were happy days for the Black Hundreds and the underworld generally. The chief of police had been present at the plundering in one section of the city, and on his appearance had been carried shoulder-high by the mob. He watched for some time, then called out good-humoredly: "That's enough, little brothers!" Thereupon the little brothers looked surprised and stopped for a moment till one of them burst out joyously: "Don't you see he's only joking?" In another part of the city the general in over-all command issued the order: "You may destroy but not plunder." When the wife of one of the plunderers held up a bale of cloth thrown out to her from a shopwindow by her husband, the general said: "Well, all right, that isn't really plunder. You found it."

More than five years had passed since that profitable *impresa,* and there had been no pogrom in Kiev or anywhere else; yet the administration was as hostile to the Jews as ever. Surely, as the leaflets said, it was time, it was time.

Not all of those who looked back wistfully to the *tempo felice* were vulgar robbers. Some members of the Union of the Russian People and the sister organizations were merely hot-eyed patriots; their interest in a pogrom was blood, not booty; their sole desire was to strike a blow for Mother Russia—under the protection of the police; and if somehow, amid the slaughter of unarmed men, women, and children, a little raping took place, what of it? But whether base material gain or high patriotic principle was the motive, everyone knew there was nothing like the Blood Accusation as a trumpet call to action; and therefore there was nothing profound or original about Detective Mishchuk's theory. However, he was not given the time to discover an important additional motive for the murder of Andryusha.

2

Andryusha's family, the Prikhodkos (the name of his adoptive father), were, in spite of Mishchuk's suspicions, what they appeared to be; they belonged to the decent poor of the slums, those who, besides being ill-housed, ill-clad, and ill-nourished, must put up with the unneighborly attentions of the ill-behaved —the little people who are pushed about by law enforcers and law breakers alike. Andryusha was the illegitimate child* of an early love affair of his mother's, and he was sometimes twitted with this by playmates and even by grownups. He had a great longing to meet his father, whom he knew only by hearsay and whom he bore no grudge for having abandoned his mother. On the contrary, he had built him up into a romantic figure and often said that if he could find him, he would leave home to join him. He knew that his father had been called up for military service, had been sent to the Far East about the time of the Russo-Japanese War, and had never been heard from again. Possibly he was dead, but his death had not been reported. The mother, too, remembered her lover kindly. At the trial the state prosecutor asked her offensively: "So he abandoned you?" She answered with dignity: "He was taken into the army."

Andryusha was always on the lookout for ex-soldiers who had served in the Far East at the same time as his father. One such man, a Jew by the name of Shneyerson, was familiar in Luk-yanovka; he used to come in to the Beilisses for meals. According to a remark Andryusha was said to have let fall, Shneyerson had promised to bring him to his father. Shneyerson denied this at the trial, denied ever having talked with Andryusha, and he may have been telling the truth; Andryusha's remark was re-ported years after he was supposed to have made it. Made or not, it was enough to turn Shneyerson into a prominent figure at the trial, and on no other evidence the prosecution persistently linked him—though he was a witness, not a defendant, and no move was made to indict him—with the murder of Andryusha. The prosecution did, however, have circumstantial evidence of another kind against Shneyerson. His name was that of an illustrious rabbinical family* (its scions still occupy a high place in Jewish religious life), and, according to the prosecution, rabbis were the leading practitioners and promulgators of the ritual murder of Christians—a reasonable conclusion if such were among the tenets of Judaism. That this particular Shneyer-son was not a rabbi but a hay and straw dealer in a small way, that he had no Jewish education, and that he was not connected with *the* Shneyersons did not count with the prosecution.

The Prikhodko family had lived in Lukyanovka until a year before Andryusha's murder. His mother had married and had borne children in wedlock. Her husband, Luka Prikhodko, was a bookbinder and a sober, reliable workman. With six working days in the week and the hours so long that he slept in the workshop together with the other employees, he earned twenty-six to twenty-eight rubles a month (the American purchasing equivalent today would be under forty dollars a week). The mother, Alexandra, helped out by selling apples, pears, and vegetables in the marketplace, getting up at three o'clock in the summer and five o'clock in the winter. Sometimes she worked at house cleaning for thirty kopeks a day; how the little ones were cared for does not appear. Food was scanty; the staple was of course borshch—the borshch of the poor, made with cabbages, beets, potatoes, and sunflower-seed oil, on rare occasions with a piece of meat. Sometimes Andryusha came to school without a lunch package, and the autopsy revealed that he was under-nourished. In his home they washed with plain water, soap was beyond their means, and they were accustomed to guessing at the hours—they had no clock.

Those who have grown up in poverty know the marvelous ingenuity of children in wringing happiness out of life under all but the most crushing circumstances, and Andryusha's home was far from the poorest in Lukyanovka or Slobodka. There was, moreover, a benefactress in the family, Andryusha's maiden aunt, Nataliya, who loved him. She earned "good money"—eighty to a hundred rubles a month—as a boxmaker. His grandmother too had a special affection for him, and had bestowed on him her second married name, Yushchinsky. She was a doughty old widow whose brief and earthy answers at the trial made the badgering state prosecutor look foolish. At the time of Andry-usha's death old Yushchinskaya was living with her daughter Nataliya at some distance from the Prikhodkos, and Andryusha stayed with them as often as at home. When he brought no lunch to school, it was usually after a night at home.

Aunt Nataliya was concerned for Andryusha's future. She would have made a priest of him and had had him coached for the preparatory religious school he was attending at the time of his death. She paid for his tuition and his uniform (and, poor soul, for his burial clothes and funeral). All in all, then, Andry-usha was better off than some of his playmates. His stepfather treated him like one of his own children, and there was little quarreling between husband and wife—little opportunity for it, too, with Luka home only on Sundays.

Andryusha's teachers spoke well of him. "A good boy, quiet, diligent, humble, frequently stayed after lessons." "No offenses, never punished, good attendance, though he lived quite far from

the school." "A fairly good student, kind, interested in things."
"Honest, never stole." "Mentally developed for his age." "Somewhat pensive." But also: "Secret and solitary." "Gloomy." "Secretive and silent in hall." "Home life unhappy"—this last referring not to ill-treatment but to his brooding over his illegitimacy and his dreams of the protective figure of his father.

His bosom friend Zhenya Cheberyak thus described him to the investigating magistrate: "A good boy . . . never fought . . . his mother used to beat him, but not badly. His stepfather did not punish him." At the trial Andryusha's schoolmates testified in the same vein. "A loyal boy, not a tattler." "Quiet, modest."

Aunt Nataliya died soon after the murder. Though she had known herself to be tubercular, she had worked feverishly to support her mother and help Andryusha, whose frightful death struck her down. Her deposition was read at the trial and, as might be expected, she had nothing but good to say of her nephew. In particular she noted with satisfaction that he and his family fasted throughout Lent, which may mean little for a family that seldom saw meat anyhow or much if the temptation presented itself at the forbidden season and was resisted.

Andryusha's grandmother, who reminds one of Gorky's as she appears in his great autobiography, survived her daughter and at the age of sixty-four or sixty-five—she was not sure which—was destitute. She and her daughter Alexandra, Andryusha's mother, were among the most moving and stirring witnesses at the trial. Illiterate, simple, straightforward, they resisted the efforts of the prosecution to pull them into anti-Semitic utterances. The mother, for whom the prosecution expressed the deepest compassion—as indeed everyone did, including those who were exploiting Andryusha's death for their own purposes—refused the role offered her by the Union of the Russian People. She took no part in the agitation. At the trial she refused to be baited by the prosecution into accusing the Jews. Defense counsel asked her: "When you were questioned, did anyone ask you whom you suspected of the murder?" She answered: "Yes, but I cannot suspect anyone"—she spoke in the present tense even after the long and relentless agitation conducted round the memory of her son as a martyr to the bloodlust of the Jews. The prosecution tried to elicit some expression of anti-Jewish sentiment from the grandmother, too; it failed.

In her deposition, read at the trial, Aunt Nataliya had stated as a simple fact that her nephew had had Jewish friends, which the state prosecutor seemed to find ominous as well as objectionable. One of the youngsters testified at the trial, and the state prosecutor questioned the grandmother about him.

> Q.: How about the Jewish boy who was just here?
> A.: He [Andryusha] used to go about with him.
> Q.: Did you mind?
> A.: No.

Here are some further exchanges between the prosecution and the grandmother:

> Q.: Did you love your grandson?
> A.: Of course. He grew up in my arms.
> Q.: Was he an obedient boy?
> A.: Very.
> Q.: In what way?
> A.: He was poor and he worked hard.
> Q.: You are crying when you speak of him. Why?
> A.: (Witness is silent.)
> Q.: So in general you were very pleased with him?
> A.: Yes.

The grandmother was asked about the toy gun Andryusha had made for himself and about his bird-snaring. (Gorky as a boy used to earn a little money in the same way.)

> Q.: I don't quite understand how he made a gun.
> A.: With his own hands. Whatever he saw, he made.
> Q.: So you lost your daughter and your grandson and now you can't work?
> A.: Yes.

Q.: How did the stepfather treat Andryusha?
A.: So-so.
Q.: Did he beat him?
A.: Heaven forbid. He loved him as his own child.

The prosecution kept harping on the sinister Shneyerson and his purported promise to bring Andryusha together with his father.

Q.: Did Andryusha wish to see his father?
A.: Certainly. Every child would be interested.
Q.: Did he ever say a Jew promised to show him his father?
A.: God alone knows. I can't recall; you can't remember everything.

The state prosecutor adverted to the rumored trust fund.

Q.: Did Chirkov [Alexandra's lover] leave her any money?
A.: Two children he left her; Andryusha and a daughter who died.
Q.: But money?
A.: Not a kopek.

The mother was questioned by opposing attorneys on the relations between her and her dead son.

Q.: How did Andryusha behave at school?
A.: Very well; if badly, I'd have known about it.
Q.: Andryusha was illegitimate. You loved him as much as the others?
A.: Best of all.
Q.: What were Andryusha's hobbies?
A.: He made a net and caught birds, made toys, made a banner from colored paper. He had a gun.
Q.: Was there any talk about you and your husband mistreating him?
A.: I don't know who said that I and my husband beat him, but it is rubbish, not true.
Q.: What did Andryusha eat that morning [of his disappearance]?
A.: I had very little. Borshch of beets and potatoes and a crust of bread, because we had nothing else.

We see Andryusha clearly. With all his repressions and reserve, he was a normal and likable boy. He was active and inventive; he had friendships and played like other youngsters. We may pause over the effect on him of his friendship with Zhenya Cheberyak, but Zhenya was shown at the trial to have been free from delinquency; indeed, he had a streak of honesty which his unspeakable home had not eradicated. Of course both boys knew something about the stolen goods that entered and left the apartment; they put the matter out of their minds. They may have seen drunkenness there, but that was common enough. In respect of the other goings on, the children seem to have remained innocent. It was Cheberyak's custom to send all of them frequently to stay with her mother—not an ideal alternative, to be sure. Zhenya's friendship was not the most helpful Andryusha could have lighted on, but neither was it as detrimental as it might have been.

The brickworks where Mendel Beiliss was employed stood a short distance from the Cheberyak home and from Andryusha's when he lived in Lukyanovka. In 1894, Nicholas II married Alexandra of Hesse and acceded to the throne almost simultaneously; and a wealthy Jew of Kiev, Jonah Zaitsev, commemorated the double event by building a hospital for the poor. He set aside an endowment fund, then founded the brickworks and assigned one half of its profits to the upkeep of the hospital. Jonah Zaitsev died in 1907, leaving behind him a reputation for philanthropy and unusual piety. Had he lived a few years longer he too would have been a figure in the world drama that centered on his property; he might also have been moved to painful reflections on the perverse destiny which sometimes waits on good deeds, for without the Zaitsev brick factory there would have been no Beiliss case.

In the yard of the factory there was a clay mixer. It consisted of a large stone receptacle into which the clay mixture was dumped and of treadles which did the mixing. The treadles were activated at right angles by a long horizontal bar that protruded from the mixer and was pulled round and round by a horse. The clay mixer was a favorite plaything of the children of

Lukyanovka, who, when it was not in use, would steal into the yard through gaps in the fence and take turns at pulling the bar and riding on it. The watchman on his rounds or a workman who happened to see them from one of the buildings would chase them away, and they would return as soon as the coast was clear. Andryusha used to enjoy this game as much as anyone else.

After his family moved away to Slobodka, on the other side of the river, Andryusha would sometimes pay a visit to Lukyanovka. It was an hour's brisk walk for an adult, but he was strongly drawn to his old playground and his friend. On the morning of his disappearance, Saturday, March 12, 1911, he and Zhenya and some other children were supposed to have gone "riding the clay mixer."

C H A P T E R   3

EGG DANCE

1

A GENIUS OF INEPTITUDE seems to have informed the Beiliss conspiracy from beginning to end, leaving us astonished at the degree of success it managed to achieve. Granted that in its early stages it was improvised in uncoordinated bits and pieces, an inspiration here, an idea there, allowing also for sabotage by recalcitrant officials and for mutual distrust and divergent objectives among the conspirators, there remains a vast residue of carelessness, shortsightedness, and fatuity throughout its development. The chief pervading defect seems to have been the inability to grasp one of the simple facts of life—that there are people who have an unconquerable aversion to skulduggery.

The task immediately before the Kiev administration was not difficult. Having decided, with the cooperation of St. Petersburg, on the elimination of Detective Mishchuk, it needed a first-class man who would find the murderers and keep his mouth shut to all but his superiors. One would think that such a task would be approached with a certain degree of circumspection; if all men are essentially scoundrels, those with superior ability are least to be trusted; in choosing an accomplice from among them one must therefore make sure of a community of interest, and this the Kiev administration in its precipitancy neglected to do. The man it picked was a detective, Nikolai Krasovsky.

Concerning Krasovsky's abilities there could be no question. He had acquired a national reputation for his solution of a number of complicated crimes and was popularly known as the Sherlock Holmes of Russia. At the time of the Yushchinsky murder he was chief of a rural police district, and the instant Mishchuk's dismissal had been agreed upon, he was summoned to Kiev and offered the case. He was to operate secretly for some weeks while the arrangements were being made (without his knowledge) for the disgrace and indictment of Mishchuk.

Lyadov, the emissary of Minister of Justice Shcheglovitov, was still in Kiev when the choice was made. He was a member of the committee that interviewed Krasovsky, the others being Chaplinsky and Brandorf, state prosecutor of the Kiev Superior Court. The inclusion of Brandorf calls for comment. He was one of the highest type of Russian officials, incorruptible and courageous, and he was soon to prove it by opposing the conspiracy and paying the penalty. Given his character, it must be assumed that there was no talk at the interview of ulterior purposes. Lyadov and Chaplinsky undoubtedly took Krasovsky's ultimate compliance for granted; and if he balked, there would be Mishchuk's example for him to contemplate.

Krasovsky accepted the assignment reluctantly. As he said at the trial: "I knew from previous experience what to expect: intrigues, unpleasantness on the part of co-workers and people connected one way or another with the case [Golubev and his fellow-pogromshchiks]. . . . I refused the offer, but I was told not to worry." He was also told that the Czar himself was interested in the case.*

As a safeguard the administration placed Krasovsky with the gendarmery instead of the regular police; his immediate superior was Lt. Col. Ivanov. Both men were instructed to work with the

utmost speed, and there is no doubt that Ivanov was as genuinely concerned as Krasovsky to follow the scent wherever it
led. There was, however, a profound difference in the texture of
the two men: Krasovsky had professional pride and integrity;
Ivanov was a timid bureaucrat. We have no reason to assume
that Ivanov did not begin the search for the murderers with
honest intent; but the record shows that before the end of the
year he had joined the conspiracy and was manufacturing
evidence against Beiliss. The administration had counted cor-
rectly on his taking Mishchuk's lesson to heart; but Krasovsky
was one of its major blunders.

2

Detective Krasovsky was tough, persistent, crafty and fore-
sighted. He took it as a tribute to his reputation that he had
been called in to replace a chief of the secret police; but he
knew that Mishchuk's displacement—and later his punishment
—was a tribute to student Golubev's political influence. Now
that he was in it, he meant to solve the crime, expose the criminals, and get the credit for it. To achieve this he had somehow
to take care of Golubev.

To declare his contempt for the ritual version of the murder
would have been suicidal; but in seeming to accept it he could
not let himself be crippled. Cooperation from Golubev's men,
who were poking around in Lukyanovka and other districts,
was out of the question; but the least he had to have was freedom from interference.

He got it by entering into an egg dance. When Golubev came
to see him, immediately after his appointment, he expressed the
view that this might well be a murder by fanatical Jews, but
it would not do to exclude the possibility that Christians had
cooperated. Golubev, who like the prosecution at the trial, did
not care who would be involved as long as the ritual character
of the murder could be established, agreed. For a month or so
Krasovsky had no trouble with Golubev.

His suspicions inclined him strongly toward Cheberyak; at

the same time he was not satisfied that Mishchuk had done a thorough investigation of Andryusha's family, and again several members—the mother was spared this time—were arrested. The unhappy stepfather, Luka Prikhodko, was subjected a second time to a brutal third degree. He was forced to assume various disguises and to submit to identification by someone who had seen a man loitering in Lukyanovka on the morning of the murder. It all led to nothing, and Krasovsky was compelled to concentrate on Cheberyak.

His situation was awkward. Golubev's men had not taken as kindly as their leader to Krasovsky's explanations. For them the only way to find Jewish culprits was to go after Jews, and Krasovsky simply had no Jew on his list. When Andryusha's relatives were exculpated for the second time, Krasovsky's obstinate preoccupation with Cheberyak added the last touch to the impatience of the members of the Union of the Russian People. They told their leader that they had another Mishchuk on their hands.

They were right, except that Krasovsky was an abler man,* more tenacious and unyielding. His ideas had a wider range and he was by nature more speculative. Examining the case as a whole he paused over the fact—of no significance to Mishchuk —that two days before the murder the Cheberyak apartment had been raided for the first time, though it had long been known as a hideout and disposal depot for gangsters; then immediately after this raid the wave of robberies that had swamped Kiev in the early spring receded, and the numbers of visitors to the Cheberyak apartment diminished in the same proportion. The scandalous immunity of Vera Cheberyak had come to an end, and the gangsters had lost their *malina* ("raspberry"— thieves' cant for hideout); and it had been such a cozy and convenient one, where pleasure could be mingled with business.

Cheberyak and the gang were bound to be asking themselves, reasoned Krasovsky, what lay behind the raid. Why had their perfect arrangement been disrupted suddenly and, what was more infuriating, without cause? For the police had found nothing, and no citizen is more outraged and indignant than a habitual criminal who is accused of a crime he does not happen to have committed—or on whom the goods have not been found. It would be hard for Cheberyak and company to believe that the police, under pressure of public demand for action, had bethought themselves of this old and, as it were, honored establishment; and harder still to believe that they had descended on it at random. Somebody had committed the unforgivable sin of the underworld: somebody had informed. But that was not enough. No one had needed to inform the police about the Cheberyak apartment; something peculiar had happened. Some reminder or nudge had been applied.

Nosing around as an itinerant workman, Krasovsky came across a story that had been making the rounds of Lukyanovka subterraneously since the time of the finding of Andryusha's body. It will be recalled that on the morning of his disappearance Andryusha had been seen in Lukyanovka by at least three persons—two lamplighters (husband and wife) and Zhenya Cheberyak. The woman lamplighter saw Andryusha and Zhenya together near the Cheberyak home at about eight o'clock; her husband saw them in the same place a few minutes later but in the company of a third boy who was never identified. The story—so everyone believed—was started by the unidentified boy.

The three boys had gone into the Lukyanovka woods and amused themselves by cutting switches from fallen branches. A quarrel broke out between Andryusha and Zhenya. Andryusha had cut himself a smooth and pretty switch, and Zhenya asked him for it in exchange for one of his own. Andryusha refused. Zhenya took offense and said: "If you don't give me your switch I'll tell your mother that you played truant this morning." And Andryusha answered: "Then I'll tell that there are stolen goods in your mother's house." Thereupon Zhenya ran home, accompanied by the unidentified boy, leaving Andryusha in the woods.

At the Cheberyak home the unidentified boy, standing at the open door, heard Zhenya tell his mother about the quarrel with

Andryusha.* There were some men with Cheberyak, and she asked them: "What shall we do with him?" One of them answered: "He must be put out of the way at once." The boy ran away, terrified, and spread the story—through whom first could not be established.

When Krasovsky heard the story for the first time, he did not yet know that the lamplighters had seen the boys that morning, the man all three, his wife only two; that came out some time later. But he knew of Zhenya's deposition before the investigating magistrate: Andryusha had come to visit him that morning, had asked him to come out to play, had gone away disappointed. That sounded unlikely, whereas the story of the switches, because of its artlessness, struck him as something that could not have been invented.

He could not get the story out of his head. Was it not possible that on hearing from Zhenya what Andryusha had said, the gang had concluded on the spot that Andryusha was the informer, or rather the particular kind of informer who, during the crime wave, would have an unusual effect on the police? The discrepancy in the timing was not important. The raid had taken place two days before Andryusha had made the threat; but if he could make such a threat, it could easily be supposed that he had already been blabbing. A youngster who knew the house and went about saying such things was even more dangerous than a grownup. And whether or not he was the direct cause of the raid, something had to be done about him.

If there was anything at all in the story, if suspicion had fallen on Andryusha just at that moment, the gang in its rage and uncertainty would not weigh the probabilities too nicely. A little questioning, half an admission, and their fury would break loose.

Later revelations were to show how accurately Krasovsky had gauged the state of mind of the criminals. These revelations are anticipated here not in vindication of Krasovsky but for chronological reasons.

At around midnight of March 12, that is, the day of the

murder, the three men that I have grouped under the name
of the Troika robbed an optical goods store on the Kreshchatik,
the principal business street of Kiev. On the following morning
they left for Moscow. There, a few days later, one of them
attracted attention in a saloon by flashing a one-hundred-ruble
note. The three of them were arrested and sent back under
guard to Kiev. Though two of them, Latyshev and Rudzinsky,
had criminal records (the third was Singayevsky, Cheberyak's
half-brother), they were released; no connection was established
at the time between them and the robbery on the Kreshchatik
or any other recent crime. It was only later, for reasons to follow,
that Rudzinsky and Singayevsky came forward of their own free
will to confess to the robbery of the optical goods store and
implicate the third member of the Troika, Latyshev.

3

The egg dance was becoming more intricate. Golubev was
beginning to share his followers' mistrust of Krasovsky, whose
excuse that he was looking for the Christians who had cooperated
with the Jewish master criminals was wearing thin. The Union
of the Russian People objected far more strongly to the "harassment" of Cheberyak than to that of Andryusha's family, and
Krasovsky's new story, that all this was only a blind, did not go
down well even with Golubev. But the more open Golubev's
dissatisfaction became, the more obstinate became Krasovsky's
conviction that the murderers were members of Cheberyak's
gang and that their principal motive had been to punish and
silence an informer, supposed or real.

On May 10, when his relations with Golubev were approaching
a crisis, Krasovsky got the first substantial confirmation of his
speculations. That morning he went with his assistant, Detective
Kirichenko, an able and honest officer who was also a pupil and
admirer of Krasovsky's, to make a thorough search of the
Cheberyak home. They were accompanied by two other detectives and a policeman. This is what Kirichenko reported to
Krasovsky and repeated at the trial: "While Krasovsky and the

others were searching the shed, I struck up a conversation with Zhenya Cheberyak and asked him about the murder of Yushchinsky. He wanted to tell me something but suddenly he stuttered and said he couldn't remember. I was sitting to one side of the door and he to the other. Cheberyak was in the next room behind the wall where I sat and listened in on our conversation. When I asked Zhenya who killed Yushchinsky, I noticed that his face went into a nervous tic. I somehow glanced round into the neighboring room at the same time as he did, and when I leaned over in my chair, I saw that Cheberyak was behind the wall and with her hand and entire body was making threatening gestures. Both Zhenya and I caught the gestures."

With the search going on throughout the house Kirichenko could not follow up the interrogation, but the incident made a profound impression on him, as it did on Krasovsky.

4

On June 9 Krasovsky and State Prosecutor Brandorf took a daring step and arrested Vera Cheberyak, placing the administration in a painful quandary. If, as Krasovsky and Brandorf expected, she would break down under intensive questioning and confess to having played a part in the murder, the first task of the conspirators would have been completed; they would have the identity of the murderers. The arrest was therefore welcome to the administration, but it had its unpleasant side. Golubev and the Union of the Russian People, who had raised such a storm over Pavlovich's arrest, would not accept Cheberyak's arrest quietly. They did not understand Chaplinsky's anxieties and those of his fellow conspirators, or if they understood, did not sympathize. They were not in official positions; they did not have to reckon with the possibility that the St. Petersburg group might still run out on the conspiracy; they had no jobs or reputations to lose. Nor could they be expected to see into the game being played by the Kiev administration. Their actions were straightforward; with them it was an article of faith that the Jews practiced ritual murder and that Andryusha was one of their victims.

To the furious protests of Golubev the administration could
reply that the blame lay with State Prosecutor Brandorf and with
Investigating Magistrate Fenenko—which it did the more will-
ingly because both of these men were resisting the conspiracy* to
the best of their ability. Technically the administration's excuse
was sound: Magistrate Fenenko had the legal right to interrogate
Cheberyak; Prosecutor Brandorf had the right to order her arrest.
Golubev knew, however, that technicalities were evasions. If
Mishchuk could be removed, so could Brandorf and Fenenko.
True, the law forbade the removal of magistrates—but what was
Shcheglovitov the Minister of Justice for? And in fact Brandorf
was dismissed from office less than three months later, and
Fenenko, Investigating Magistrate for Important Cases, was replaced in this, one of the most important cases that had come his
way, by a Shcheglovitov man from St. Petersburg. Taking the case
out of Fenenko's jurisdiction, however, took some time; he remained in charge of it for another year.

Fenenko was to testify later: "Shortly after I started the investigation, I began to suspect Cheberyak as an accomplice in Yushchinsky's murder. . . . It was clear to me that the murder of
Yushchinsky had been committed in Cheberyak's tenement, and
I began, therefore, to collect all the facts that might expose her."*

Brandorf was to testify: "Parallel with the official investigation
was a private one, carried on by Golubev with the knowledge
and consent of Chaplinsky. He [Golubev] was the inventor of
the Beiliss case . . . he often visited Chaplinsky and brought
him various bits of information. . . . I many times pointed out to
Chaplinsky that this was an impossible situation, that according
to my information Golubev was using illegal methods, inten-
tionally hindering the activities of the police . . . and not re-
fraining from disreputable means to obtain testimony. . . .
Chaplinsky told me that if I did not want to ruin my career I
must not tell Shcheglovitov that there were no features of a ritual
murder* in the Yushchinsky case."

Finally, Krasovsky was to testify: "My investigations led me to
the conviction that the murder had been committed by an organi-

zation of thieves led by Vera Cheberyak. When I reported this to Chaplinsky, he ignored the material* I had collected along these lines."

"Pretended to ignore" would have been more exact; Chaplinsky was vitally concerned with the material, but the closer Krasovsky came to the truth, the more ticklish became the position of the administration. Within a few days of the dismissal of Brandorf in September, Krasovsky was abruptly transferred back to his rural post. But many things happened between June and September; here only two will be mentioned.

Vera Cheberyak was released after five weeks of detention. She had finally admitted to having seen Andryusha the morning of the murder, but she had not confessed to participation in the murder; nor had the most important evidence against her yet been collected. It might have been better for her to have confessed to Chaplinsky, who could then perhaps have done more to protect her and her Troika. But she too must have had her calculations; she stood in somewhat the same relation to the Kiev administration as the latter to St. Petersburg: she could not trust her protectors. By fighting the investigation she prolonged it. True, she did receive full protection when the administration was finally convinced of her guilt, but much that was revealed about her to the public might have remained a secret. Above all, her guilt might not have been exposed.

MENDEL BEILISS

1

HE WAS THIRTY-NINE YEARS OLD at the time of the trial, an ex-soldier, and the father of five children. His photographs show a man of medium height and stocky build; in normal condition his face was rather full and heavy, adorned with a short, black beard. He wore glasses, but on him they did not suggest a reading man. All the descriptions agree on one point: there was nothing to remember about him except that he was Mendel Beiliss.*

His full given name was Menachem Mendel, his father's Tevyeh. Menachem Mendel and Tevyeh happen to be the names of Sholom Aleichem's two most brilliant creations, but these were given to the world more than a decade before Beiliss attracted any attention outside the little circle of his family, his fellow-workers, and his friends. Possibly the genius of Sholom Aleichem could have turned Beiliss into a "character", if so, it would have had to be in a non-Sholom Aleichem genre. For Beiliss the Russian Jew did not belong to the world of Sholom Aleichem, except perhaps as a peripheral figure; there was little of the folk coloration in him.

He worked as a dispatcher at the Zaitsev brickworks, where he had been employed for fifteen years. Kiev, and therefore Lukyanovka, were outside the notorious Pale of Settlement, the area to which most of Russia's six million Jews were restricted by law. There were, however, some categories of Jews who were admitted to other areas, and Kiev had a Jewish population of some twenty thousand out of a total population of four hundred thousand. Beiliss belonged to one of the "permitted" categories and lived on the premises of the brickworks.

On his return from military service at the age of twenty-two, Beiliss had married and settled in a town not far from Kiev, where he had found employment in a brick factory. Within a short time he was offered a better position in the much larger brick factory founded by Jonah Zaitsev. It was a wonderful opportunity, and the manner in which it came his way has a bearing on our story.

Beiliss's father, no longer alive at the time of the case, had been a pious Jew with some pretensions to learning and had been an occasional visitor at the home of old Zaitsev. One cannot talk of "friendship" between the Jew of the lower middle class and the sugar magnate, but there was mutual esteem, which was rather unusual because of a special circumstance: Beiliss *père* had been a member of the Chassidic branch of Judaism; Jonah Zaitsev, equally pious, had not. In Sholom Aleichem's world, to which these men distinctly belonged, the Chassidim and their opponents, the Misnagdim, were still very much at loggerheads, though less so than a generation earlier. The mutual esteem between Beiliss *père* and old Zaitsev therefore speaks well for both men. It was through his father that Mendel Beiliss got his job at the brickworks, and he counted himself a lucky man. The pay was better than anything he could expect elsewhere; he was receiving, when his employment was abruptly terminated, forty-five rubles a month and free quarters, which kept him within lower middle-class standards. When he began he may have hoped for more: the patronage of the great Zaitsev was something to build on.

But Jonah Zaitsev died in 1907, Beiliss's line to the seat of power was cut, and he never got to be manager. Even if he had been pious and scholarly, it would not have brought him into contact with the younger generation of Zaitsevs. Their way of life was quite different from their father's, who in his latter days had been an isolated figure in his own home. They had not by any means abandoned Judaism, but their notions of it were remote from his. They served ham and other forbidden foods in their homes and were strangers to the devotional minutiae that had been precious to him. Nor could they boast of the kind of learning that had created the bond between the heads of the older generation.

Beiliss, too, had fallen away from his father's religious standards, and for Jewish learning he had never shown any aptitude. He could *davven*, that is, read the Hebrew prayers, and of course he knew something about the ceremonies and the more common religious prescriptions. He could read and write Yiddish, but in spite of his three years in the service he spoke Russian poorly, could barely read it, and wrote it not at all. As for his piety it is enough to say that he worked regularly on the Sabbath and on all the holy days except the New Year and the Day of Atonement; to which must be added—inscrutable are the ways of Providence—that this was a fortunate circumstance for him, for Andryusha was murdered on a Saturday morning, and Beiliss was mingling with the workmen on that day.

It must be said for the younger Zaitsevs that while they did not follow in their father's ways, they respected his memory. Also, for all the laxness of their ritualistic observance, they went on occasion to synagogue, and on Passover they ate *matzos,* but whether with or without forbidden food is not recorded. Their *matzos,* too, were of the ordinary variety, whereas their father's had been scrupulously prepared with supererogatory regard to ancient prescriptions. It was old Zaitsev's custom to grow the wheat for his *matzos* on his own estate, under the twenty-four-hour guard of special watchmen; the *matzos* were also baked under special surveillance, and every Passover old Zaitsev sent two tons of them to his family and friends. After his death the children were content to buy their *matzos* from the regular dealers, which is what the vast majority of Jews do, and Mendel Beiliss was relieved of his annual duty of attending to their distribution. That this had been his duty until 1907 was a tremendous matter for the prosecution: *matzos*, it contended, had to contain Christian blood, Beiliss had had something to do with *matzos*, Andryusha was killed shortly before the Passover—an irresistible sequitur.

A similar chain of significant associations was exposed by the prosecution to connect Andryusha's murder with Jewish ritual. The younger Zaitsevs had decided to honor the memory of their father by founding an old people's home in his name. They attended the laying of the cornerstone and invited to the religious ceremony prominent local officials and leaders of Russian society who, with the exception of a medical officer and two or three doctors, declined the invitation. The cornerstone was laid on March 7, 1911, only five days before the murder of Andryusha. To the prosecution it was obvious that Christian blood was needed to complete the sanctification of the new building.

It was a striking aspect of the Beiliss case that none of the Jews accused, directly or indirectly, of complicity in a crime of religious fanaticism was particularly religious or particularly versed in the tradition. The principal figure was an ordinary workingman whose life was taken up with tugging at ends that could barely be made to meet. Devoid of higher ambitions for himself, he had them for his oldest son, whom he was sending to the local *gymnaziya*, or high school, though to do so he had to sell his cow, while his wife cooked for boarders. He worked twelve hours a day supervising shipments, keeping the accounts straight, and attending to a variety of chores. Only an old-world Jew of iron determination—there were such, but Beiliss was not of them—could under such conditions have found time for the minimal hours of study demanded by the tradition.

Such was the religious background of Beiliss and the younger

Zaitsevs. There was even less of it to Shneyerson, the hay and straw dealer who was supposed to have promised Andryusha to find his father and thus to have lured the boy to his death. Shneyerson is described as young, plump, beardless, and dressed like a laborer. He did not know that he bore the name of an illustrious rabbinical family; he had never heard of the Shneyerson (originally Shneor Zalman) who had founded the great Chabad branch of Chassidism. He was questioned in court on his religious affiliations. He had none. Did he ever visit the graves of his parents, as many people do, and Jews particularly during the penitential days preceding the Day of Atonement? He answered: "I never do," then added gratis a summary of his philosophy on such matters: "Dead is dead."

In two respects Beiliss was fortunate: the friendliness of his disposition and his good relations with his neighbors. They called him *"nash* Mendel"—our Mendel—and at the trial they had nothing but good to say of him; the child witnesses smiled at him in court. He was on friendly terms with the parish priest, for whom he had done more than one service. When a local parochial school was being built, the Zaitsevs, at Mendel's instance, supplied the bricks at less than cost, while the other local brickmaker, a Christian, had refused to abate the price by as much as a kopek. The same priest had asked the same Christian brickmaker for permission to let funerals pass through his yard as a shortcut to the cemetery and had been turned down; an alternative shortcut ran through the Zaitsev yard, and Mendel obtained the permission. Even the local members of the Union of the Russian People felt differently about Mendel. During the pogrom of 1905 they and the priest had come to assure him that no harm would befall him and his family; nor did it.

The role that the prosecution tried to thrust on Beiliss, that of the fanatical killer of Christian children and drinker of their blood, had something ludicrous about it in the midst of its obscenity. Had it at least been some picturesque and exotic figure, some beetle-browed, white-bearded *exalté*—but *nash* Mendel! Nor was he cut out for the role in which others tried to cast him, that of the hero and unflinching martyr. Martyr he was, perhaps the more so because he was precisely a simple, good-hearted, worried, bewildered workingman who struck no poses and made no speeches. He was not the kind that mounts the pyre or scaffold with unfaltering steps to sanctify the Name and inspire posterity. He did not want to be in history; he wanted to be let alone. Yet assigned this part—unimaginable to him—he carried it off honorably. He complained but he did not grovel. A Russian journalist wrote from the courtroom: "What can one say about him, this very ordinary, middle-aged Jew whose face has become familiar to everybody? . . . He is pale and thin. . . . Yet his self-control is amazing. . . . At no trial have I seen a quiet, defenseless, and frightened man surrounded by so many soldiers."*

This was after he had spent twenty-six months in a filthy jail among thieves, spies, and murderers. In the course of the thirty-four days of the trial he wept into his hands three or four times. And once he laughed out loud: that was when a witness for the prosecution said that among the factory workers he had had the reputation of a *tzaddik*—a saint and pietist.

2

Until his arrest and even for a brief period after it Beiliss no more imagined that he was to be mixed up in the Yushchinsky murder than he foresaw that some two years later his picture would appear in all the principal newspapers of the world. There had been inquiries at the factory; all sorts of people—reporters, detectives, members of the Union of the Russian People—had been in and out; but there had been inquiries everywhere in Lukyanovka. The arrest of the Prikhodkos, who had been neighbors until the year before, and then of Cheberyak, still a neighbor, and a very unwelcome one, had kept tongues wagging for months. Those who had known the quiet, hard-working Prikhodkos were amazed and incredulous, and they heard with indignation that when Alexandra had appeared in the market after her release, stones had been thrown at her and there

had been cries of "Murderess!" They were not at all amazed
when Cheberyak was arrested; it was rather her release that
amazed them. The story of the switches had become folklore
in Lukyanovka.

The manner of Beiliss's arrest was, to say the least, unusual.
Cheberyak and the Prikhodkos had been taken into custody in
the routine fashion by a policeman or two; to bring in Beiliss
it was thought necessary to mobilize in the dead of night a
small expeditionary force of fifteen gendarmes headed by the
local chief of the *okhrana*, Colonel Kuliabko. The paramilitary
preparations were made at the direction of Chaplinsky, who
invoked Article Twenty-one of the ordinance known as the State
of Reinforced Protection—a device for the suspension of a number of civil rights and under certain circumstances, for the declaration of martial law.

Exactly what this raiding force expected to find, what massive
resistance it anticipated, is hard to imagine. The only persons
on the premises were Beiliss, his wife, and their five children,
who were routed out of bed in their night clothes. A thorough
search was made; no arms were found, no subversive literature,
no secret chambers, no instruments of torture, no indications of
bloody rites. It was just an ordinary workingman's home. At
three o'clock in the morning Beiliss and his oldest son, the
gymnaziya student, were taken to *okhrana* headquarters. No
reason was given then or later why the boy was arrested, but
within two days he was sent home and Beiliss was transferred
to the city prison, where he remained two years and two months
before he was put on trial.

In spite of its spectacular nature the arrest attracted none of
the attention that attended the arrests of Cheberyak and the
Yushchinsky family. No one associated it with the murder.
Arnold Margolin, Beiliss's first attorney, recalls: "The Kiev
newspapers reported that a certain Jew, Mendel Beiliss, an
employee of the Zaitsev brickyards, had been arrested without
a warrant because of some misunderstanding about his right of
residence in Kiev. At the time nobody paid any attention to . . . a

case which was so common in the practice of the police authorities at that period." *The Jewish Chronicle* of London, which had been reporting since April on the ritual murder agitation, first mentioned Beiliss in its issue of September 15.

The date of Beiliss's arrest was July 22—it happened that year to follow the day of the Black Fast for the destruction of the Temple—and he was not charged with illegal residence or anything else. It was not until August 3 that, to his stupefaction, he was charged with the murder—"ritual" was not mentioned— of Andryusha Yushchinsky. Even then he and his family were the only ones to be alarmed; Margolin was still sure that there was a "misunderstanding" and that Beiliss would be released shortly. It was only in late September, after an interview with Investigating Magistrate Fenenko, who, together with Krasovsky and State Prosecutor Brandorf, had been present at the astonishing arrest, that Margolin became alarmed and realized that something more than a "misunderstanding" was afoot, something reaching out far beyond Beiliss. A Jewish committee of notables* was formed in Kiev to help Beiliss and his family and to plan action against the ritual murder conspiracy.

THE LAMPLIGHTERS
AND THE
WOLF-WOMAN

1

THE LAMPLIGHTERS Kazimir and Yuliana Shakhovsky were well if not favorably known to the residents of Lukyanovka. Officially only the man was the district lamplighter, but as he was often drunk and his wife, if not herself also drunk, would take over for him, they were regarded jointly as "the lamplighters." They were not considered "bad" characters, though the man was given to pilfering. The woman was feeble-minded. Theirs was the testimony that led to the arrest of Beiliss.

Nearly four months passed before Kazimir Shakhovsky admitted to Detective Krasovsky that he had seen Andryusha and Zhenya on the morning of the murder. Brought before the investigating magistrate* on July 9, the man made a rambling statement in which he offered a reasonable explanation for his long silence: "I am illiterate and don't read the newspapers. I didn't want to give evidence because I am out in the streets early in the morning and late at night and someone who didn't like my testimony might knife me." He serviced the petroleum lamps in the streets where electric lighting had not yet been installed. He remembered March 12 because on that day his employer had advanced him a ruble on his salary, and he remembered the hour because he had just finished extinguishing the lamps on his beat; it must have been a little after eight o'clock, because he noticed that the liquor store under Cheberyak's apartment was already open. "I saw Andryusha and Zhenya a little farther up the street and about fifty yards away another boy [this was the boy to whom the story of the switches was attributed] whom I didn't recognize. . . . I don't know where the boys went. Andryusha was dressed in a jacket and a regulation cap with an emblem. He had no overcoat and no books." Then the lamplighter added a personal opinion: "I advise you to check with Vera Cheberyak—the neighbors will tell you what kind of woman she is."

Yuliana Shakhovskaya deposed that separately from her husband she had seen Andryusha and Zhenya that same morning at the same place and at about the same time. She saw no third boy; Andryusha was without his overcoat, but he was carrying a strapful of books.

Vera Cheberyak, who at the time of these first depositions of the Shakhovskys was still in prison, now admitted to having seen Andryusha on the morning of March 12; she admitted further that he had left his overcoat in her apartment and that she had burned it: she had lied, she said, because she had been afraid of being dragged into the case. But she denied that Andryusha had left his books in her apartment.

Thus on July 9 weighty circumstantial evidence was piled up against Cheberyak. The books were a far more serious matter than the overcoat; for the notebooks had been found with Andryusha's body, and only the murderers could have placed them there. If the Shakhovskys' testimony about the books was as reliable as their testimony about the overcoat, it was obvious that the woman had seen the boys first and that Andryusha had returned to the house to leave the books together with his over-coat.

A highly complicated situation had developed. Cheberyak had been arrested on the kind of warrant that made her release mandatory at the end of a month unless a new order was issued. Brandorf, Fenenko, and Krasovsky wanted a new order issued. So, no doubt, did Chaplinsky and the administration; they were still not sure of Cheberyak's guilt. But student Golubev, who had been outraged by the arrest, was becoming unmanageable. On July 9 Brandorf issued the new order, and on the thirteenth Golubev appeared before Chaplinsky with a vehement demand for Cheberyak's release, declaring: "She belongs* to the Union of the Russian People." Whether he meant that she was a member of the organization or had been taken under its wing is not clear, but on July 14 she was released. However, the pull-devil-pull-baker contest was not quite over. Brandorf had her re-arrested on July 29; Chaplinsky had her released on August 8. That was Cheberyak's last arrest in connection with the Yushchin-sky murder; and in the meantime there had been other strange developments.

The first depositions of the Shakhovskys had been valueless to Golubev, since there was no mention of a Jew in them; in so far as they seemed to implicate Vera Cheberyak he, unlike Chap-linsky, really ignored them. For a time Golubev had had an eye on Mendel Beiliss. As far back as May Golubev had expressed the opinion that the murder had been committed on the Zaitsev grounds where Beiliss was employed and that it was a ritual mur-der. Chaplinsky had reported this to Minister of Justice Shcheg-lovitov, who in turn reported it to the Czar on May 18. But there was no evidence, nor was there any by July 9; but by July 20 enough, in Chaplinsky's opinion, was supplied by the Shakhov-skys to justify Beiliss's arrest.

It came in stages. On July 18 in his second deposition Shakhov-sky offered only general information, hinting at new possibilities. "The place where Cheberyak lives is separated from Zaitsev's factory by a fence. On March 12 you could pass from one place to the other because the fence was damaged. . . . Work at the factory usually started Easter [i.e., after the date of the murder], and on the day of the murder the factory was empty and no workmen were there. . . . Going from the Cheberyak place you could see a large number of kilns for making bricks. . . . In charge of the whole grounds was the clerk Mendel Beiliss, who lived at the other end of the grounds. He was a very good friend of Vera Cheberyak and used to visit her."

This is the first mention of Beiliss in the magistrates' records, and its context calls for attention. Having previously hinted that Cheberyak was probably in the know about the murder—"I advise you to check with Cheberyak, the neighbors will tell you what kind of woman she is"—the lamplighter now links Beiliss's name closely with hers: "a very good friend . . . used to visit her . . . on March 12 you could pass from one place to the other because the fence was damaged."

The man was driving at something. If Andryusha was killed in the brickyard, his body could easily have been carried out through the gap in the fence to be deposited in the cave. Cheberyak and Beiliss—it was an attractive combination: the notorious woman and the Jew, the very good friend who used to visit her.

But the combination was no sooner suggested than it was abandoned, to be revived tentatively and again abandoned at the trial. Beiliss carrying on with the Cheberyak woman couldn't be made to stick; it could never have remained a secret in Lukyanovka, and no one had ever heard of such a thing. It is true that none of the other evidence against Beiliss could be made to stick, either. It was easily established, for instance, that work was going on at the factory on the morning of March 12; bricks were being carted away, and receipt slips for the shipments, countersigned by Beiliss, were produced. But the administration, fumbling about for a line, decided on the whole that Beiliss and Cheberyak as intimates and as accomplices in the murder of Andryusha was just too obviously a fantasy.

On July 20 Yuliana Shakhovskaya deposed that her husband

had told her that he had seen Beiliss carrying or dragging
Andryusha away toward the kilns, and on the same day Shakhovsky himself made his third deposition:

"I forgot to add an important fact. About Tuesday of the week
following the Saturday on which I saw Zhenya and Andryusha,
I ran into Zhenya at my aunt's house and asked him how things
went that Saturday morning. He told me that a man with a
black beard chased them away from the kiln at Zaitsev's and
they ran off in different directions. I feel sure that Andryusha
was killed in the kiln at Zaitsev's. Today [i.e., July 20, 1911]
my wife met Vera Cheberyak on the street and she said: 'Because
of that shit Zhenya I have to be questioned now.' I then remembered Zhenya's story about the bearded man at the factory, and
that was Mendel Beiliss."

Here at last was what Golubev, Chaplinsky, and the administration had been waiting for. It was not much, and it was soon to
become less, but they considered it good enough for the arrest—
not just the questioning but the arrest—of Beiliss in the manner
described.

The order was issued on July 21; the mobilization, the raid, and
the arrest were carried out before dawn on the twenty-second.
The administration might have waited for something better if
it could have foreseen what was to happen later in the day.

Krasovsky learned of the lamplighter's third deposition on the
day it was made, July 20. Greatly perturbed he began an intensive questioning in Lukyanovka about the lamplighter's character.
Among those he questioned there was one man who deserves a
special place in this chronicle. He was the shoemaker Nakonechny, who had his shop in the same tenement as Cheberyak.
He knew Cheberyak, of course, and he knew Beiliss; he also knew
the lamplighter, and what he heard from Krasovsky was too much
for him. Like every inhabitant of Lukyanovka, he dreaded contact
with police no less than with gangsters, and most of all he
dreaded the thought of meddling in the Yushchinsky murder. But
he was one of the little people who are ready to come out for
their kind against injustice in high places. This is what Krasovsky

testified of him at the trial: "Nakonechny became very upset and excited. He told me: 'This is horrible! Shakhovsky's statement to the magistrate is absolutely false. He lives near the factory and sometimes steals wood from there, and sometimes boards and planks. Beiliss caught him at it, and since then he hates Beiliss.' When I [next] went to the magistrate Nakonechny had already been there."

The courageous voluntary intervention of the shoemaker had its effect. On July 22 and 23, with Beiliss and his son already in jail, the lamplighter made his fourth and fifth depositions:

"I never told my wife I saw Mendel dragging Andryusha toward the kiln. I saw Nakonechny at your office; I never told him that Beiliss has to be implicated, even though Beiliss did tell the police that I stole wood."

"After my confrontation with Nakonechny I will say the following: All that I have told about seeing Andryusha, and so on, was the honest truth. I added nothing. Zhenya told me that he and Andryusha rode on the clay mixer, but they couldn't explore any further because they were chased away by someone. Zhenya said nothing about a bearded man. I added that myself because no one but Mendel could be on the factory premises. I did this because I was coached and pestered by the detectives. I admit that I said to Nakonechny that I would implicate Beiliss because Beiliss said I had stolen wood. Everything else I said was true."

Asked what detectives had pestered him, the lamplighter named a certain Polishchuk and a partner. Polishchuk, an agent of the secret police, had been attached early in the case to Detective Krasovsky, and to all appearances was working loyally with him. It was Polishchuk, in fact, who as we shall soon see, brought in a seriously damaging report on Cheberyak. But his more important job was to steer the investigation toward a Jew, and to this end he alternately threatened and cajoled the lamplighters, plying them meanwhile with vodka.*

Thus, behind Krasovsky's back, Polishchuk had been pushing the couple to drag Beiliss into the murder. From Yuliana he obtained a story that contradicted her husband's but also pointed at Beiliss as the murderer. A third story, contradicting the other two, purportedly came from a woman known as Anna Volkivna, or Anna the Wolf-Woman (her real name was Zakharova), a pitiful old derelict who got this nickname not because of lycanthropic hallucinations but because in the summer she used to sleep under the open sky in a place called Wolf's Ravine. Which of the stories the prosecution was going to use was none of Polishchuk's business. Oddly enough it used all three.

Yuliana Shakhovskaya's first deposition also contained the following details: "I am thirty years old, cannot read or write, Orthodox, married two years. . . . I knew Andryusha for a long time as *Domovoi* [Goblin]. . . . On March 12, at about eight o'clock, I went to the grocery store. . . . Near my aunt's house I saw Andryusha and Zhenya. [Here follows mention of Andryusha's overcoat and books, already quoted.] The day before yesterday [i.e., July 7, 1911] I saw an old friend of mine, Anna, known as Volkivna, who said that although I live near the cave and she far away from it, *she* knew everything. She said that Andryusha and Zhenya and another boy were playing in the factory yard and a man with a black beard seized Andryusha and carried him off to the kiln while the other boys ran away. She didn't tell me who the man was."

In her second deposition Yuliana Shakhovskaya added these details: "The day before yesterday, at [Detective] Polishchuk's request, I tried to find Volkivna but could not. Polishchuk, my husband, and I drank vodka, and I don't remember what I said to him [Polishchuk] later. I forgot to say that when Volkivna told me about the man carrying Andryusha, she was slightly drunk."

The depositions of the Shakhovskys were read out in full at the trial. Then Yuliana was put on the stand and a determined effort was made by the judge and the prosecuting attorneys to get a coherent account out of her. The result was only greater confusion. She repeated the story that she said she had heard from the Wolf-Woman, and she repeated also that the Wolf-Woman was tipsy when she told it. But she denied ever having relayed the story to Polishchuk; she had relayed it to other people but definitely not to Polishchuk. Then she retracted; yes, she had told

the story to Polishchuk when he was plying her and her husband
with vodka. She had done it because Polishchuk had mentioned
a reward if she would change her testimony. Polishchuk wanted
her to accuse Beiliss. No, she said a few minutes later, this was
not so. Polishchuk did not want her to accuse Beiliss. Her testimony became so self-contradictory from sentence to sentence that
what emerged was a haze of Polishchuk, vodka, Wolf-Woman,
Zhenya, Andryusha and a man with a black beard who might be
Beiliss. She remained consistent only with regard to one point:
she had seen Zhenya and Andryusha together on the morning of
March 12. That seemed to have made an indelible impression on
her.

Yuliana Shakhovskaya was a profound disappointment to the
prosecution at the trial, but disappointment is too feeble a word
for the performance of Anna the Wolf-Woman, who went on the
stand two days after Yuliana Shakhovskaya. In spite of all that had
gone before, the state prosecutor seemed to repose the highest
hopes in the Wolf-Woman; for as she approached the stand, he
rose with a vehement gesture, like a man certain of victory and
impatient of delay. The questioning was begun* by him and the
presiding judge.

JUDGE: What do you know of this case?
WITNESS: Do I know anything? I don't know a thing.
JUDGE (to prosecutor): Do you have any questions?
PROSECUTOR (to witness): Please look at the man sitting there in
   the dock between the two armed guards.
W.: Little father, which way should I turn?
PROS.: Turn to the right and you'll see a man sitting there. Whom
   do you see there?
W.: What do you mean, whom do I see? There's a man sitting
   there, with one soldier at his right and one at his left.
PROS.: But who is the man? Do you recognize him?
W.: How should I recognize him? He looks like one of those Yids.
PROS.: But do you know *this* Yid?
W.: What are you talking about, little father? Do I know all the
   Yids? It seems that he's a Yid, and that's all.
PROS. (turns to court): I request that a transcript of her deposition
   before the investigating magistrate be read to the witness.

The presiding judge reads out the deposition, and the state prosecutor resumes his interrogation of the Wolf-Woman.

PROS.: Have you heard?

W.: I have heard.

PROS.: Well, then, you stated that you saw the Jew Beiliss carrying on his shoulders the [Russian Orthodox] Christian boy Yushchinsky at twelve noon to Zaitsev's factory.

W.: Did I say that? I didn't say a thing. Do I know such a Yid? I don't know anything.

PROS.: But you saw with your own eyes a Jew carrying on his shoulders a Christian boy.

W.: Did I see that? I didn't see a thing. Is it possible to see such a strange sight as a Yid carrying on his shoulders a Christian person?

PROS.: But it is written here that you said it.

W.: What are you talking about, dearie? Did I write that? I didn't write it. Do I know how to read and write?

PROS. (to court): No more questions.

The interrogation is taken over by another member of the prosecution.

Q.: Did you know Yushchinsky?

A.: Which Yushchinsky?

Q.: The Christian martyred boy who was tortured by the Jews.

A.: I didn't know him, my benefactor and protector; I didn't know him, may his soul rest in peace in the kingdom of heaven.

Q.: And didn't you see how they dragged him?

A.: I didn't see it, little father, I didn't, may he rest in the kingdom of heaven.

Q. But it is written here that you said these things to the investigating magistrate, that you saw it with your own eyes. Recall this, please. Perhaps you have forgotten. Surely we are sorry for a Christian soul gone to the great beyond.

A.: Of course we are sorry, greatly sorry, good, kind sir. There is nothing to say, but did I say anything? I didn't say a thing. Did I see? I didn't see a thing. Did I write? I wrote nothing.

Q.: How did it happen that the investigating magistrate wrote in your name things that you didn't say? Do you know what an investigating magistrate is?

A.: Do I know who wrote and why he wrote? Do I know what an investigating magistrate is? They called me, so I came. They wrote what they wrote, and then they told me to leave, and I left.

The interrogation is resumed by the presiding judge and the state prosecutor.

JUDGE: You were questioned by detectives?
W.: Yes, they asked me what I told Yuliana [Shakhovskaya] and I said I didn't tell her anything and didn't know anything.
PROS.: So Yuliana invented it all?
W.: That's right.
PROS.: And you never invent stories?
W.: No, I don't.

Yuliana is recalled for a confrontation with the Wolf-Woman.

JUDGE (to Yuliana): Is this the woman who told you that a black-bearded man dragged Yushchinsky away?
W.: Yes, it is.

The women exchange remarks inaudible to anyone else. Laughter in the court.

JUDGE: Zakharova [i.e., Volkivna], what did you say?
W.: That I don't know why she is saying this about me.
JUDGE: You, Shakhovskaya, affirm that she told you about the black-bearded man who dragged the boy away?
W.: Yes.
JUDGE: And you, Volkivna, say you didn't say so?
W.: Yes.

There the matter rested. That night the London *Times* correspondent cabled: "Anna the Wolf denies the whole story. It seems incredible that the Imperial authorities will allow the nauseous case to proceed further." The trial continued for another twenty-seven days. Neither of the two women was called again, but in his summation to the jury the state prosecutor returned to the Wolf-

Woman's reported story, expressed his faith in it, and asserted that she had retracted under duress.

2

From the foregoing it is clear that Polishchuk's efforts to get Beiliss's name linked with the murder had not gone too well. Ironically enough he did much better in implicating Cheberyak. The evidence he collected against her was not decisive, but added to the evidence already collected and to that collected later by Kirichenko, Krasovsky, and others, it had a powerful effect.

We will recall that in the tug of war between Brandorf and Chaplinsky, Cheberyak had been arrested on June 9 and released on July 14; she was rearrested on July 29 and released on August 8. During her second and shorter spell in prison her three children, Zhenya, Valya (Valentina), and Lyudmilla, fell ill, apparently of dysentery. Zhenya was taken to the hospital, and the little girls remained at home, looked after haphazardly by their father and neighbors. Zhenya and the younger girl, Valya, aged four, sank rapidly.

By August 8 Zhenya was in a dying condition, and on that day Cheberyak went straight from the prison to the hospital to take him home. The doctor expostulated that the boy was in no condition to travel across the city, but Cheberyak was obdurate. She told the doctor she wanted her son to die at home.

He did not die in peace. All that day and the next Krasovsky, Kirichenko, and Polishchuk were in and out of the house trying to speak with him. Most of the time he was in a delirium, but very close to the end he had a lucid spell, and of the detectives only Polishchuk was present.

A priest, Father Sinkevich,* had been called in to administer extreme unction; he was a prominent monarchist, a president of the Double-Headed Eagle, and the author of a number of anti-Semitic articles—circumstances which add significance to the account he gave at the trial of Zhenya's last moments.

There were present at his death the priest, the mother, and Polishchuk. The record does not mention where the other children were at the time. At the trial the priest testified: "I was called in to administer the holy communion to the sick boy Zhenya. After I had done it he called out to me: 'Father,' trying apparently to tell me something . . . but he couldn't say anything."

> Q.: What was your impression?
> A.: I think he was going through a very complicated psychological process.
> Q.: Was his mother present?
> A.: Yes, standing behind me. Perhaps she was giving him some signal.
> Q.: The boy knew he was dying, and still he didn't dare to talk to you?
> A.: That is right.

Polishchuk's account of the death of Zhenya had to be dragged out of him. What he had told his superiors freely as long as Cheberyak's involvement was to be a secret, came out grudgingly and haltingly in court. But the defense knew the original story and knew, therefore, what questions to ask.

> GRUZENBERG: How do you explain that the mother prevented him [Zhenya] from answering questions asked of him?
> POLISHCHUK: Because it was hard for him to talk and the mother didn't want him to be molested.
> Q.: But didn't she say to him: "Tell them, my child, that I had nothing to do with it"?
> A.: Yes, she said that.
> Q.: What did the boy reply?
> A.: He didn't say anything.
> Q.: But didn't you say on a previous occasion that the boy said: "Leave me alone, mother"?
> A.: I don't remember.

Stroke by stroke the picture was limned in before an appalled courtroom: the watchful priest, the relentless detective, the equally relentless mother trying to extort from her dying son a word of exoneration. From time to time, when Polishchuk put in a dangerous question, the mother leaned over and covered the boy's mouth with a kiss. Very close to the end Zhenya suddenly shouted: "Don't scream, Andryusha! Don't scream!"

Zhenya died on August 8, his sister Valya a few days later; Lyudmilla recovered. There was much talk then and later of poisoning, and the anti-Semitic press went into a frenzy. "The Yids," wrote one paper, "call this poisoning mysterious. But what is there mysterious in this fact? The elimination of important witnesses is the usual means employed by this blood-thirsty race. . . . It is evident that the Yids decided to kill all those who might say a single word about the kidnapping of Andryusha by Beiliss."*

The administration, of course immediately informed of the deathbed scene, considered it "more than likely" (as Shcheglovitov's confidential agent wrote him) that Cheberyak herself had poisoned the children. This is impossible to believe; what remains certain is that while the Jews were accused by their enemies, Cheberyak was suspected by her better-informed protectors, and most outspokenly by Colonel Ivanov.

C H A P T E R 6

CONCOCTING THE
EVIDENCE

1

To Beiliss it seemed that the world had collapsed about him. It was all very well for his attorney, Margolin, to declare that the evidence on which he was being charged with the murder of Yushchinsky was the merest rubbish and that the "misunderstanding" would soon be cleared up. How soon was soon? The summer passed, the misunderstanding somehow persisted, and every day was a nightmare. The cold weather set in, the nights grew longer, and at best a Russian prison was not a home away from home. Forty prisoners shared Beiliss's cell; the floors and walls were filthy, infested with rats and vermin; the food, usually watery borshch followed by weak tea, was served in three or four buckets and the prisoners helped themselves with ladles. The strongest naturally took their share first. On Sundays prisoners were allowed to receive parcels; but only a few, Beiliss among them, had interested friends or families able and willing to use this privilege. The arrival of parcels was followed by a general scrimmage in which the recipients were left with nothing except—if they protested—bloody noses and bruised bones; and woe to him who dared to complain to the guards.

Fortunately for Beiliss there were some decent elements among the prisoners; if he could not be protected from the toughs, he at least found someone to talk to and keep him from brooding perpetually over his inexplicable fate. In a few weeks it was his good luck to be transferred to a smaller cell that housed only a dozen men. There he became greatly attached to a fellow prisoner, Kozachenko, about thirty years of age, and to him he poured out his heart. Kozachenko was endlessly attentive to Beiliss's needs; young, healthy, strong, he did what he could to make Beiliss's life bearable.

Kozachenko said that he was being held on a charge of theft, but he was sure that he would be acquitted at his forthcoming trial; once he was out he would make it his mission to get Beiliss out, too. He was only a plain, simple person, like Beiliss himself; but he was a true Ukrainian, he could mingle with the kind of people Beiliss's attorney could never reach, he could find out things; and the more Beiliss listened, the more grateful he was to Providence for this chance encounter.

Kozachenko's trial approached and, presumably, his release. It became necessary to prepare a letter to be smuggled out, recommending him to Beiliss's wife. But as Kozachenko was illiterate, and Beiliss nearly so in Russian, a problem arose. Beiliss wanted Kozachenko to know every heartfelt word in the letter, so Yiddish would not do. They had to find a third prisoner who would write at Beiliss's dictation in Kozachenko's hearing. The letter was read out at the trial:

> The man who will bring you this note was in prison with me. . . . Please, dear wife, treat him as nicely as possible—if not for him I would have perished in prison. Don't be afraid of him—tell him about those who gave false testimony against me. . . . Everybody knows I am not a thief, I am not a murderer. . . . If this man asks for money, give it to him. He might need it. Is there anyone trying

to get me out on bail? Those enemies of mine who gave false
testimony want to take revenge because I did not let them walk
through the factory grounds. I send my best wishes to you and the
children.

How was the unhappy, bewildered Beiliss to guess that
Kozachenko was a convict spy planted in his cell by Colonel
Ivanov, who was then directing operations in person? It was on
Ivanov's instructions that Kozachenko took the letter to Mrs.
Beiliss after he had shown it to the prison authorities. The prose-
cution placed great emphasis on the letter as proving that
Kozachenko had been on terms of close intimacy with Beiliss,
and was entitled to belief when, immediately after leaving the
prison, he made the following deposition before the investigating
magistrate:

> Beiliss had a talk with me, without witnesses. He asked me to see
> the factory manager and one of the owners. These people were sup-
> posed to collect money among the Jews, enough to pay me for
> poisoning two witnesses, a lamplighter, whose name he did not give
> me, and another one called "Frog." Beiliss said I could give them
> some vodka with strychnine. I consented, but of course I did not
> intend to do it. I did not want Jews to drink Christian blood. . . .
> According to Mendel Beiliss "Frog" and the lamplighter could not
> be bought. I therefore had to use the strychnine.

With the lamplighter Shakhovsky the reader is by now familiar.
"Frog" was the nickname of the honest shoemaker Nakonechny.
If Kozachenko's deposition, solemnly read forth at the trial, were
not completely daft anyhow, we might ask why Nakonechny,
who had so valiantly intervened for Beiliss, should have been
given the same summary treatment as Shakhovsky. Trying to
disentangle what was going on in the minds of the lowest eche-
lons of the administration's agents is an unrewarding pursuit.

Kozachenko did not appear at the trial; he was one of several
witnesses who "could not be found" by the administration. However, it was reported that after making his deposition Kozachenko
went round among the Jews collecting money "to help Beiliss."

He met with no success. A worker at the Zaitsev factory had this
to say of Kozachenko: "He comes from my district. When I
stayed with my father in the village I used to see him. One
Sunday he came to me in the village, very drunk. We went for
a walk and came across a Jewish wedding. There were many
Jewish children around. He started chasing them and beating
them up. He also tried to pick a quarrel with the Jews, told them
there would soon be a revolt against them."*

Colonel Ivanov admitted at the trial that he had employed
Kozachenko, and admitted further, in a remarkable understatement, that the man "was not always to be trusted." What Ivanov
refused to admit was that after reading the deposition, he had
summoned Kozachenko and demanded an explanation and that
Kozachenko had gone down on his knees and confessed to having
made the whole thing up from beginning to end. But Ivanov
had told the story in confidence to Trifonov, an editor of the
Kievlyanin, the anti-Semitic monarchist daily, and was confronted with it at the trial. Ivanov's behavior is one of the
riddles of the Beiliss case. We can only surmise that when he
first read the Kozachenko deposition late in 1911 he was still
struggling with his conscience. At the trial two years later the
struggle was over, and in Kozachenko's arranged absence he
pretended to take the deposition seriously.

The administration managed to add one more document to its
Beiliss dossier before that year ended. On December 20, 1911,
four months after Zhenya's death, his father deposed before the
investigating magistrate that some days before the murder (he
was not sure exactly how many—"four days, perhaps seven")
Zhenya came running home with a story that he and Andryusha
had been chased out of the brickyard by Beiliss.

We may now sum up all the evidence collected against Beiliss
until December 1911: the hodgepodge of depositions made by
the lamplighters and the Wolf-Woman; Kozachenko's story;
Vasily Cheberyak's deposition. Nothing more was added until
nearly a year later.

2

It was clear by now that the objective of the administration fell into two halves of unequal importance: first, to prove that Beiliss was guilty of the murder of Andryusha Yushchinsky; and second, to prove that the murder was ritual in character. The second half was obviously far more important than the first; there was no mass propaganda value in an ordinary murder committed by a Jew, even if the victim was Christian. In a pinch one could even forego the first half. It would be a great pity of course; with no Jewish murderer named, a valuable, personalized focus of public fury would be lacking. But the ritual murder was the thing, and the more so because once established it would create an atmosphere helpful toward the conviction of the Jew.

On the other hand, the conviction of the Jew would predispose a jury—and the public—to believe in the ritual character of the murder. The two halves interacted.

But the ritual murder half of the program ran at once into difficulties of its own, born in part of the haphazard, uncoordinated origins of the conspiracy. Much depended on the autopsy report. The ritual murder leaflets had based themselves on the first autopsy, that of City Coroner Karpinsky made on March 24, but had done so by obvious distortion; nothing in the report lent itself to such an interpretation. The Union of the Russian People, its kindred organizations and their press could—and did—go on distorting, but the administration wanted a better text for the trial.

We may now recall that a second autopsy was performed on March 26 by Professor Obolonsky and Anatomist Tufanov, members of the faculty of medicine of Kiev University; and we may also recall that whereas the city coroner issued his report within two days, Obolonsky and Tufanov took a month to issue theirs. We have to guess at the reason for the delay, but the following helpful facts are in the record:

On March 31, before the conspiracy had been taken up by the administration, the Kiev Metropolitan, Flavian, an outspoken anti-Semite, wrote as follows to the religious authorities in St. Petersburg: "I consider it my duty to inform the Most Holy Supreme Synod of the sad case of Andrei Yushchinsky, a pupil of the preparatory class of the Sophia Ecclesiastical School of Kiev, who was criminally murdered. . . . The official autopsy in the anatomical theatre showed that the murderer cruelly tortured the defenseless victim. After this, on the demand of the State Attorneys, a second autopsy was made on the corpse of Yushchinsky. . . . Both the first and the second autopsies refuted the theory of a sexual or ritual motive in the crime."*

The Obolonsky-Tufanov report, though not published till April 25, was therefore completed by March 31. Flavian's use of the word "refuted" in connection with the theory of a ritual murder is significant because the leaflets of the Union of the Russian People had been distributed on March 27. In spite of this imprudent letter, made public years letter, Metropolitan Flavian became a supporter of the conspiracy.

Within a few weeks the extreme Rightist press was everywhere proclaiming that *both* autopsies pointed to a ritual murder—though the first did nothing of the sort and the second had still not been published. The obstreperous Brandorf wrote to Chaplinsky in Kiev and to Minister of Justice Shcheglovitov in St. Petersburg protesting against the propaganda: "Such an opinion of experts is not yet present in the dossier of the investigation. . . . Anyhow, many of the assertions in these articles are not in accord with the truth, as is evident from the preliminary information I have received from expert Tufanov. . . . In particular the statement in the newspaper articles that the wounds were inflicted while the victim was still alive does not correspond to the findings of the autopsy, for the punctures in the heart and chest were inflicted after death." *

The Obolonsky-Tufanov report, when finally issued on April 25, was a blow to the administration. Like the first autopsy, it was lacking in the three essential data pointing to a ritual murder. It did *not* show that all the wounds were inflicted before death so that the killers could obtain the maximum amount of blood, which, as the prosecution asserted, was the purpose of a ritual murder; it *did* show that some internal organs were pierced before death, and that the blood collected in them was therefore lost to the killers; it did *not* show, by the presence of marks on the skin, that the killers had used a suction or drawing instrument without which a quantity of blood, spurting or flowing at random, would also be lost.

Thus by the time the administration was fairly committed it did not have even a minimum of medical backing for the ritual murder theory. But something of the sort had to be inserted in the indictment. The administration turned to I. A. Sikorsky, professor emeritus of the University of Kiev, widely known as a psychiatrist and a lurid anti-Semite. From him it obtained a thoroughly satisfactory statement. Quoting from the indictment:

> Professor Sikorsky, basing his opinion on considerations of a historical and anthropological character, and judging by basic and other indications [in the autopsy] considers the murder of Yushchinsky typical of many similar murders which occur from time to time in Russia as well as in other countries. The psychological basis of this type of murder, according to Professor Sikorsky, is "the racial revenge and vendetta of the Sons of Jacob" directed against the persons of another race; and the typical resemblance in the way this revenge manifests itself in all the countries can be explained by the fact that "the nationality which commits this horrible deed, being scattered among other nations, brings with it the traits of its racial psychology." The crimes, similar to Yushchinsky's murder, Professor Sikorsky says further, cannot be explained by racial revenge alone. From this point of view the torture and killing are understandable, but the fact of choosing young victims and also the letting out of their blood, according to Professor Sikorsky, are the result of other considerations which perhaps have to the murderers the significance of a religious act.

This attestation, dated May 8, greatly encouraged the administration. Still, its position needed a little strengthening; Sikorsky was a specialist in psychiatry. The administration looked round for a medical man, and found him in the person of Dr. Kosorotov, professor of forensic medicine at St. Petersburg University. His

statement was not as wholehearted as Sikorsky's, though it cost
more; for while Sikorsky acted out of pure idealism, Kosorotov
had to be given 4,000 rubles.* The indictment quotes him as
follows: "The wounds were inflicted during the life of the victim . . . the arrangement of the wounds does not show that
torture was the main purpose. . . . The body was left nearly
bloodless. . . . All this makes one think that the wounds were
inflicted with the purpose of obtaining the biggest quantity of
blood, possibly for some special purpose."

The administration felt that something ought to be done now
about the autopsies themselves. Karpinsky, the city coroner,
being of inferior scientific status to Obolonsky and Tufanov, the
administration urged the last two to reconsider. It is not unreasonable to suggest that the month-long delay in the official
issuance of their report was due to pressure from the administration. But Obolonsky and Tufanov could not change the text of
their report because they had already shown it around unofficially, as we know from the letters of State Prosecutor Brandorf
and Metropolitan Flavian. However, on December 23 Obolonsky
and Tufanov added a number of supplementary statements to
their original report as issued on April 25. These too fell short
of Sikorsky's thoroughgoing blast, but they did something to
correct the impression produced by their original report. The
operative sentences were: "We believe that A. Yushchinsky died
of severe blood loss resulting from his wounds. . . . The blood
loss was so severe that the body was almost completely drained
of blood. . . . The last wounds were made in the area of the
heart. . . . Inasmuch as the most severe hemorrhaging was in
the left temple region . . . we must assume that it would have
been more convenient to collect blood from Yushchinsky's body
from these wounds, if blood actually was collected."

In the document—read at the trial—from which these crucial
sentences are excerpted, Obolonsky and Tufanov nowhere state
what caused them to change their minds at the end of six months;
they could not of course have performed a third autopsy. The
importance of their statement lies in the categoric conclusion

that Andryusha died of blood loss, which would be characteristic of a ritual murder. The qualification "if blood was actually collected" was a hypocritical bow to scientific propriety. They had no business to raise the subject of "collection of the blood" unless they could point to marks indicating the use of a suction or drawing implement, which they could not. The same sneak quality of innuendo, of suggestion and hasty qualification—"I'm not saying, you know"—characterizes Kosorotov's "biggest quantity of blood probably for some special purpose." "Special purpose" was not within his competence as medical man, nor "if blood was actually collected" within the competence of Obolonsky and Tufanov.

3

Early in 1912 the medical opinions collected by the administration in support of the ritual murder theory were made public. Interest in the Beiliss case had by then spread to the Western world, and the documents were scrutinized by fourteen leading medical experts* whose comments were published in the same year.

The response of the foreign scientists was a unanimous hoot of derision. For the most part the hooting was decorous and academic, so to speak; it was nonetheless devastating. Only one scientist sank to the level of forthright ridicule. "Professor Sikorsky," he said, "was supposed to give his opinion on the psychiatric-psychological aspect of the case. He does so in a fashion which makes it difficult for one not to become satirical. One hardly knows which to marvel at more, the naïveté or the prejudice of the psychiatric expert." The attestations of the Western scientists constitute a withering denunciation of the prostitution of science to a political purpose.

The reader will properly ask whether the administration did not collect a parallel body of scientific opinion in refutation of the denunciation. In three years of research I have discovered no reference to such a collection, nor even so much as an individual addition to the medical evidence supporting the prosecution's case.

Within Russia, too, protesting voices were raised, and Sikorsky was the chief target because he was the best known of the administration experts. The Kharkov Medical Society passed a resolution that "it considers it shameful and degrading to the high standards of a physician to display racial and religious intolerance and to attempt to base the possibility of 'ritual murders' on pseudo-scientific arguments."* Two days later the activities of the Kharkov Medical Society were suspended by the governor of the city. In St. Petersburg a special committee was appointed by the Society of Psychiatrists to analyze Sikorsky's attestation. The chief of the Military-Medical Academy sent for two members of the committee and warned them that if disturbances occurred among the students in connection with Sikorsky's expert opinion they [the committee members] would be removed from their positions.

Sikorsky complained to the administration that the attacks on him, "surpassing in their sharpness and passionate tone all else that is published in the press, have a depressing effect on the Russian population, while they also excite the Jewish masses."* The local governor assured St. Petersburg that measures would be taken "to influence the Kiev papers . . . in case the abuse of Professor Sikorsky is not discontinued."*

4

The administration foresaw the need to arm itself with religious as well as scientific experts. Here its efforts to enlist a respectable figure were futile. No Russian scholar of standing could be cajoled or bribed into a defense of the ritual murder legend. The first catch made by the administration is recorded for May 3, 1911, and reads in part as follows:

I, the Archimandrite Ambrosius, am of the Orthodox faith. I have not personally studied the sources of ritual murder of Christians by Jews, but during my stay at the Pochayevo-Uspensky monastery from 1897 to 1909, I had numerous occasions to talk on this subject with various people, and in particular with two Orthodox monks who had been converted from the Jewish religion to the Christian. I also had occasion to speak about these matters in

Kiev, where I live at present. All these discussions, as far as I can recall, gave me reason to believe that among the Jews, especially the Chassidim, it is the custom to obtain blood, particularly by the murder of Christian boys. This blood is required for the preparation of Paschal *matzos* for the following reasons:

According to the Talmud blood is the symbol of life; the Jews are the sole masters of the world and all other peoples are simply their slaves; and so the blood of Christian boys in the *matzos* symbolizes that to the Jews is given the right to take the lives of those slaves. . . . The Jews want this to be known by non-Jews, too, and that is why the body of a Christian from which the blood has been taken must not be completely destroyed. . . . When such bodies are found, the Jews have arranged it so that there is no clue to the place where the murder was committed, but the non-Jews who find the body are made to remember that the Jews have a right to their lives as masters of life and death. . . . At the committing of the crime a rabbi must be present to read specially prescribed prayers, and must finish them while the victim is still alive and bleeding.

This deposition was made before Magistrate Fenenko, who was compelled to enter it into the dossier. A year later Fenenko, shortly before he was taken off the case, called Father Ambrosius back, and obtained from him a supplementary deposition. It was brief:

The two monks who had converted from the Jewish to the Orthodox faith were Cantonists [Jews who as young boys had been impressed into the army for a period of twenty-five years and who nearly always lost all touch with their early lives],* people who were not very well educated. In conversations with me these monks did not show a background of reading from Jewish books of ritual, but simply gave me their observations from life.

What the second deposition brings out is that the Jewish converts, the Cantonists, were repeating the folklore they had picked up in their army years and elsewhere; the value of the Ambrosius deposition lay in its "explanation" why Andryusha's corpse had been left in a place where it was bound to be discovered and why the identifying notebooks had been left with it. But the explanation was double-edged: in a simulated ritual murder this

piece of folklore could be a guide for murderers belonging to
the uneducated or semi-educated classes.

For its showpiece expert the administration finally had to
content itself with an obscure Catholic priest, Father Justin
Pranaitis, whom it discovered in, of all strange places, Tashkent.
This man had a curious history. In 1893, living at that time in
St. Petersburg, he had written a pamphlet, *The Christians in the
Jewish Talmud, or The Secrets of the Teachings of the Rabbis
about Christians*, to prove that the practice of ritual murder was
advocated by the Jewish religion. The pamphlet attracted a
modicum of contemptuous attention at the time and was then
forgotten. Pranaitis got into trouble with the police on an unrelated matter—attempted extortion—and betook himself to
Tashkent, where he remained until 1911. In February of that
year he returned to St. Petersburg, where he distributed copies
of his pamphlet at the seventh annual Congress of the United
Nobility.

In his later years—he was in his sixties—he could still dream
of coming into his own. The Jewish question was again to the
fore, and the United Nobility, a replica among the lesser squire-
archy of the Union of the Russian People, took a leading part in
the battle against the amelioration of the Jewish position. Its
views on the subject were reflected in the address of its principal
orator, Duma Deputy Markov II: "All the Jews must be driven
within the Pale of Settlement—this is the first act. The second
act is to drive them out of Russia entirely. . . . There must be
no Jewish physicians, no Jewish lawyers, no Jewish artisans; they
must not act as jurymen, and obviously they must not be admitted to governmental service. This is the minimum demand
which the nobility must present to the attention of the Government."* In the Duma Markov expressed himself even more
forcefully:

> You all know my views on the Jewish race, a criminal race, and
> one that hates mankind. . . . If such is the fact, as it undoubtedly
> is, then they must remain subject to all those restrictions which
> were established in the past. . . . The Jews were restricted not

because of the wickedness of other nations, including the Russian, but because all the states of the world, all the nations, defended themselves against the attacks of the criminal Jewish race on their well-being, their very souls. . . . The Russian people are not yet able to defend themselves against the Jews by the same means. The Jewish force is extraordinary, almost superhuman. . . . I assert, as I have always asserted in the past, that in the case of the Jews the suppression of a separate nationality is never in contradiction to the ideals of sound statesmanship.*

Father Pranaitis, who had taken his life into his hands by writing his pamphlet—he solemnly declared in it that he would be killed by the Jews—risked it a second time by distributing it to the Congress of the United Nobility. His heroism did not meet with immediate reward. For some reason or other the pamphlet did not move the Congress to acclaim him as the God-sent deliverer of Russia. No reprint was ordered; nor was Pranaitis crowned with that higher reward—martyrdom. He returned to his little flock in the capital of Turkestan, and it was only a year later that someone in the Kiev administration remembered his pamphlet and sent for him to act as the prosecution's expert on the Jewish religion.

CHAPTER 7

UNEASINESS IN KIEV

IN SEPTEMBER 1911 the Czar paid his promised visit to Kiev to unveil the statue of his grandfather, Alexander II, whose assassination just over thirty years earlier had stamped itself fatefully into the next two generations of Romanovs. This was the gala visit for the honor of which student Golubev had consented to postpone his pogrom—a pogrom that (it might as well be stated) never came off. Amid the flowers and the fireworks Chaplinsky was particularly happy to inform the Czar that there had been distinct progress on the Yushchinsky case, which had now become in fact the Beiliss case. There was evidence of a kind—all it consisted of at this time was the depositions of the lamplighters and the Wolf-Woman—pointing to Beiliss as the murderer. This was the third report received by the Czar; the other two had been submitted by Minister of Justice Shcheglovitov.

A tragic incident marred the festivities. A young Jew, Dmitri Bogrov, shot and killed Premier Pyotr Stolypin at a command performance in Kiev's principal theater. The motive of the assassination was unrelated to the Beiliss case, which, still in its embryonic stage, had not yet come to the attention of the Jewish community. But there was a relationship of effect. It was remarked with horror that Bogrov might as easily have aimed his pistol at the Czar as at Stolypin. If the profoundly anti-Semitic Czar had until then been deeply interested in the development of a ritual murder case, the assassination of his premier by a Jew—and that in the imperial presence—must have turned his interest into something like a mania; and such must have been the reflections of Chaplinsky, Shcheglovitov, and their accomplices. The fact that Stolypin, whose conservatism bordered on reaction, was detested by the extreme Rightists almost as much as by the Liberals and Leftists, and who nevertheless was out of favor with the Czar for a suspected taint of liberalism—not to mention Nicholas's congenital dislike of able men—did not interfere with extreme Rightist denunciation of the Jewish assassin and of Jews in general. All in all, the incident shone like a good omen for the conspirators. The Czar's patronage of the case was dramatically reinforced, and a favorable atmosphere for the trial was in the making.

At the end of November Chaplinsky scored another triumph. He forwarded to Minister of Justice Shcheglovitov the deposition of the convict spy Kozachenko, who had been planted in Beiliss's cell by Colonel Ivanov with the results that we have seen; Shcheglovitov was able in turn to report to Nicholas that "direct indications have been obtained that the Jew Mendel Beiliss was one of the participants in the crime."*

The Kiev conspirators now considered St. Petersburg fairly committed, and some of them could now voice their hitherto suppressed misgivings with a certain amount of freedom. On February 14, 1912, Colonel Shredel, head of the Kiev gendarmery and Ivanov's immediate superior, unburdened himself to the vice-director of the Department of Police in St. Petersburg. The letter was marked: "Personal; top secret: to be delivered into his own hands."*

The case will probably be put on trial in April or May of this year and will last about ten days. At the present time further inquiries into the murder of Andrei Yushchinsky are being made by my assistant, Lt.-Col. Pavel Ivanov. . . . These inquiries are mainly centered around Vera Vladimirovna Cheberyak . . . and around professional criminals closely associated with her. . . . The latter are [here follow seven names, among which are those of the Troika—Ivan Latyshev, Pyotr Singayevsky, and Boris Rudzinsky].

It is a probable assumption that the boy Yushchinsky was an involuntary witness to one of the criminal acts of this band and that on account of fear it was necessary to do away with him. . . .

Considering the insufficiency of the evidence against him, and the universal interest in the case which has acquired almost European prominence, the accusation of Mendel Beiliss may cause a great deal of unpleasantness to the officials of the Department of Justice and may lead to just rebuke for the hastiness of their conclusions, nay, the one-sidedness exhibited during the investigation.

A month later Colonel Shredel wrote to the same official in a similar vein (again: "Personal; top secret, etc."):

I merely wish to add that it is now clear that the indirect evidence gathered against Beiliss will entirely fall to the ground. . . .

By the method of exclusion we must concentrate on the investigation of the activities of the professional criminals Ivan Latyshev, Boris Rudzinsky . . . and also Pyotr Singayevsky [i.e., the Troika].

We must interpret these letters in the light of the following facts: the valuelessness of the evidence against Beiliss was known to the Kiev administration as far back as the fall of 1911; in June it had received Kirichenko's report on Cheberyak's behavior during the interrogation of her son Zhenya; in August it received Polishchuk's grisly report on Zhenya's last moments. Colonel Shredel, the highest gendarmery officer in Kiev, was kept abreast of all developments and was in many cases their initiator. Why does he write, in February and March 1912, in this queer vein, as though he had only just made his disquieting discoveries? We would not be able to understand if we did not know that to the very end, up to the trial and beyond, Colonel Shredel went along with the conspiracy and that these "absolutely secret" communications came to light only when the February Revolution of 1917 threw open the archives.

There was uneasiness in Kiev by the beginning of 1912. The thing had grown too big for the local administration. Indirectly, through his confidant, Shredel warned the Department of Justice of a possible fiasco with, possibly, "a great deal of unpleasantness." If St. Petersburg were thinking of getting out from under, he had placed himself on record as having reported the real state of affairs.

He was not the only one to smell danger. The Governor of Kiev, Girs, who cannot really be called a member of the conspiracy except in so far as he seems to have remained silent throughout it, wrote to the Deputy Minister of the Interior on April 19:

> As is known to Your Excellency, the Beiliss case has attracted universal attention not only in Russia but abroad, and therefore the trial of this case will undoubtedly arouse great social interest, threatening to divert the attention of society from all other things. The outcome of this dreadful case is bound, however, to make a very disagreeable and distressing impression upon the Russian population. On the other hand, an acquittal of the defendant may evoke unheard of jubilation and joy among the minority groups and especially among the Jews. Considering that at the time when the Beiliss case may be expected to be put on trial the elections to the Imperial Duma will take place in this province . . . I deem it my duty to suggest that it might be advisable not to set the above case for trial before the end of the elections in my province.

Makarov, Minister of the Interior, wrote to Shcheglovitov direct, copying word for word many of the phrases in the letter his Deputy Minister had received from Girs: "The Beiliss case has attracted universal attention not only in Russia but also abroad. The possible outcome of the case in an acquittal, etc. . . . I have the honor most humbly to ask Your Excellency whether you would think it advisable to give an order to put the Beiliss case on trial not before the end of the elections to the Imperial Duma in the Kiev province."

Makarov, too, does not seem to have been an active participant in the conspiracy. Like Girs he stood aside and condoned by silence. Neither he nor Girs dared to go so far as to call for the discontinuance of the case and the release of Beiliss. In feeble extenuation of Makarov it should be said that the first steps in the conspiracy were kept secret from him, but by the beginning of 1912 he had all the information he needed to put a stop to it. However in December of that year he was replaced by N. A. Maklakov, a careerist devoid of principle who found his highest happiness in meeting the wishes of the Czar. (His brother, V. A. Maklakov, a moderate liberal, was to be one of Beiliss's defense attorneys—the most brilliant of a notable team.)

Chaplinsky seems to have been the only consistent proponent of the trial. He was more deeply committed than anyone else in Kiev, and as Shcheglovitov's local key man he dared not voice any irresolution he may have felt. Still, he could not pretend that he was wholly happy. On May 28 he wrote Shcheglovitov: "This is a very unfortunate case, and great pressure is being brought to bear on all sides. Many persons of solid position are trying hard to persuade me that the Beiliss case must be dropped, that such is the desire of our Minister [of the Interior, Makarov], and so on. . . . Naturally I am not caught with this bait and drive away my well-wishers."

If the trial was finally held, it was because the forces for it, "full of passionate intensity," were stronger, more insistent than those against it. There was, however, a postponement of more than a year, for reasons that will be given.

The incriminating letters quoted in this chapter can be explained as precautionary maneuvers between mutually suspicious accomplices; what we cannot explain is why the recipients kept them—"secret," "to be handed over in person," etc.—and carefully filed them away in the archives. No doubt they did not expect the revolution to take place in their time, but neither did they expect to remain in office forever. Why did they pass on to their successors such a damning record of their rascalities?

Perhaps it was, at least in part, the pride of the bureaucrat, whose status symbol is the thickness of his dossiers. At the last moment, when the judgment burst upon them, they made an effort to destroy the record, but it had grown to such dimensions that they would have needed another tenure of office to complete the task. And given another tenure of office, they would have continued to add documents.

PART TWO

EMPIRE IN

SENILITY

CHAPTER 8

THE ANGEL

1

THE BEILISS case may be described as a drama—or comedy—portraying how a somnambulistic emperor, a scoundrelly minister of justice, and a homicidal underworld slut entered into a combination that made an unexpected and not negligible contribution to world history. To understand how this came about and what the ending of the play meant, one needs to know something about the general background, and this can best be reviewed through the characters of the first two figures.

In the language of the theater it can be said that Nicholas II was the "angel" of the play—he provided the backing; Shcheglovitov was the producer—he provided the machinery; and the Cheberyak gang came up with the gimmick—it provided the plot line. The Beiliss trial, as distinguished from the Beiliss case, is a play within a play and is highly interesting in its own right.

To continue the metaphor, in the interior play there were two important props, human to be sure, but props nevertheless, two objects pushed about, either physically or symbolically, placed now front, now upstage, lighted in a variety of colors according to mood, and sometimes kept off stage for long intervals. One of them, Andryusha Yushchinsky, put in only a brief and partial appearance; he was represented by some of his viscera preserved in bottles and submitted as material evidence. The other, Mendel Beiliss, was alive, though not in the best condition after twenty-six months of imprisonment before his trial. He was off stage for long stretches only in the mental sense; physically he was there all the time but mostly forgotten or ignored. In the interior play Vera Cheberyak was the star performer.

Returning to the exterior play, the stage of which was not the crowded courtroom in Kiev but the Russian empire and the Western world, we may briefly sum up the motives of the three principals: Nicholas was thinking of his throne and the eternal sanctity of autocracy, while longing above all for a quiet life; Shcheglovitov was thinking of his career, which he thought to further by playing up to Nicholas's obsessions; Cheberyak was thinking of her skin.

2

Hardly anyone knows the last two names today. Nicholas is of course remembered, and not a few are familiar with his character. Nevertheless we must reintroduce him at some length, for without him Shcheglovitov would not have been prompted to do what he did, and, without Shcheglovitov, Cheberyak would not have become a historical curiosity. But Nicholas's inspirational connection with the Beiliss case has to be seen in the light of the man as a whole and his contribution to the fall of the czarist regime as well as to what came after. His anti-Semitism, the matrix of the Beiliss case, is an instructive showpiece both with regard to its personal development and its public effects; for granting much to the view that individuals do not make history, it is not unreasonable to suggest that the last seventy years would have been very different if Nicholas II had been another kind of man.

As to the kind of man he was, opinions vary, though within a narrow range. "He was fit only to live in a country house and grow turnips"* was the verdict of his fellow Emperor, Wilhelm II,

who spent the last twenty-three years of his life in a country
house sawing wood. Others, kindlier, are of the opinion that in a
private station Nicholas would have done very well, passing for
a decent, likable, and respected neighbor; his misfortune was to
have been born to the purple. It was also his country's misfortune,
and the world's.

Certainly he was a loving father and a doting husband; he
found complete fulfillment in the family circle, and his highest
pleasure was to read to his children. He was pious, too, with
more than a touch of superstition; he was attentive to anniver-
saries and namedays; he was fond of hunting and skating, and
he was a great observer of the weather. Apologists and critics
agree that he was possessed of considerable charm; the critics
add that he was least to be trusted when he was most charming.

But if we are to imagine Nicholas as a respected country gentleman, we should have to make a crucial additional change, namely,
in the wife he chose of his own free will and in the face of much
initial discouragement. Here he displayed a pertinacity so out of
keeping with his notoriously feeble will that it bespeaks a
desperate need rooted in a fatal defect. No one, not even among
those that loved him, ever failed to concede that Alexandra (nee
Alice) of Hesse-Darmstadt, the German princess he married, was
a calamity for him. We would say nowadays that she was the
expression—as she was ultimately to become the fulfillment—of
his deathwish; and it is not enough to say that he doted on her
—he was besotted.

So, all the evidence shows, was she, and the relationship lasted,
unmarred by a cloud, for two and a half decades, from the day of
their betrothal and before it until the time of their murder. It
glows in their correspondence and in the diaries he kept, which
she used to read and annotate.

"Darling boyse," she writes (in English), "me loves you, oh, so
very tenderly and deep."

He (in the same language): "I am indescribably happy with
my Alix. It's a pity that business takes up so many hours which
I would desire to spend only with Alix."

She: "How intensely happy you have made your wifey—God

bless you, my own, true, beloved husband—daily purer, stronger, deeper."

He: "My ownest darling . . . my little bit of heaven."

She: "Your little wife loves you."

He: "My happiness knows no bounds."

She: "Never did I believe that there could be such happiness in this world between two mortal beings."

He: "It is inexpressibly delightful to be able to be together at night in peace, disturbed by no one."

She: "Wifey must try to be as good and kind as possible. Let me help you, my treasure. . . . All my soul will follow and surround you everywhere. . . . Angels guard thee day and night, and Sunny [his favorite name for her] prays earnestly for your happiness."

Without going further we get the feeling that these infantile exchanges, unfalteringly sustained into middle age, are the expression of a sickly relationship not helpful to the ruler of an empire, or even to the administrator of a country estate. But if we do go further, we perceive that Alexandra was a sweetly and ferociously dominating woman who needed that kind of husband as much as he needed that kind of wife—"needed" may be taken both simply and ironically. Parallel with the note of almost unbearable connubial bliss runs, on her side, the insistent note of "I know best what's good for my boyse." And she began early, before their marriage. When his father, Alexander III, lay dying and Nicholas was standing around helplessly—that is, normally—she wrote him: "If the doctor has any wishes, make him come direct to you. Don't let others be put first and you left out. . . . Show your mind, and don't let others forget WHO YOU ARE." (The emphasis is hers.) When with little stomach for the job he had ascended the throne, she wrote: "If you could only be severe, my love. They must tremble before you." "Be more autocratic, my very own sweetheart." "Be firm, remember you are the Emperor." "Oh, my boy, make them tremble before you."

As the years went by she moved in more massively. She had her strong views (not altogether her own, as we shall see in a

moment) on ministers and generals. She demanded—and got—
the dismissal of the commander in chief of the armies. She was
infuriated by the nationwide clamor for a representative government: "That horrid Rodzyanko [president of the Duma] is asking
that the Duma be called. Oh, please, don't. . . . Russia, thank God,
is not a constitutional country." "Sweetheart, let me guide you
more."

We read with some surprise the observation by Sir Bernard
Pares, an authority on the Russia of those days: "This is not a
nagging wife, but one who is heart and soul" devoted to Nicholas.
So she was, as the alligator is to the strayed buffalo, and Nicholas
had about as much chance against her. Only once do we come
across a flicker of self-assertion. "You write about my being firm, a
master. That is quite right. Be assured that I do not forget; but
it is not necessary to snap at people right and left every minute.
A quiet, caustic remark or answer is quite enough to show a person his place." Poor devil! He was incapable of caustic remarks.
Face to face with anyone he had to be charming, but a minister
going home elated after an enchanting audience with Nicholas
might very well arrive there to find a letter dismissing him from
office.

There was another side to Alexandra's character that fortifies
her position as history's outstanding gift to misogynists. She was
insanely superstitious, so much so that Nicholas seems almost a
rationalist by contrast. She brought into the palace an assortment
of saintly fools (*yurodivy*), imposters, and charlatans that would
have made a laughingstock of any husband. They succeeded each
other with some rapidity until the ineffable Rasputin displaced
all rivals soon after his appearance at court in 1905, to relinquish
his command of the Empress only on that day in 1916 when a
group of monarchists, among them two members of the imperial
family, assassinated him.*

Like Nicholas, this remarkable man is well remembered. He
capers onto the stage like a satyr, unwashed, illiterate, insatiably
lecherous, a roisterer in public places, a lover of wine and gypsy
music, crafty, patriotic after his peculiar fashion, possessed of

hypnotic powers and endowed with such physical stamina that his assassins had to shoot him several times after he had swallowed, unawares, enough potassium cyanide to kill a horse: a singular illustration of the adage that what you don't know won't hurt you. Finding the unanimity of his detractors suspicious as well as tedious, I turned to René Fülöp-Miller, one of his defenders—or so he calls himself: "Even his own wife and daughters were convinced of his powers to banish the devil of sensual desire," and "she bore her husband's infidelities calmly, patiently and unreproachfully, for in her mind Grigory Efimovich [Rasputin] had been entrusted by God with a holy mission and his debaucheries, therefore, served a holy purpose."* This unusual husband-wife adjustment, so different in its way from the imperial example, is almost the sole ground for his "defense." As to the rest, Rasputin's unconscionable interference in state affairs is not denied, while his ineffectual and tainted virtues are admitted by all his serious critics. He was opposed to religious persecution and to the oppression of religious minorities; but what could such opposition amount to in a rogue dedicated to the support of an all-autocracy on which he battened?* It was suggested*—such was his power—that he be approached to intervene against the continuance of the Beiliss case, but decent people shrank from contact with him and it was doubtful that he would oppose a project so dear to the Emperor's heart.

Rasputin was suspected of belonging to a branch of the *Khlysty*, and preached the attractive doctrine attributed to some of the Gnostics of antiquity that the subdual of the flesh can best be achieved by uninhibited surrender to its temptations. If the suspicion was well founded, he was by far the most distinguished member of that Russian sect in the diligence and capacities he brought to its practices, the world-wide reputation and permanent fame he acquired, and the social eminence of his spiritual beneficiaries. His ministrations extended to some of the highest ladies of the court, and it was rumored that the Empress herself was not a stranger to them. This suspicion, denounced with horror and indignation, would be unworthy of mention if it had not been thought necessary to denounce it. Whatever were the undercover religio-sexual by-products for the Empress, it is unthinkable that there was any impropriety, as the word is usually understood, between her and Rasputin.

We are left with a curious picture: the chaste, idyllic home life of the imperial family, with the Empress befriending a coarse and boisterous voluptuary who turned the court into a national and international scandal—*Little Women* and *Fanny Hill* in peaceful coexistence under the same high patronage (this is not altogether fair to *Fanny Hill*, which is free from drunkenness and political knavery). But it was the imperial family alone that Rasputin left untouched, for this weird *religieux* finally achieved almost complete control of ministerial and other appointments, exercising an irresistible pressure on Nicholas through the Empress.

"All my trust," writes the Empress to Nicholas toward the end of their reign, "is in our Friend [Rasputin], who thinks only of you, Baby [the czarevitch, the long-prayed-for and only son] and Russia, and guided by him we shall get through this heavy time. It will be a hard time, but a man of God is near to guide you safely through the reefs, and little Sunny [herself] is standing as a rock behind you, firm and unwavering." The mixed metaphor fails to conceal the fact that she is standing behind Rasputin, who, if I may so put it, is standing behind her. She adds: "Had we not got him, all would long ago have been finished." All was finished very soon after she wrote those words.

We are concerned with Rasputin only in so far as he serves to reconstruct the times and elicit the character of the angel of our play. To the Empress one did not dare to breathe a word against the *Starets*, the holy sage. She believed with all her soul that the life of her sickly son and that of the empire depended on his mysterious influence. To the enemies of Rasputin she ascribed all Russia's misfortunes, and with perverse and self-fulfilling intuition she foresaw that his death would bring ultimate calamity. She had his bullet-riddled body, satiated at last, buried in the royal park, and came to pray nightly in the chapel she had erected over his grave. Within two months of Rasputin's death the throne was overturned; within a year and a half Alexandra and Nicholas and the czarevitch, of whose well-being Rasputin had been the divinely sent guarantor, were massacred together with the rest of the family. We may be fairly sure that even in the last moments it did not cross her mind that toward this frightful denouement she and Rasputin had contributed more than any other two individuals in the empire.

What was passing through Nicholas's mind in those last moments is beyond surmise. Did he at any time between his dethronement and his death catch a glimpse of his own guilt, of Rasputin's, of his wife's? Did it occur to him that he had gone through life a sleepwalker into whose dreams reality had penetrated only fitfully, and then completely transformed? At one point shortly before his abdication he clutched his head and cried: "Is it possible that for twenty-two years it was all a mistake?"* If the question was not rhetorical, was he referring to his strategy or his principles?

He had much time for reflection in the eighteen months of displacements, successive humiliations, and increasing discomforts before he and his family were awakened one night in their last place of exile—on the threshold of Siberia (the miserable justice of it!)—rushed down into the cellar, and shot and bayoneted to death. We are told that he and the Empress conducted themselves throughout their long ordeal with a dignity that could only have come from a clear conscience and an original fineness of character corrupted absolutely by absolute power. Yet there is evidence that Nicholas may have had something on his conscience; he had not always been convinced of the sanctity and indispensability of the man who had been the beacon light of the Empress. He acknowledged that Rasputin with his hypnotic gift had been able to help the czarevitch when the doctors were at a loss; but not less important to Nicholas was the tranquilizing effect on the Empress and the domestic atmosphere; and between them these two meant everything to him. Still, one could talk to him about Rasputin's demoralization of the government and the country. He would listen, ill at ease, and on one occasion he answered sheepishly: "Better one Rasputin than ten hysterics a day."*

3

If there is pathos in Nicholas's attachment to his family, and dignity in the closing months of his life, there is, I think, much nonsense in the widely accepted notion that he was a kindly man. Whatever he may have been as a child, as an adult he was a sentimentalist in the most objectionable sense of the word. His nerves could not bear the sight of suffering; to suffering at a distance, even if inflicted by him, he was callous. He could summon up a vague benevolence where his interests as he conceived them were not adversely affected; the moment he was called upon to make a personal sacrifice or to suffer an intrusion into his dream life of all-autocracy his benevolence evaporated. "When it came to defending his divine right," says Alexander Kerensky, "he became cunning, obstinate and cruel, merciless at times."*

His very coronation supplied a symbol of the man and his rule. At the celebrations in Moscow a dreadful disaster occurred. Half a million citizens were gathered "as the guests of the Czar" in a field outside the city—they were to receive packages of sweets and food—when the collapse of some barriers precipitated a stampede in which more than two thousand persons were crushed to death. The news spread instantly to every end of the city; it reached the ears of the Czar in the midst of the entertainments, but he gave no public sign of having been affected. Count Witte was present that afternoon at a concert to which Nicholas came two hours after the frightful incident. He records a conversation with the Chinese ambassador, who had taken it for granted that Nicholas had not been told, and was astonished to learn the contrary. "A gorgeous evening party," continues Witte, "had been arranged that day by the French ambassador. We expected it to be called off because of the disaster. It took place as if nothing had happened and the ball was opened by Their Majesties dancing a quadrille." At that hour hundreds of thousands of Muscovites were milling about in the darkness looking for loved ones among the living or among the corpses as these were unpiled by the police; and Moscow never forgot Khodynka Field. It is fair to suppose that Nicholas was particularly anxious not to spoil the evening for his young wife.

We stare at some of his memoranda and cannot decide whether they indicate frivolity or want of imagination. Following the abortive revolution of 1905, which saddled Nicholas with a Duma—Russia's first national parliament, but one with limited powers—disorders broke out in many parts of the empire, particularly among the subject peoples. They were repressed savagely. In one of the Baltic provinces the brutality of the expeditionary army was such that the local governor appealed to St. Petersburg against a commanding officer who was executing without trial people who offered no resistance. The report was sent to Nicholas, who entered into the margin: "Fine! A capital fellow."*

Two years later an unsuccessful attempt was made on the life of Dubasov, governor-general of Moscow. Witte tells us:

> I went to see Dubasov several hours after the attempt. He was perfectly composed. The only thing that worried him was the fate of the young man who had shot him. . . . He read me a letter he had written the Emperor begging him to pardon the young terrorist. His Majesty replied the next day that he had not the right to change the automatic and immutable course of justice. . . . I scarcely know whether to qualify this as Jesuitical or puerile.

By way of contrast we have an incident following the assassination of Premier Stolypin. An attempt was made, on ample grounds, to indict the principal security officer in Kiev on the charge of criminal negligence. Nicholas knew him and forbade the indictment. He told one of his ministers: "I see him at every turn. He follows me about like a shadow, and I simply cannot see this man so oppressed with grief."*

But Nicholas did not see the young terrorist, or the corpses and the frantic crowds on Khodynka Field, or the unresisting people shot down in the Baltic province, or the children—to speak only of them—impaled or disemboweled in the pogroms. Of these last, one of the worst took place in Gomel in 1905. Witte managed to force an investigation which revealed that the pogrom had been organized by the secret police. The Council of Ministers recommended nothing more severe than the dismissal of the responsible official, one Count Podgorichiny. On the margin of the council minutes, Nicholas, with the power of life and death in his hands, wrote: "How does all this concern me?"*

But pogroms did concern him, for when told about them he answered that he would always treat with leniency Russians who committed that kind of crime. At the Ministry of Justice there was in fact a regular "clemency form" for such cases; only the name had to be inserted before the document was forwarded to the Czar. The above-mentioned Podgorichiny was transferred with a promotion.

We shall be reminded that Nicholas was a leading spirit in the calling of the two Hague Conferences of 1907 and 1912, where several important conventions on international arbitration, the conduct of war, and world peace were adopted. But he could with a word have prevented the outbreak of the senseless Russo-Japanese War; instead he let himself be dragged along by a group of courtiers who had interests in the Far East and who argued that a quick, glorious, and inexpensive war was just what the masses needed to revitalize their loyalty to the throne.

Count Witte makes a feeble effort to find some good in Nicholas; it collapses before it gets off to a start. "A ruler who cannot be trusted, who approves today what he rejects tomorrow. . . . His outstanding defect is his lack of character. Though benevolent and not unintelligent, this shortcoming disqualifies him entirely as the unlimited autocrat of the Russian people." One cannot help asking what it did qualify him for. How could Witte, a man of immense energy, vision, and ability, feel anything but contempt for Nicholas, and how could Nicholas fail to be uneasy in his presence, or in that of any man of exceptional force and ability? Witte writes: "To the Japanese the Emperor was in the habit of referring as macacoes [monkeys], using this

term even in official documents. The English he called Yids."
"'An Englishman,' he liked to repeat, 'is a *Zhid.*' His Majesty
expressed himself to the effect that the Russians had badly defeated the Japanese." Witte's "not unintelligent" amounts to what
has been called "the medium man"—no great sage and no
small fool.

As we have seen, Witte was appalled by Nicholas's enthusi-
astic endorsement of organizations like the Union of the Russian
People and the Association of the Archangel Michael. With all
this, in composing his sketch of Nicholas, Witte had never seen
the famous private diaries, published after the revolutions of
1917. They are among the curiosities of history.*

The editor of the French translation summarizes them thus:
". . . Little daily notes which are put down pell-mell, almost as
it were, mechanically, the shabbiest and most insignificant details
side by side with events of the most decisive and grievous character . . . noting down minutely and with puerile vanity the
trophies of the chase at the moment of the most disastrous news
of Mukden and Tsushima." (At Mukden the Japanese crushed
the Russian army; at Tsushima they sank practically the whole of
Russia's Baltic fleet, which had been sent half way round the
world to attack them.)

Here are a few entries made in the course of the Russo-
Japanese War:

> April 20, 1904: At one o'clock in the morning I went hunting
> and killed two pheasants. I returned to the house at five o'clock.
> Rain fell all night long: also during the day, but it was hot.
> April 21 [after a particularly severe defeat reported by
> Kuropatkin, commander in chief in the East]: Painful and dolorous
> news! The weather was grey and a strong wind blowing. [I re-
> member out of my boyhood a German pun that was current
> in our circles. Kuroki was a Japanese army group commander,
> and we called Kuropatkin "Kuroki-pakt-ihn"—Kuroki nabs him.]

Reading the diaries I had an odd sensation, something like
the minor annoyance of an unresolved association. Then one
evening it was cleared up when I heard over the radio: "Stay

tuned for the weather report, won't you?" Wherever Nicholas
fails to mention the weather in his diaries I went over the
passage a second time, fearing I had been inattentive.

> Mama returned from Denmark. . . . At the fortress a funeral
> mass was celebrated for the memory of my unforgettable father.
> Ten years have passed since the time of his cruel death and how
> complicated everything is! How everything has become difficult.
> But God is merciful; after the trials he has sent us calm days will
> follow. [Nicholas is now thirty-six years old.]
>
> October 21: It is grey outside and cool. At 11 o'clock I went to
> church. . . . I received Mirsky [Minister of the Interior]. I took a
> walk with him and at six o'clock received Kokovtsev [Finance
> Minister]. I read a lot. I had dinner in my bedroom. The offensive
> by our troops has been stopped by the Japanese. . . . Our losses
> are great, it appears.

The years brought no change in the tenor of the diaries.

> April 27, 1907 [by this time the land was to all appearances
> quiet and resigned after the abortive 1905 revolution]: The night
> was clear and there was some frost. I killed two cocks. I saw a lot
> of them running along the ground. They were terribly agitated.

A run-of-the-mill haruspex could have told Nicholas that the
pheasants knew more about the real state of the country than he.

Nearly ten years later, toward the apocalyptic ending of
World War I, when the army had begun to disintegrate and the
country, hungry, desperate, infuriated by the incompetence and
corruption of the court camarilla and the footling ministers
manipulated by Rasputin, was ripe for revolution, the Empress
wrote Nicholas of "the great and beautiful times coming for your
reign and Russia." "Now comes the reign of will and power. . . .
He [Rasputin] has kept you where you are. . , , Only believe
more in our Friend. . . . Draw the reins tightly which you let
loose. . . . I am your wall behind you. . . . Russia loves to feel
the whip." ". . . Listen to me, which means Our Friend." "Be
the Emperor, Peter the Great, Ivan the Terrible, the Emperor
Paul—crush them all under you—now don't you laugh, naughty

one. . . . I kiss you, caress you, love you, long for you, can't sleep without you, bless you." In reply Nicholas bleated: "Tender thanks for your severe written scolding. . . . Your poor little weak-willed hubby."

Five weeks before the abdication Nicholas wrote to her: "Sincerest thanks for your dear letter, which you left in the coupé. I read it with avidity before going to sleep. It was a great comfort to me in my loneliness, after spending two months together. . . . I greatly miss my half hour of patience in the evening. I shall take up dominoes in my spare time." And two days after the abdication he wrote in his diary, resumed after a ten-year lapse: "I slept well. . . . At midnight I went to meet dear Mama, who was arriving from Kiev. We talked for a long time. Today at last I received two telegrams from my dear Alix. I went for a walk. The weather was dreadful."

4

Nicholas came by his anti-Semitism naturally. His father, Alexander III, a born autocrat, conscientious, industrious, of iron physique and will, had watched with equanimity the pogroms of 1881 and 1882. Under his rule the position of the Jews, which had considerably improved under the reign of his father, Alexander II, deteriorated rapidly. But Alexander III's anti-Semitism did not addle his mind. Witte, who served him for many years, and for the Russia of those days could hardly be called anti-Semitic at all (his wife came from a converted Jewish family), took talent where he found it and employed such a large number of Jews that the Emperor once asked him bluntly: "Is it true that you are a supporter of the Jews?" Witte writes:

> I told His Majesty that I found it difficult to answer his question and asked his permission to answer with a question. Permission being granted, I asked whether he could drown all the Jews in the Black Sea. If he could do so, I would understand such a solution of the problem. If he could not, then the only solution was to enable them to live, and this was possible only through the gradual abolition of the special laws created for the Jews. His Majesty said

nothing in reply and retained his benevolence toward me till the day of his death.

The home, then, was Nicholas's first school in anti-Semitism. To the home was added the influence of his tutor, Pobedonostsev, the able, scholarly, and absolutist Procurator of the Holy Synod. Pobedonostsev was referred to by the Jews as the modern Torquemada. He is credited with a special version of the Final Solution, which, unlike Hitler, he was reasonable enough to modify in one important respect and to limit to the Jews of his own country. His famous formula was: "One third will convert, one third will emigrate and one third will die out." Pobedonostsev's influence continued well into Nicholas's reign. (He died in 1907 at the age of eighty.) Another influence must have been a certain writer, Hippolyte Lyutostansky, who merits a little attention for that reason.

He was a Catholic priest who had been unfrocked and handed over to the civil authorities for various misdemeanors, including attempted rape. He was then (1868) thirty years of age. He converted to the Orthodox Russian Church and in 1869 prepared for his baccalaureate a paper, *The Question of the Use of Christian Blood for Religious Purposes Connected with the Attitude of Judaism toward Christianity*, which, he confessed in a newspaper article in 1905,* he copied word for word from a forgotten manuscript in a Moscow library. He took his own manuscript, he further relates, to a Moscow rabbi and offered, for a consideration of 500 rubles, to destroy it. Rejected, he submitted the paper and got his degree. He then printed the paper as a pamphlet and sent copies to various personages, among them the Crown Prince (our Nicholas) and the chief of the gendarmery, who ordered 800 copies and had them distributed to the chief provincial officials throughout the empire. From 1876 or 1877 on, Lyutostansky produced six volumes on the Jews and Judaism, finding time in 1880 to appear in vaudeville, where he gave "comical recitations" on Jewish life. He was apparently not a success, for before he published his first volume he made another rabbi an offer to publish a pamphlet refuting his earlier one, and was sent packing a second time.

The gist of Lyutostansky's views, and the level of his scholarship, may be gathered from a few quotations: "The Talmud is built upon falsehood and contempt for work; filled with immoral and anarchistic tendencies, the Talmud is the offspring of the most contemptible of all revolutions which ever degraded mankind by its stupidity and bloodshed. Insolence and cunning, crafty casuistry," etc., etc. "We must ask all the Jews to go back to Palestine, but as they will not go of their own free will, we must force them to do it." Then follows a series of prescriptions designed to make life impossible for Jews in Russia. They are more or less an anticipation of the Nuremberg laws.

One passage is so close to Nicholas's view on the English that it establishes a direct influence. "The English are pure-blooded Israelites. . . . The clearest characteristics of the Israelites are well known all over the world and the same characteristics are to be found in the English people . . . the universal business greed of the English people, their political greed," etc. The theory that the British are the lost Ten Tribes is widespread among certain cranks, but it is usually couched in laudatory terms.

This queer creature was still alive at the time of the Beiliss trial, where he was frequently quoted by the prosecution as a leading authority on Judaism. There was some talk of having him appear as the expert for the prosecution, but he was passed over in favor of Pranaitis.

Lyutostansky's dissertations on the Talmud found approval and support in various high quarters. In 1905 the Ministry of Education promised to take up the question of a subsidy for the indigent scholar, while Major General Sukhinsky wrote him from the Ministry of War that volumes one to five had been approved for distribution in the military schools. With all this he remained a very poor man and died in obscurity.*

Nicholas, by nature neither a hater nor, in spite of his superstitious inclinations, a fanatic in religion, gave no evidence of rabid or hallucinatory anti-Semitism before he ascended the throne in

1894, and little of it in the eleven years that followed, that is, until the revolution of 1905, which he saw as a Jewish plot. But the revolution was an attack on the sacred principle of all-autocracy, and to this he responded with the wild fury of the timid. He was deeply convinced that if left alone the Russian people would never have dreamed of such unnatural behavior.* The revolutionaries were responsible, and for him the revolutionaries had always been the Jews and their hirelings or dupes.

It would have been idle to tell him what every halfway-informed Russian knew, that the liberal and radical socialist movements in Russia were native, born in the early part of the nineteenth century without Jewish participation. There are no major Jewish figures among the Russian revolutionaries prior to the 1870's. One observes in reading the elder Kennan's work, *Siberia and the Exile System*, which made an enormous international impression in its day, the almost total absence of Jews among the many revolutionaries whose maltreatment he describes so indignantly. Yet the material for this work was collected by him, on the spot and with heroic exertions, between June 1885 and March 1886. (He is particularly instructive on the mounting interaction between terrorism and undiscriminating repression.) Even in the late nineteenth and early twentieth centuries there are no Jews among the writers, the Tolstoys and Gorkys and Chekhovs and Korolenkos, to name only a few, whose works, eagerly read in open or clandestine circulation by hundreds of thousands of Russians, were the spiritual force behind the libertarian movement. From the seventies on the Jews appeared in increasing numbers till they represented, and for good reason, a disproportionate ratio of the activists; still, they never achieved anything like a similar ratio among the literary inspirers and ideologues.

Nicholas, as we have seen, was something of a reader. His favorite authors were Marie Corelli (*God's Good Man*), Florence Barclay (*The Rosary*), and Ella Wheeler Wilcox, whom some of us remember with a slight shudder. With a touch of genius for self-disclosure Nicholas has left to posterity a remarkable observation on another literary figure. On November 11, 1910, he wrote to his mother: "As you must have heard, Tolstoy is dead. This event is being much discussed and written about—a great deal too much, in my opinion. Fortunately he was buried quickly, so that not many people were in time for the funeral."

We cannot doubt that Nicholas read *The Protocols of the Elders of Zion* soon after its appearance. His private copy of the 1906 edition, in the imperial binding, was discovered among his effects, and found its way into the Library of Congress in Washington. It was on such stuff that he brooded when he looked for a means of stabilizing the empire.

5

Two half-forgotten incidents, one diplomatic, the other (to coin a word) prediplomatic, give us an additional insight into the dream world that was Nicholas's natural habitat.*

In July 1905 Nicholas met with Wilhelm II at Björkoe, a Baltic coastal village. Wilhelm had been visited by a dazzling inspiration. Why should not he, *Der Allerhöchste*, and Nicholas, the all-autocrat of the Russian empire, become the dam against the flood of anarchy which was rising all over the world? Were not God and history beckoning to them, the two great carriers of the principle of absolutism, to assume this role before it was too late?

To be sure there were some minor complications. France would have to be drawn in, so as to isolate England, Nicholas's land of the "Yids," and there was some incongruity in an alliance between the absolutist monarchical order and the republican country whose official motto was *Liberté, Egalité, Fraternité*. But the incongruity was already there; an old alliance with France had already been negotiated by Nicholas's father, after whom the French had named one of the Seine bridges. Again, England herself was a monarchy, not a republic, but to Nicholas and Wilhelm a constitutional monarchy was perhaps more hateful than an avowed republic. It does not say much for Wilhelm that he could have conceived this plan. The Anglo-French

Entente had already been established, and there was that matter
of 1870, which France could not forget; it says even less for
Wilhelm that he should have believed Nicholas to be in a position, or to have the capacity, to further the plan.

But Nicholas was captivated. Here was not only a magnificent
idea; it was a magnificent opportunity to do something on his
own and show "Sunny" that her admonitions had borne fruit.
He would make "them"—in this case the English—tremble.

The only high official accompanying Nicholas on this rendez-
vous was the Minister of Marine, and it is his signature that
appears below the Czar's on the "treaty." He later offered the
following explanation: "I do not deny that I signed an apparently important document. This is how it happened. His Majesty
summoned me to his stateroom and asked me point-blank: 'Do
you believe in me, Alexei Alexeyevich?' Naturally there could
be only one answer. 'In that case,' His Majesty went on, 'sign
this paper. It is signed, as you can see, by the German Emperor,
and countersigned on Germany's side by the proper officials. Now
the German Emperor wants it countersigned by one of my Ministers.' Of course I applied my signature to the paper."

The treaty of Björkoe might just as well have been drawn up
by two students on a binge. The "prediplomatic" incident is even
more fatuous and more illuminating: and it was Nicholas's brain-
child. Whether or not conceived at Björkoe, it followed close on
the meeting and consisted of a proposal for a Triple Alliance
of another kind, with the Holy See replacing France. It was to
lead a crusade against international Jewry, which, according to
the long preamble, was fomenting revolution everywhere, particularly in Russia, through its two wings, Jewish capitalism and
Jewish socialism.

Touching on the spontaneous world-wide Jewish collections
for the victims of the 1903–6 pogroms and for the arming of
Jewish self-defense groups, the preamble says: "This connection
between the Russian revolutionary movements and foreign Jewish
organizations . . . is confirmed by the wholesale importation of
arms into Russia which is carried on via England." On which

Lucien Wolf, the Anglo-Jewish historian, comments icily: "The self-defense groups . . . and indeed, the Russian revolutionaries themselves, found it quite easy to purchase arms from the Imperial Russian magazines." The preamble continues:

"Nor can it in any way be doubted that the practical direction of the Russian revolutionary movement is in Jewish hands. . . . We also discover with great probability the organizing and intellectual centre where the main supports and feeding organs of the militant hostility to the Government of Russia are hiding themselves. This is the famous pan-Jewish union, the Alliance Israélite Universelle, which possesses gigantic pecuniary means, disposes of an enormous membership and is supported by Masonic Lodges of every description. The principle of the Alliance Israélite Universelle—the all-around triumph of anti-Christian and anti-monarchical Jewry (which has already taken practical possession of France) by means of Socialism which is to serve as a bait for the ignorant masses—could not but find in the State system of Russia an obstacle in its path. That is also the chief watchword of this inexorable campaign at the present time for universal, equal, direct and secret suffrage. . . ."

To the document Nicholas added, immediately above his signature: "Negotiations must be entered into *immediately*. I share entirely the opinions expressed herein" (emphasis in the original).

The signature below the Czar's is that of Count Lamsdorff, Minister for Foreign Affairs. How it comes there is a puzzle, as Lamsdorff, though no *Kirchenlicht* as a statesman, was not of subnormal intelligence. Possibly he was confronted with the same challenge as the Minister of Marine and met it in the same way. On the other hand, Nicholas himself could not have drawn up the document, for though it echoes the ravings of *The Protocols of the Elders of Zion* it is written in impeccable bureaucratic jargon. Whether negotiations were entered into immediately, or ever, is not known. Only one copy of the document, the original with the two signatures, exists; it was found in the Czar's archives.

In his particular brand of anti-Semitism Nicholas did not represent the large majority of Russian conservatives. He sympathized
with the bloodthirsty variety, but added a touch of mysticism
issuing from his deeply religious nature, which was tinged with
pessimism. The Jews were at once a present menace and the ever-
lasting deniers of salvation. When as monarch he sometimes
had to receive representatives of his six million Jews he acted
the gentleman. He was bloodthirsty only by proxy; what his code,
or rather his nerves, forbade him to do, he had others do for him.

If Nicholas did any coherent thinking about Russia's treatment
of the Jews, it was probably along the lines expressed by one of
his Ministers of the Interior, von Plehve, who had been an
instigator of pogroms. Von Plehve's offer to the Jews was succinct,
cynical, and inane: "Give up your revolutionary activities and
we will stop the pogroms." Von Plehve was perfectly aware that
the young Jews were as often in rebellion against their elders
as against the regime; the old generation could do nothing with
them, while the government could easily have put a stop to the
pogroms, as in fact it did later. But by "revolutionary activities"
von Plehve meant also the mildest form of liberalism. He was
assassinated in 1904 in the midst of the series of pogroms for
which he shared so much of the guilt, and even the London
Times, conservative in spirit and favorably inclined toward the
Russian-oriented British policy, would not condemn the assassination.

To complete this unavoidably long but still sketchy picture of
the background something must be said about the massive inefficiency of the machinery of the czarist regime, the butt of so
much Russian satire. It was grounded partly in sheer inertia and
indifference, partly in a tradition of corruption and tyranny on
all levels, and partly in the native character of the bureaucrat,
here developed into unrivaled perfection. Obviously there must
have been many loyal and passably able, even exceptionally able
officials, or the machinery would have been incapable of moving;
but loyal officials were often driven to give government employment to "subversives," or were themselves at odds with the gov-

ernment's barbarous policy. Reading the life of Tolstoy one is alternately staggered by the pettiness of the censorship and bewildered by its liberality. The Rightist hand does not seem to have known what the Leftist hand was doing. Harmless little stories are suppressed, novels like *Resurrection* passed with clumsy cuts that scarcely interfere with the impact of the story; and as with Tolstoy, so with Gorky, Andreyev, Korolenko, and others; and supreme irony, Marx's *Das Kapital* was sold legally.

Thus it was also in other spheres of administration. A single instance will suffice to mirror the state of affairs. Joel Carmichael writes in his introduction to Sukhanov's *The Russian Revolution*: "One of the entertaining oddities of this period, with its characteristic Czarist combination of oppressiveness, mildness and inefficiency is illustrated by his [Sukhanov's] employment during the period of the First World War in the Czarist Government itself, in a section dealing with the irrigation of Turkestan, while at the same time he was being looked for by the police because of his subversive activities. His superior knew quite well who Sukhanov was, but in accordance with the Witte tradition of employing political suspects because of their ability, he willingly protected him. . . . Thus, while Sukhanov was signing his own articles 'Sukhanov' in Gorky's paper *Letopis*, he was dodging the police at home and reporting for work regularly under his real name of Himmer."

These "entertaining oddities" were created to a considerable extent by something other than the desperate shortage of ability, a something already noted by Kennan a generation earlier. Among entrenched bureaucrats there were many who recoiled from the cruelties of the regime; either on principle or out of simple decency they evaded their official duty and in their own way added to the over-all helplessness of the administration.

CHAPTER 9

THE PRODUCER

1

"IT WAS my opinion," said ex-Minister of Justice Shcheglovitov* before the revolutionary board of inquiry in 1917, "that in view of their religious peculiarities the Jews were not fit for judicial work."

A member of the board, who happened to be a Jew, asked: "You found it possible to include this opinion of the Jewish faith in your program as Minister of Justice?" and he cited a number of cases in which this opinion had been implemented.

"I don't know what to say," answered Shcheglovitov.

It was a pity that he lost his tongue at this point, for an explanation would have been of psychological interest. He had not always held such views. At one time he had been a liberal, almost a Leftist, but with his appointment to office in 1906 such a sudden change came over him that he was politically unrecognizable. Overnight the constitutionalist was transformed into a black reactionary, a rabid anti-Semite and an infatuated advocate of absolutism.

Of Shcheglovitov's ability and industry one cannot say enough —nor of the shambles he made of the judiciary, giving rise to the byword "Shcheglovitov justice." Witte wrote of him in 1912: "This has been the most terrible of appointments since my resignation. Shcheglovitov, it may be said, destroyed the courts. It is impossible to tell now where the courts end and where the police and the Azevs begin [Azev was the master, *hors concours*, among the double agents of the security police]. . . . I am convinced that he will be remembered with a curse for many decades to come."

Shcheglovitov's usual nickname was Red Vanka (Johnny), a reference only to his hair, which had not undergone a parallel transformation with his political views; another nickname was Vanka Cain, a reference to a famous Russian bandit-turned-policeman of the seventeenth century. Witte's opinion of Shcheglovitov was colored by personal animosity, but one of the reasons for this animosity certainly imparts some objectivity to the opinion.

Witte was loathed by the reactionaries, for he was a great modernizer, to be ranked in that respect with Peter the Great and Alexander II. To him more than to any other man Russia owed the considerable industrialization she had achieved under Alexander III and the early years of Nicholas II. For Witte, however, modernization meant government as well as industry, and in 1905 he sided with the revolutionary demand for a national legislative body. This was a direct affront to the absolutist principle, which was for Nicholas and the reactionaries the only conceivable foundation of government. Witte was dismissed from office after fifteen years of incomparable service to his country.

It was not enough, however, to dismiss Witte, who at fifty-six was in the prime of life; it was necessary to make sure that he would never return to office and there was only one way of doing this. Anthony, Archbishop of Volhynia, was a man of understanding; in his opinion the struggle against revolution had to begin with the irrevocable elimination of Witte. "Appeals, clever speeches, books are good," wrote the perceptive cleric, "but the first act must be this execution."*

An assassination was attempted, without success. An inquiry was opened, and when Witte asked for a report he was told by the state prosecutor that he could not pursue the matter beyond a certain point because it would lead into high places. "If we arrested such persons and searched their homes," he reported, "we do not know what we should find. . . . Let the Minister of Justice [Shcheglovitov] tell us that we do not have to feel under any restraint, that we may arrest the highly placed . . . and that we should not be held accountable for these acts."*

The stupefying frankness of this communication, addressed as it was to Russia's leading statesman, conveys accurately the spirit brought by Shcheglovitov into the judiciary system. The courts had been the one branch of the government of which Russians could be justifiably proud. Of the great reforms brought in by Alexander II* only the Law Statutes of 1864, pertaining to the organization and procedures of the courts, had remained relatively untouched. In the other branches of government Russia had been going backward while Europe had been going forward. It was Shcheglovitov's determined aim to bring the judicial system into line with the other branches of the government.

Under him judges were appointed, shifted to obscure posts, or driven to resignation by humiliations and harassments according to their views on the sanctity of the autocratic principle: "Judges," he wrote, "are first of all servants of the State . . . and have to reckon with the general interests of the State." But "the general interests of the State" as seen by a man like Shcheglovitov did not necessarily coincide with justice as between private citizens, and so one did not have to be a Jew or even a liberal to fall victim to "Shcheglovitov justice." A judge who dared not risk the displeasure of Shcheglovitov was powerless when any defendant had effective enough connections with the "right-thinking people," and

> *Ein Richter der nicht strafen kann*
> *Gesellt sich endlich zum Verbrecher.*

> (A judge without the power to punish
> Becomes the criminal's accomplice.)

Among the countless witnesses against Shcheglovitov I single out Vladimir Nabokov (father of the poet-novelist-scholar-lepidopterist), to whom the son pays manly and loving tribute in his autobiography. Something of a *grand seigneur,* Nabokov inherited a family tradition of high culture, liberal thought, and public service. His father had played an important part in the judicial reforms that Shcheglovitov was bent on nullifying; and he himself represented the considerable group of upper-class Russians who struggled for several generations for the methodical creation of a democratic order.

Nabokov's protests against the Russian government's vicious attitude toward the Jews long antedated the Beiliss case. His flaming article "The Blood Bath of Kishinev," following the ghastly pogrom of 1903, created an immense sensation. For his membership in the Constitutional Democratic Party, his son tells us, he had "contemptuously forfeited his court title. After he had refused to drink the Czar's health at a certain banquet he coolly advertised his court uniform for sale in the newspapers."

Reviewing the legal story of 1913 in the annual of *Rech* (*Speech*), the widely read liberal newspaper of which he was co-editor, Nabokov cites instance after instance drawn from trials in the principal cities of Russia of the bullying tactics employed by judges and prosecutors against juries refusing to follow tendentious instructions. Under such conditions, protests Nabokov, "relations between governmental organs and the jury can become absolutely abnormal." In one case the foreman of a jury lodged a complaint that the "nervousness" of the judge, as he prudently called it, had a disturbing effect on the jury. "In case after case the Presiding Judge makes derisive remarks about the jury after an acquittal of the accused." In April of 1913 "there were several conflicts between the Presiding Judge and the jury." A foreman "asks the Presiding Judge not to interrupt the attorney for the defense because it prevents the jury from concentrating on the case." "Members of the jury asked for protection against the insults of the Assistant Prosecutor." Since when, asks Nabokov (that is, since the appointment of

Shcheglovitov), "did such cases become possible? . . . And can
we say that the higher authorities react to such cases in the
correct and desirable way? Alas, we cannot."

What Nabokov thought of the behavior of the court in the
Beiliss trial, which he attended as special correspondent, will
appear below.

The board of inquiry referred to at the beginning of this
chapter was set up after the February 1917 revolution. Its
official title was the Extraordinary Commission* of the Provisional Government (I shall refer to it as the Commission) and
its purpose was to look into the derelictions and delinquencies
of the overturned regime. The Commission sat until the Bolsheviks took over in October of that year, and the testimony was
published in seven volumes under the title of *Padeniye Tsarskovo Rezhima* (*The Fall of the Czarist Regime*). The men who
appeared before it were a mixed bag of bumbling officials and
of rascals of high and low degree, and one looks in vain for an
example of dignity in adversity. Almost literally overnight the
masters of the millions, strutting about with such assurance in
the panoply of office, become the confused and hangdog testi-
fiers to their own depravity and nullity. Shcheglovitov wriggles
and blusters; Beletsky, the once dreaded Chief of Police, breaks
down and snivels: "I blush for myself. . . . I am glad to confess
. . . I have a little girl of fifteen at school, a son; his schoolmates
may tell him about this."

"Glad to confess" is touchingly hypocritical. Like the others,
Beletsky tried hard to lie his way out and broke down only
under relentless probing and when he was confronted with
official documents he had either forgotten or hoped had been
destroyed.

Shcheglovitov and Beletsky are our two most important witnesses on the Beiliss case, but Shcheglovitov is especially interesting because of the light he throws on the condition to which
he had reduced the courts. He understood with perfect clarity
the meaning of his general policy and of his role in the Beiliss
case. We may say that the frame-up of Beiliss was the climax

of his career, and it was characteristic of the man that in the very year of the Beiliss trial he could, in an ecstacy of mendacity, repeatedly boast before the Duma and the Conference of Judges that he had inspired the Russian judiciary system with a nobility of spirit it had never known before. "Russia," he cried, "is now reaching the peak of modern scientific justice, and in the nearest future it will stand on a level unreached by Western European states which entered on the road of civilization long before us."*

Shcheglovitov's conception of "modern scientific justice" may be gathered from his own words in the stenographic report of the Commission.

"My main purpose [in assuming the post of Minister of Justice] was to keep the Department on the high level required by the Statutes of 1864."

By what means? asked the chairman of the Commission. By the selection of the right kind of functionaries, answered Shcheglovitov. What were the criteria? He chose, said Shcheglovitov, "persons of firm character and with monarchical principles, capable of safeguarding the law." But such qualities, objected the chairman, belonged in politics, not in the courtroom. "Undoubtedly," answered Shcheglovitov. The stenographic report unfortunately does not indicate the effect produced by this candid admission.

So far, however, it was plain sailing. Shcheglovitov recognized freely that as Minister of Justice he had played the politician. But when the chairman got down to cases, disarming candor gradually gave way to equivocation and lapses of memory.

"When naming or dismissing judges, weren't you guided by the opinions of private persons?"

"I don't remember."

The chairman pointed out that if judges throughout Russia were to follow the example of the Minister of Justice, conditions "could become intolerable for the Russian people. . . . You have written on law, you have been a professor of law." Yes, admitted Shcheglovitov, "it was a dangerous road."

Then what about the automatic recommendations for pardon that he submitted for the Czar's signature on behalf of members of Rightist organizations charged with various crimes? "That," answered Shcheglovitov, "was so to speak the political tendency of the times." However: "This is probably one of the big mistakes of my life."

The chairman pressed in closer. "How did it come about that in asking the Emperor to exercise pardon you sometimes offered as motivation [of the crimes]: 'They acted out of animosity toward the Jews'?"

Shcheglovitov's answer to this question is a curiosity of judicial reasoning. "This, probably, is explained by the fact that animosity against the Jews exists in certain classes of the population; this could lead to certain excesses, in which hatred and passion overpowered reason. . . . This explains such expressions in my reports to the Emperor." The robbing, beating, and even murder of Jews is thus represented as part of a folk tradition that had to be taken into account; it would follow that the more the folk hated the Jews the less reprehensible would be the murder of Jews. However, Shcheglovitov omitted the crucial point, his eagerness to please the Emperor; it was the Emperor's animosity against the Jews that was the deciding factor in Shcheglovitov's calculations, particularly with respect to the Beiliss case.

The Commission reverted to Shcheglovitov's pressure on judges. He had made it a practice to send inspectors or agents to attend trials of a political nature and report to him on the attitude of the judges. He wanted to be informed, as he put it, "whether they had been sufficiently severe." Leniency could result in transfers or dismissals—"with their consent," he added. "Of course," said one member of the Commission who had been sentenced to imprisonment for protesting against the Beiliss trial, "according to law you could not act otherwise; but we see that very often it was a forced consent." "There were cases," answered Shcheglovitov, coyly, "where I had to persuade the judge personally to change his post."

"As a result of your inspectors' reports?"

"It could be."

2

Beletsky's testimony before the Commission is somewhat less offensive than Shcheglovitov's because he was not an initiator of evil. As head of the police he had inherited the system of double agents and *agents provocateurs* that imparted a special character to the Russian government. The trouble with double-agentry in Russia was (1) that the police agents could, in their eagerness to ingratiate themselves with subversives, overdo their role and become subversives themselves; (2) that subversives could join the police force and get jobs as double agents. One of the products of the system was the famous Azev, already mentioned. He arranged for the assassination of high personages (e.g., the Czar's uncle, Grand Duke Sergei Alexandrovich) in order to consolidate his position with the terrorist revolutionaries, and betrayed revolutionaries to consolidate his position with the *okhrana*. There are various theories as to whom Azev was really working for, or meant to work for, besides himself, some inclining to the view that at least toward the end he lost track. Beletsky pleaded that he had modified the system insofar as it applied to the army, for there it had resulted in demoralization; as an afterthought he conceded that the system was immoral as well as self-defeating.

Why, then, did he consider the system justifiable as applied to the civilian population? There was no other way, he explained, of getting at the identity or plots of the revolutionaries; moreover double-agentry was a standard practice in civilized countries, including republican France. This was a partial truth; all countries use double agents to ferret out subversives, though not in anything like the numbers used in Russia. Peculiar to Russia, however, was the use of the double agent as *agent provocateur*. As the latter he not only spied on revolutionaries but he also looked for individuals who might be susceptible to liberal ideas and coaxed them into imprudent or careless expressions of opinion. Or he would inspire revolutionaries to acts of terrorism, in the attempted performance of which they would be seized by the police—or perhaps not, when it was an Azev engaged in more complicated maneuvers.

One brilliant police performance in Beletsky's time was its cooperation in the election to the Duma of a certain Malinovsky.* Special measures had to be taken by the government to regularize his candidacy, as he happened to be facing a charge of burglary at the time. As a member of the Duma Malinovsky was charged by the *okhrana* with the duty of delivering extreme Leftist inflammatory speeches, the purpose of which was to discredit the Duma and make it unworkable. This may or may not have fallen in with Malinovsky's own inclinations. After the revolution he claimed that he had always been a good Bolshevik, which in itself may have meant nothing, but the great Lenin himself vouched furiously for Malinovsky's honesty, directing the usual stream of invective at his detractors. In the end Malinovsky was executed by the Bolsheviks, which is certainly no proof that he had not been a good Bolshevik.

Perhaps, as in Azev's case, one will never know if Malinovsky had any political intentions at all. He did in fact help to make the Duma unworkable, but that was wanted by both the extreme Right and the extreme Left.

It was a bad system, confessed Beletsky. "I have always reproached myself with it." But he pleaded that he had done what he could under it. Besides removing the *agents provocateurs* from the army he had, after some delay, corrected one of the ugliest practices of the *okhrana*, namely, the training of political spies among high-school students. Their function had been to keep an eye on their fellow students and to act as "collaborators" with those who expressed liberal or revolutionary opinions.

At this point in the inquiry the chairman of the Commission, a respected jurist, who had maintained a judicial calm throughout, could no longer contain himself. "There were secret agents of the *okhrana* in the high schools? And for a whole year you tolerated this in the senior classes? Didn't it occur to you that the enrollment of secret collaborators among the students of high schools was in itself a crime, quite apart from the moral aspect, the corruption of family life?"

Beletsky, who had shown such lachrymose concern for the moral stability of his own family, and particularly for that of his son and daughter, both high-school students, could only beat his breast again.

At national headquarters Beletsky played a part second only to Shcheglovitov's in the setting up of the Beiliss case. That too we shall examine in due course.

CHAPTER 10

THE UNTEACHABLES

...ts across the Beiliss
Beiliss case is part
with which we al-
vestigating Magis-
mery, Ivanov; the
o—he who made
del Beiliss in the
course is Czar
N   and who later,
ou   dictment of the
pr   But the central
figu   o direct con-
nec

Tl   ost strangely
for tl   of Dostoevsky.
The l   respected Jewish family of
Kiev,   into what he himself described as an

Anarchist-Communist, with complicated views on the subject of means and ends. He was for several years in the pay of the Kiev security police, under the direction of Colonel Ivanov. Why Bogrov took a spy's money—it was a paltry amount for a man of his means, a hundred or a hundred and fifty rubles a month—has not been explained; he himself refused to explain it. According to Ivanov his services were not worth even that amount.

From Bogrov's own depositions, made between his arrest and the day of his execution, it is impossible to fathom his motives. On the one hand he declared that in 1907, when he was twenty-three years old, he had already formed the idea of assassinating a high official as a spectacular protest against the regime; on the other hand it appeared that he committed the crime in order to rehabilitate himself with the revolutionaries. But why had he entered Colonel Ivanov's service in the first place? He told Investigating Magistrate Fenenko: "Soon after joining the anarchist group, I became disappointed with their activities. . . . Being still a party member, I decided to inform the Kiev *okhrana* about their activities. This decision was due partly to my desire to have more money. I refuse to explain why I wanted that money." Actually he was never short of money, and regarding his first venture into double-agentry he said: "When I came to St. Petersburg in 1910, I decided to join the *okhrana* in order to be *au courant* with its activities"—and this was after he had been in Ivanov's employ.

Whatever else was going on in Bogrov's mind it seems certain that he was also occupied if only peripherally with the Jewish question. When he was asked why he did not shoot the Czar, which he could have done by simply turning his pistol in the direction of the imperial box a few feet away, he answered: "I am a Jew; if I had killed Nicholas there would have been a pogrom."* Certainly the assassination of the Czar by a Jew might very well have unleashed a series of pogroms; but the assassination of Stolypin was, as we shall see, no great service to the Jews.

The manner in which Bogrov was able to enter the theater

with a pistol concealed under his coat gives us an additional glimpse—if one were needed—into the confusions and labyrinths of cross-purposes in which the conspiratorial worlds of government and revolutionaries were trapped. Colonel Kuliabko, one of the subordinate security officers, was in charge of admissions. To him Bogrov unfolded a cock-and-bull story of a couple who had come to Kiev for the purpose of assassinating one of the ministers who would be present at the performance; only he, Bogrov, would be able to identify the couple, who had somehow obtained admission tickets. On the strength of this story Bogrov himself obtained an admission ticket from Kuliabko. Such, at any rate, was Kuliabko's explanation; honest or not, its absurdity was such that rumors were immediately born—and they have never died—that Stolypin's assassination had been the work of the police, at the instigation of extreme Rightists. The rumors can only have gathered vitality from several circumstances: the hostility displayed by the extreme Right toward Stolypin; the decline of Stolypin's popularity with the Czar; the Czar's protection of the officer in over-all charge of security at the assassination; and, finally, the extremely mild punishment visited on Kuliabko. He was merely dismissed from the service, and I have been told* that this Napoleon of the Lukyanovka turned insurance agent— an odd transformation, all things considered.

One of the reasons for Stolypin's growing unpopularity with the extreme Right was undoubtedly his refusal to play up to its rabid anti-Semitism. A thoroughgoing realist, Stolypin understood that the excessive repression of the Jews harmed the country at home and abroad. As early as 1906—the year he was called in by Nicholas to head the government—he had moved the Council of Ministers to recommend a mild improvement in the status of the Jews. Nicholas's response was immediate and drastic. He wrote Stolypin: "An inner voice more and more resolutely tells me not to take the responsibility for this decision. . . . I bear before God and the country the responsibility for all the government powers established by me, and I am always ready to give an accounting for everything to God."* The inner voice Nicholas heard was reinforced by two hundred telegrams from Rightists protesting against the recommendation of the Council of Ministers.

Stolypin had not been able to make any headway against the anti-Semitism of Nicholas and the extreme Rightists, but he had been a restraining influence. With him gone there was a perceptible deterioration in the Jewish position and an intensification of the continuous cold pogrom, taking the form of increased expulsions of Jews from towns and villages into the crowded area of the Pale of Settlement. These measures were ostensibly intended to deliver the local populations from the hands of the Jewish mercantile class, the theory, or pretext, being that the non-Jewish mercantile class was less profit-conscious. It was, however, demonstrated over and over again that true-Russian merchants were certainly not less apt than their Jewish competitors to exploit villagers and townsmen. There were occasional protests by peasants: they got better and cheaper service from the Jews, and they derived no satisfaction from being rooked by their blood brothers.*

Then, as if to advertise its obsession to the world, the administration sharpened its discrimination against foreign Jews visiting or seeking to visit Russia, either refusing them admission or placing them under travel restrictions not applied to non-Jewish foreigners. This practice had already been protested by a number of countries; in 1911 it led to a humiliating rebuke from the American government, when President Taft declared it to be in contravention of the commercial treaty of 1832.

One cannot help wondering whether the Beiliss conspiracy would ever have come to a head if Stolypin had remained alive and in power. Shcheglovitov could not have managed it without the active assistance of the Department of Police, which was a section of the Ministry of the Interior. Beletsky, the Chief of Police, willingly cooperated with Shcheglovitov, but the first phases of the conspiracy were kept a secret from Makarov, the Minister of the Interior. Later, when Makarov was replaced by N. A. Maklakov, there was no need for secrecy. But even with the Czar's encouragement the ignorance or connivance of the

Minister of the Interior was not enough; the Prime Minister too
had to be kept in ignorance or won over. It is difficult to think
of Stolypin as conniving at the ruinous imbecilities of the Beiliss
conspiracy; with the nonentities who followed him it was
different.

2

Seen in retrospect, the assiduity of the Russian imperial administration in the pursuit of self-destruction is an awesome thing;
and nowhere does it stand out more strikingly than in the
grouping of forces round the Beiliss case.

The extreme or radical Right on which Nicholas and the
administration placed their ultimate hopes owed its existence as
a parliamentary bloc to Stolypin. When Nicholas was forced by
the revolution of 1905 to grant the country a constitution, the
first two Dumas elected under it were predominantly liberal and
Leftist. Both Dumas were dissolved in a hurry by Nicholas, and
between the second and third Dumas Nicholas, with Stolypin as
his strong man, subverted the constitution, or Fundamental Laws,
as they were called, on which the Duma rested. The new constitution contained this preamble: "The supreme autocratic power
belongs to the Emperor of all the Russias. Acceptance of his
authority is dictated not alone by fear and conscience, but also
by God Himself." But more important than even this ominous
declaration, which unlike the English king's "Defender of the
Faith" was meant literally, was the sweeping and illegal change
in the electoral laws, the purpose of which was to favor the
Right, and which resulted in the return of a bloc of fifty
Rightists to the Duma.*

It is possible that Stolypin arrived too late on the scene to
save Russia; it is possible that he chose the wrong methods; but
he was a considerable figure, determined, courageous, and persistent. He aimed first at the pacification of the country by the
crushing of the terrorists of the Left, and to that end set up a
legalized terrorism of the Right. He resorted to an unparalleled
use of the emergency measure known as the "State of Reinforced

Protection"—we have noted it as the law under which Beiliss was arrested—and of field courts-martial that superseded the civil courts in any area designated by the administration. In this way the administration could deal summarily with Leftist political offenders of all shades. In the use of these measures Stolypin proceeded with craft and ruthlessness, and his devious methods led to the coining of the word *Stolypinshchina*—"the Stolypin way" —while a phrase to which his hanging propensities gave currency was "the Stolypin necktie."

Stolypin had creative plans, too. He was aware that the condition of the vast majority of Russia's hundred million peasants had become unendurable, and he was concerned to prevent an explosion. He exerted himself with some success to create a landowning middle- and upper-class peasantry as a stabilizer; and according to his biographer—an apologist, to be sure—he hoped some day to liberalize the constitution. But what he is remembered for is his subversion of it and his bloody concessions to the extreme Rightists.

But extreme Rightists are not won over by concessions; with them it is always *va banque*. Stolypin was a disappointment to Nicholas and his supporters; with all his subversion of the constitution, with all his ruthless repression of the Left, there was a taint of reasonableness in him—witness his tentative move in favor of the Jews; and while discounting completely the rumors that his assassination was arranged by Rightists, there is good ground for believing that if he had lived he would not long have remained in power.

He had lost the support of the Czar and the Rightists, and in his wooing of them he had alienated the genuine conservatives. His ruthlessness had also helped to bring the liberal spirit out of the stupor into which it had fallen when the country failed to rebel against the subversion of the constitution. Now the elections for the fourth Duma were at hand, and the Rightists, having tasted blood (this hackneyed phrase has a certain inverse aptness in connection with the Beiliss case), wanted more. The Jewish question was bound to come to the fore as one of the

symbols, perhaps the most characteristic, of the renewed struggle.
Kennan thus describes the situation as it was seven months
before Stolypin's assassination in September 1911:

> The attitude of the Government was determined partly by the
> personal hatred of the Czar for the Jews and partly by considera-
> tions of a political character. The Ministry at that time did not
> have a trustworthy majority in the Duma. The Octobrists [moderate
> conservatives] . . . who held the balance of power were dis-
> appointed with the repressive measures of Stolypin and were show-
> ing a disposition to join the Constitutional Democrats [liberals].
> In February 1911 . . . 166 members of the Duma united in a
> bill for the complete abolition of the Pale of Jewish Settlement. . . .
> This seemed to the Czar and the Ministers a very disquieting
> symptom of disaffection.

The bill died in committee. It stood no chance of being passed
if it had reached the floor. But there it was, a sign that the
liberal spirit was returning. The extreme Right, impatient with
what it believed to be the inadequacy of Stolypin's counter-
terror, was looking for some slogan, some issue, that would provide a knockout blow to Liberalism in the coming elections. And
just then, a month after the contumacious bill had been proposed
in the Duma, came the Yushchinsky murder and the Blood
Accusation clamor raised round it by Golubev and the Kiev
reactionary organizations.

This might be the thing! There were the exchanges we have
noted between the Golubev-Chaplinsky combination in Kiev and
the Shcheglovitov-Beletsky combination in St. Petersburg. At
first with a certain degree of caution, and then with increasing
recklessness, the administration flung itself into the conspiracy.
With the death of Stolypin—the man who was its last chance
if it had any chance at all—the administration proceeded enthusiastically to cut its own throat.

Some years ago, in Durban, South Africa, an attendant in the
city zoo showed me how monkeys were captured. A narrow
opening, just wide enough to admit a monkey's extended paw,

is bored in a heavy coconut, which is then left on the ground in any area frequented by wild monkeys. One of them comes upon the coconut, inserts his paw with difficulty, and grabs a fistful of pulp. He cannot withdraw his paw without opening it and relinquishing the pulp, and this he will under no circumstances do. As the captor approaches, the monkey tries to make off, dragging the heavy coconut with him. Thus encumbered, he is easily taken. Captured, he still refuses to open his fist, and the coconut has to be smashed.

PART THREE

THE SECOND

PHASE

CHAPTER 11

RE-ENTER
KRASOVSKY

1

By THE SPRING OF 1912 the Kiev administration was as we
have seen taking a dim view of the case against Beiliss. All it
had was the collection of weird depositions obtained from the
lamplighters and the Wolf-Woman, to which it had added the
even weirder testimony of the convict spy Kozachenko and, by
way of climax, the deposition of Vasily Cheberyak. As Governor
Girs wrote the Deputy Minister of the Interior on April 19: "It
is certain, according to the information in my possession, that
the case will end in the acquittal of the defendant." But the initiative was no longer with Kiev, and perhaps not even with
Shcheglovitov. The issue had been taken up nationally by the extreme Right; the Czar had been practically assured by Shcheglovitov that Beiliss was one of the murderers. There was nothing
the administration could do but go forward, hoping that some-

thing plausible could still be improvised. And, in any case, the conviction of Beiliss was a secondary objective. It would still be a great victory if the jury could be persuaded that a ritual murder had taken place and if such a verdict were issued to the Russian people and the world.

Meanwhile it was a vital part of the strategy to cover up the administration's moral certainty that the murderers were Cheberyak and the Troika. The acquittal of Beiliss might indeed, as Colonel Shredel wrote, "lead to a just rebuke for the hastiness of their [the administration's] conclusions, nay the one-sidedness exhibited during the investigation"; but that would be nothing compared to the scandal which would follow if it were revealed that the administration had deliberately suppressed the overwhelming evidence pointing to Cheberyak and the gang. For then it would not be simply a question of collusion and perversion of justice; the whole legend of the Blood Accusation would be imperiled; its manufacturers or perpetuators would be shown up, caught red-handed, and instead of a storm of anti-Jewish feeling there would be a wave of disgust and a knitting of brows: "So that's how it was done!" Even the incorrigibly hallucinatory anti-Semites would be infuriated and would cry: "Clumsy idiots!"

Hence the dismissal and persecution of Detective Mishchuk and, more drastic, the dismissal of an important figure like Prosecutor Brandorf. Hence also the removal of Detective Krasovsky from the case and his reassignment to his rural post. But hence, too—and this was the inescapable predicament— Kiev's need for a good man on the job to collect the final proofs against Cheberyak, to be held in reserve as a measure of self-protection.

The third one to be given the Beiliss case was Detective Kirichenko. It was he who had interrogated Zhenya Cheberyak and had caught the mother signaling frantically to her son. I do not pretend to understand this extraordinary choice. Surely anyone, even if a second- or third-rater, would have been better than the pupil and admirer of the man who was disgraced for refusing to sell out his talents and his office to the conspirators.

But there it was; Kirichenko, like Krasovsky, took over and worked under the direction of Ivanov.

2

But they were not content to leave ill enough alone. It irked them that Krasovsky should have been let off more easily than Mishchuk and Brandorf, and he the slyest of the three, pretending at first that he put stock in the ritual murder theory. The official statement of Krasovsky's transfer reads: "He resumed his former position as Head of Rural Police."* There was no hint of punishment in it, and that could not be allowed to stand. For four months they left Krasovsky alone, then in January 1912 he was thrown out of the service, thereby releasing from official restraints an able and resourceful detective who had two powerful motives to resume the Beiliss investigation in a private capacity: embitterment, and the determination to vindicate himself.

For another three months Krasovsky remained in his rural home, brooding. In April 1912 he reappeared in Kiev as a private investigator, and his activities became extremely dangerous. It was suspected, and the suspicion was later shown to be well founded, that he got in touch at once with his former pupil Kirichenko and that Kirichenko was helping him clandestinely; thus Krasovsky had the double advantage of freedom of action and access to the plans of the administration.

There were some downright pathetic scenes at the trial, more than a year later, when the cooperation of Kirichenko and Krasovsky came into the open. State Prosecutor Vipper could not get over the knavery of it. Addressing Kirichenko he said: "You informed Krasovsky about the investigations? And you knew at the time that Krasovsky was an ex-detective? He recommended you as his outstanding pupil*—and here you divulge to an unofficial person information which should be divulged only to an official?"

> KIRICHENKO: I was acting only in the interests of the case, and since Krasovsky, as my former superior, had been on it, I informed him.

PROSECUTOR: And so, in the interests of the case, you informed your former boss? I don't quite understand.

Nor did Golubev and his aides understand Krasovsky's perfidy in pretending to go along with the ritual murder version. At the trial Krasovsky was able to declare openly: "I could see that Golubev and the others belonging to the monarchists believed fanatically in ritual murder, and they made an uproar when opposed. All the papers were printing articles about it, and I thought it wiser not to object, but just to say: 'It might be so.'" Golubev's right-hand man, a certain Rozmitalsky,* a shady character, almost wept on the stand. He had been "stunned," he said, by Krasovsky's trickery. He had been taken in completely; he had been immensely pleased by Krasovsky's stand: "It looked ideal to me. It was in the spirit of the articles in the papers."

Soon after his reappearance in Kiev, Krasovsky was summoned by the investigating magistrate. The man in charge of the Beiliss case was no longer the honest and obstinate Fenenko; he had at last been taken off it, replaced by a notorious anti-Semite, Mashkevich, sent down by Shcheglovitov from St. Petersburg. Mashkevich wanted to know what was going on, and to him Krasovsky said boldly: "Owing to the interference of the Rightist organizations this case could not develop along normal lines. The Rightist organizations think that this is a ritual murder, and I am convinced that this is an ordinary murder, committed by ordinary criminals from motives of revenge."*

Four days later Krasovsky was arrested on the charge of embezzlement while in office. It was alleged that in 1903—that is, nine years earlier—he had defrauded a prisoner of the sum of sixteen kopeks (eight cents). On this charge he remained in jail for six weeks, was tried in the Kiev District Court, and acquitted. He resumed his investigations with increased vigor and notable results.

3

The figure who now enters the Beiliss case may serve as a general warning that the recommendations of even the most foolish busybody cannot always be safely ignored in the pursuit of a serious and difficult objective. The journalist Brazul-Brushkovsky* (hereinafter Brazul) was employed by the Kiev liberal daily *Kievskaya mysl* (*Kiev Opinion,* literally *Thought*). He took it into his head and persuaded his employers that he could get to the bottom of the Beiliss case, and he was assigned to it toward the end of 1911.

Brazul was a Russian with a Jewish wife and there were idealistic motives in his determination to clear Beiliss and expose the ritual murder charge as a conspiracy; he was also hopeful, as he admitted at the trial, of achieving fame and an increase in salary. He must at least be credited with pertinacity; he was on the case for nearly a year.

As a journalist Brazul was moderately gifted; as a detective something of a joke. He began by cultivating Vera Cheberyak, on the theory that she was not a participant in the crime, but could find out through her connections in the underworld who the murderers were. For six months he wined and dined her and doled out to her small sums of money in the belief that she was genuinely concerned in helping him. He put implicit faith in her word, and continued to do so when everyone else who had had anything to do with her regarded her as, among other things—all of them unsavory—a pathological liar. A newspaper colleague to whom he introduced her at a restaurant warned him, after spending half an hour with her: "This woman probably always lies. She lies even when she tells the truth, and if she talks in her sleep she probably lies then, too." But Brazul's faith in Cheberyak could not be shaken. He said in court: "She created a kind of atmosphere which made me trust her."

And so he believed her when she told him that Miffle, her youthful French lover, was one of the murderers, and that she was going to get him because of the beating he had given her and also because it was Miffle's sister who had poisoned her children. He also believed her when she said that one of the key men in the murder was to be found in Kharkov, and if Brazul would take her to Kharkov she would get some valuable information.

Had Brazul been the only one to swallow the Kharkov story no harm would have been done. Unfortunately he managed to persuade Arnold Margolin, who was then (December 1911) Beiliss's attorney, that this was a crucial development and that it was essential for Margolin himself to be in on it. This was about as foolish a step as Margolin could have taken. As a lawyer he knew that if the report of a meeting between him and Cheberyak got about he would forfeit his right to represent Beiliss at the trial. And get about it did; Cheberyak saw to that.

Her version of the meeting as she repeated it at the trial created a sensation. She denied that she had suggested the Kharkov trip; on the contrary, it was Brazul who had coaxed and bullied her into it; he had promised to introduce her there to "an important personage," a member of the Duma, who would help her husband to get back his job, which he had lost because of the notoriety attaching to his home. She said that she went to Kharkov tearfully, timidly, reluctantly, suspecting she knew not what. When she got into her hotel room she quickly wrote her name on an inconspicuous part of the wall, and tore a page out of the hanging calendar to be able to prove she had been there—hardly the precautions a tearful and terrified woman would think of.

In court she told the following story: from her own, more modest hotel she was conducted to another, the best in Kharkov, and there she met the "member of the Duma," who was none other than Margolin, "the man sitting there" in court. He had not wanted to meet her in Kiev, so he had asked Brazul to arrange the meeting in Kharkov. And why had he wanted to meet her? In order to offer her 40,000 rubles if she would take the murder of Yushchinsky on herself. He, Margolin, would see to it that she would never be brought to trial. Let her only sign the paper he had brought along, confessing her guilt; the greatest lawyers in the country would be placed at her disposal to protect her from indictment.

Margolin, on the stand, admitted freely that he had talked with Cheberyak in Kharkov. He had gone there on business unrelated to the Beiliss case, and he had agreed to the meeting against his better judgment. He had yielded to the importunations of his old friend Brazul, who was an honorable man but one quite incapable of conducting this sort of inquiry, which ought to be left to professionals.

The Kharkov incident was played up for all it was worth by the prosecution, and it was a field day for the Rightist press. A wealthy Jew in a secret meeting with the state's key witness, Beiliss's counsel barred from defending him, etc., etc. The story would have been rather more effective if Cheberyak had not as a liar lacked all sense of proportion and form. That Brazul had been a ninny and Margolin imprudent the defense could not deny; but the idea of offering Cheberyak, the smalltime underworld trollop, a fortune for a promise that she would have been an idiot to keep once she got the money, the idea that she would trust Margolin to deliver the money and provide for her immunity—even the prosecution had to sweat blood pretending to take it seriously. Still, it had the satisfaction of giving Margolin a miserable time of it on the witness stand.

What Cheberyak hoped to get out of the Kharkov trip beyond a little junket we do not know;* nor why she suddenly came up with the preposterous story that Miffle was one of the murderers and that Miffle's sister was the poisoner of the Cheberyak children. But the gullible Brazul snatched at it, and in January 1912 submitted to the investigating magistrate "serious evidence" of the guilt of Miffle and—once again!—some members of the Yushchinsky family. The document was not worth a second glance; but it got into the papers somehow, and it understandably sent Miffle into a fury. This, unlike the sulfuric acid his sweetheart had thrown at his face, was carrying a lovers' quarrel too far, for squealing is the one unforgivable crime in the underworld. Miffle appeared before the investigating magistrate and denounced Cheberyak for a number of petty crimes which had never been solved. In the tangle of official forces at play, Cheberyak, in spite of Golubev's and Chaplinsky's protection, was indicted for theft and served a short prison term in 1912.

We note with some astonishment that the wretched husband could not appeal to them for a job: they could not even prevent the eviction of the Cheberyaks from their old apartment.

These *gaffes* of Brazul's, like many others he committed, are irrelevant to the main course of our narrative; I have introduced them only as another reminder of the mysterious ways of Providence. It was through the artless Brazul that the clinching evidence against Cheberyak and the Troika came into the hands of Krasovsky, compelling the administration to retract its first indictment, call off the trial scheduled for May 25, 1912, and look around for new material and new methods for framing Beiliss.

4

Until the spring of 1912 when Krasovsky returned to Kiev as a private investigator, Brazul had worked alone, with the not very brilliant results just outlined. It is not surprising that Krasovsky wanted Brazul out of the way and rebuffed his suggestions at cooperation. Fortunately Brazul had one great asset —the insensitivity that is the first prerequisite of the inquiring reporter. He refused to be rebuffed. He had found another lead —or rather, it came to him without his seeking—and he pestered Krasovsky into following it up.

In the winter of 1911–12 a young man by the name of Sergei Makhalin was living in a village near Kiev. He was a revolutionary with no particular party labels, or perhaps with many labels, simultaneous or successive. From his voluminous testimony at the trial we gather only that he loved the plain people and hated the regime. As a boy of thirteen or fourteen, he told the court, he had witnessed a pogrom, and though he was not a Jew the horror of it had sunk deep into him, changing forever the direction of his life. At the age of sixteen he was an "activist," and had been arrested for taking part in an "expropriation," the trade name for robbery for the benefit of revolutionary parties. By the time he had reached his majority and came into the Beiliss case he had served three prison sentences.

He had been a railroad hand, a student at an agricultural college, and a private tutor. His life's ambition, unusual among revolutionaries, was to become an opera singer; and what was not so unusual among revolutionaries, he had been a double agent, serving, like Bogrov, under Ivanov in Kiev. Unfortunately this episode in Makhalin's life was suppressed at the trial in order to spare Ivanov, and it only came out during the investigations of the Commission in 1917. However, this connection had been terminated by 1911, when Makhalin was living in the village, supporting himself by giving private lessons. He found the going hard because he could never refuse a pupil too poor to pay and, as he said at the trial, "spreading sparks of light" meant more to him than bread and butter. However, toward the end of that year he came into a small legacy from a grandfather, and without modifying his principles or abating his activities he gave rein to another somewhat unrevolutionary ambition, which was to cut a dash as a dandy. His foppish turnout at the trial moved the state prosecutor to sarcastic comment.

Makhalin first heard of the Beiliss case in September 1911 and his interest was aroused by its ritual murder aspect. A common murder was no business of his, but the provocation of pogroms touched him on the raw, plunged him back into the nightmarish experience of his boyhood and set off in him a compulsion to do something about it.

But, again like Bogrov, he had a particular personal motive, namely, to clear himself in the eyes of fellow revolutionaries who suspected that as a double agent he had really worked for the *okhrana*; and it occurred to him that nothing could serve his purpose better than helping to expose the government's Blood Accusation conspiracy. That it was a conspiracy, regardless of whether or not Beiliss had been one of Yushchinsky's murderers, he took for granted. However, he had to move into the case with great caution, and he hesitated for months, waiting for some kind of opening.

In January he read Brazul's report denouncing Miffle and the

Yushchinsky family. He then remembered having met Brazul once, and he wondered whether the bourgeois journalist would consent to work with him. A month later he decided to risk it, arranged a secret meeting with Brazul in Kiev, and offered his services.

It was as he had expected. Brazul received him coolly; an extreme Leftist, undoubtedly with an ax of his own to grind, was not the kind of collaborator he needed. Nor did the youthful Makhalin impress Brazul with his personal qualifications; against which it must be said that Makhalin's impression of Brazul was even less favorable. "A flippant man," he told the court, "devoid of discretion or experience." Nevertheless Makhalin was insistent and Brazul yielded. Actually Makhalin was not thinking of either himself or Brazul as the *deus ex machina*. He had someone else in view, a friend of his, one Karayev, a revolutionary like himself, and not much older, but with an extraordinary personality and history.

In Karayev we again meet a figure straight out of Dostoevsky's *The Possessed*. In his deposition to the investigating magistrate made a year before the trial he described himself as a "nobleman" (a member of the gentry) and native of the Caucasus, brought up in the Orthodox faith. His police record, as read out at the trial itself, portrayed him as a man in furious revolt against the existing order. At twenty-five he had already served four prison sentences, from several months to three and a half years. His own crimes were political, but in his passionate sympathy for the underdog he made no distinction between political and ordinary criminals; anyone who fell foul of the system was its victim; to be in prison for any reason at all was to be a rebel against the system, that is, a revolutionary.

Before Karayev was twenty-five he had become a legend in the underworld. Whether or not the gangsters, pimps, thieves, con men, and the like who repeated with awe the tales of his exploits quite grasped his philosophy, they admired him extravagantly, and most of all for his arrogant bearing toward authority. Krasovsky, reading out Karayev's police record in court, reported: "He never bowed to anyone and was always rebellious." On one occasion when he was being interrogated in prison he complained of toothache and the warden laughed at him; thereupon he seized the lamp on the table and dashed it to the floor. Later he killed the warden, was tried for it, and acquitted. It is next to impossible to believe these stories: yet they were told in court and passed unchallenged.

This was the man needed in the Beiliss case, said Makhalin; he spoke the lingo of the underworld, he moved in it freely, an honorary member, and he knew its ways, its lines of communications. He had only to ask who had done the job.

Karayev, having recently completed a prison sentence, was also living near Kiev. Like Makhalin and Bogrov he had (of course!) been, or was accused by some fellow revolutionaries of having been, a double agent (one wonders occasionally how anyone in the *okhrana* or the revolutionary movements ever trusted anyone else), and he too was looking for rehabilitation. But, as Makhalin was soon to discover, he drew the line at playing the stool pigeon and betraying murderers who loved and trusted him to that enemy of mankind, the police.

When the two young men met in a hotel room in Kiev and Makhalin explained what he had not been able to explain in letters, Karayev almost jumped out of his skin. He drew a Browning, as if he intended to shoot Makhalin, and stormed up and down the hotel room, waving the weapon while he expressed his unbounded disgust and resentment at the suggestion. He could not, he would not do it; this was not rehabilitation, it was adding real treachery to the fictitious treachery he was being charged with. And the mere thought of how it would have to be done, the lying and pretending and setting a trap for "fellow revolutionaries"—though of the second grade, as it were—was utterly revolting.

Finally he calmed down, and Makhalin presented his side of the case. These men, the murderers of Yushchinsky, were not ordinary murderers, unfortunate victims of the system; they had become part of it, they were working with it in a frightful plot against the masses, they were the willing instruments of the pogrom-makers. If they had simulated a ritual murder they were the lowest of the low among the reactionaries and had forfeited every claim to consideration as ordinary, decent murderers; and if they had not deliberately simulated a ritual murder, it was their business to come forward and confess rather than let the hideous conspiracy take its course. If he, Makhalin, could play the part, he would never have asked Karayev to do it; but he was a stranger to the underworld, and what with his upper-class speech and his fastidious manners, which he could not conceal, it would be ridiculous for him to try and enter it. He had only to open his mouth and they would fall upon him like a pack of wolves.

In the end Karayev accepted.

Thus through Brazul, Krasovsky was brought into contact with Makhalin and through him with Karayev. The revolutionaries and the ex-detective approached each other warily. On his side Krasovsky, now working reluctantly with the credulous and garrulous Brazul, understood how perilous it was for him to get mixed up with revolutionaries. On their side Makhalin and Karayev would have had an intense aversion to someone with Krasovsky's past. But Krasovsky used an assumed name and assured them—truthfully as it happened—that he too was a private investigator. It did not take them long to discover who Krasovsky was, namely, the famous nemesis of criminals; but by then the dirty work had been done and the most impressive single piece of evidence against the Troika had been brought in.

It was the good fortune of the three private investigators that they had only one member of the Troika to deal with, and he Singayevsky, the lummox. Latyshev was dead and Rudzinsky was serving his term in Siberia for armed robbery. There was of course Cheberyak—as we have noted, she no longer lived in Lukyanovka, her long-suffering landlord had at last managed to get her evicted—but she was a tough customer, whereas Singayevsky was approximately half-witted. The state prosecutor himself described him succinctly at the trial: "Gentlemen

of the jury, you have seen him; one does not have to be a
psychologist to figure out what sort of person he is. He is a
stupid fellow; he couldn't even be taught to read or write; he is
a thief, but also a splendid picklock. . . . He would, of course,
trust Karayev."

"Trust" was hardly the word. Singayevsky was utterly overwhelmed when an intermediary introduced him to the legendary
Karayev. How had he deserved this honor, and what did
Karayev want of him? There was a job, Karayev told him, something big, a "wet" job; a famous prisoner was to be sprung,
some ten people would have to be killed; he needed "men whose
hands don't tremble." There was money in it, too. Overawed,
delighted, Singayevsky promised to find an additional man whom
he could vouch for with his life. And, alone with Karayev, he
began to blabber that the police were trying to pin the Yushchinsky murder on him and on his two pals, Rudzinsky, who was in
Siberia, and Latyshev, who was dead.

Karayev broke off the conversation at this point. He wanted
a witness to the anticipated confession, and when the next meeting took place in his hotel room Makhalin was present. It was
then, after some preliminary talk about the "job," that Karayev
returned to the Yushchinsky murder. Addressing Makhalin and
pointing to Singayevsky, Karayev said: "There's the real murderer of Yushchinsky." Then he turned to Singayevsky and said:
"Isn't that the way it happened?" To which Singayevsky answered: "Yes, it was our work."

He went on blabbering, and blamed Rudzinsky for botching
the murder. The "bastard's" body should never have been hidden
so close to the Cheberyak home; it should have been thrown
into the Dnieper. Karayev asked, offhandedly, as it were, why
they had made such a messy job of it. Why the butchery?
Singayevsky answered, with heavy sarcasm: "It was Rudzinsky,
with his ministerial brain, who planned it all that way."

Nevertheless Singayevsky had to admit that at one point
Rudzinsky had shown himself truly ingenious. That was before
he committed the armed robbery for which he was now doing

time in Siberia. The Troika had felt from the beginning that the murder had been a clumsy hugger-mugger affair. There were two girls—*shmary*, floozies, Singayevsky called them—who knew too much, Katherine and Ksenya Diakonova. They had to be put out of the way—they, and certain others: Singayevsky wanted quite a number of people put out of the way. But meanwhile the Troika had needed a good alibi, and it was Singayevsky who had thought it up for them.

This was the manner of it. On April 18, 1911, five weeks after the murder, Rudzinsky, then still at large, had been present at a mass for the soul of Andryusha, and there the erroneous statement was made that the murder had been committed on the *night* of March 12. Thereupon Rudzinsky was struck by a brilliant idea. If that was what the police believed, the members of the Troika had only to confess* that on the night of March 12 they had been busy robbing the optical goods store on Kiev's main business street, a considerable distance from Lukyanovka. "Better," said Singayevsky, cunningly, "four years for robbery than twenty for murder."

So it was agreed. At the proper time Rudzinsky appeared before the investigating magistrate, Singayevsky before the state prosecutor and confessed to the robbery on behalf of the Troika. The three men were now in the clear, or so they thought until they discovered that the statement made at Andryusha's mass (it was widely circulated, and even appeared in *The Jewish Chronicle* of London) that the murder had been committed on the night of March 12 was contrary to what was known to the police. The autopsy revealed that the murder had been committed four hours after the boy had eaten his breakfast, which had been at six o'clock in the morning. Thus their alibi was not at all the safe though rather costly bet it had seemed to be. Still it was something, a partial alibi: they had committed a burglary that night—was it likely that they could have committed a murder the same morning?

But the complications this confession ran into were such as no ministerial brain, and perhaps not an entire cabinet, could have anticipated. It was thrown out of court. At the trial Singayevsky and Rudzinsky were again to insist, and to prove with a multitude of details, that they had indeed committed the robbery on the night of March 12; but there the record was: the confession had not been accepted.

The conversation in Karayev's hotel room was reported in detail by Karayev in his deposition to the investigating magistrate on July 18, 1912; it was read out at the trial and corroborated there by Makhalin. But Karayev himself was not permitted to appear at the trial. He was considered too dangerous by the administration. Shortly after making his deposition he was arrested by administrative order and sent to the province of Eniseisk in Siberia, where he was kept under close surveillance. Nor were the demands of the Beiliss defense of any avail; in defiance of the law the local governor refused to release the most dangerous of all the witnesses in the Beiliss case, and behind the governor stood Shcheglovitov.

This detail of the conspiracy, too, came out before the Commission during the interrogation of the cautiously penitent Beletsky. The chairman of the Commission asked him: "Were the police acting on their own initiative [in refusing to obey the subpoena] or was it with the knowledge of both Ministers or of one of them?"

BELETSKY: I don't remember it now, but I know that all the orders were given as a result of the agreement of the Ministers [of Justice and of the Interior], and the Department of Police played only an executive role.

CHAIRMAN: Do you remember that Karayev was exiled? On your instructions a letter to Krasovsky was intercepted. In that letter Karayev says that he is worried. . . . He knows a lot about the Beiliss case. . . . He decided to [escape and] go to the trial and testify even if he were to be re-arrested after it.

BELETSKY: If I am not mistaken, there is information that Karayev's testimony would not have been valuable to the defense.

CHAIRMAN: But in your actions you were not guided by the idea that the witness would have harmed the defense. . . . First, you have the order to intercept Karayev's registered letter; second, you sent a telegraphic order to prevent Karayev's escape. The point is that Karayev could not have harmed the defense, but that he could have harmed the prosecution.

BELETSKY: Of course! I don't remember everything about Karayev.

The administration did well to keep Karayev from attending the trial. With his utter fearlessness, his arrogance, his contempt for authority, and his inside information, he would have been a disaster for the prosecution. Why, then, did it permit the appearance of Makhalin who, if a less formidable figure than Karayev, was armed with the same information? We might of course just as well ask why the administration did not suppress all the adverse witnesses and conduct a Stalin trial. The answer would be that it could not. Russia was not yet a totalitarian state; there was a limit to what the administration could do overtly by way of fixing the trial. Covertly it could and did go much further, but even that had its limits in a country with a liberal press, capable journalists and editors, and a disaffected sector of the administration.

Actually there was violent disagreement among the conspirators as to what those limits were. Colonel Ivanov was for keeping Makhalin, too, away from the trial, but he gave in on one condition: on the witness stand he, Ivanov, was not to reveal that he had once been Makhalin's employer. Makhalin naturally would not want to mention it; apart from the effect in revolutionary circles, his value as a witness would be much diminished, if not totally destroyed, if he admitted in court that he had been a police spy. But for that very reason Zamyslovsky, Golubev's patron and the ablest of the prosecuting attorneys at the trial, wanted to make it public that this idealistic revolutionary, with his passion for the common people, had taken *okhrana* money; and he wanted it all the more because next to Karayev, Makhalin was the witness most dangerous to the prosecution. Zamyslovsky did not get his way, and almost withdrew from the case.

5

The publication of Brazul's inane accusation of Miffle and the Yushchinsky family in January 1912 had no effect on the admin-

istration's arrangements to open the trial on May 25. But the
situation was transformed when early in May, Brazul began the
publication, in the *Kievskaya mysl,* of a series of articles in
which he named Cheberyak and the Troika as the murderers.
The administration was faced with the shattering news that the
defense had hit on the very persons it itself strongly suspected,
and might very well have clinching evidence. There was a flurry
of consultations with St. Petersburg; the May 25 date was called
off and the case was returned to the state prosecutor's office
for a second preliminary examination, thus relieving the anxiety
of Governor Girs and Minister of the Interior Makarov about
the effect of a probable acquittal of Beiliss on the impending
elections.

The dismay in the administration may be gauged by the
reaction of Ivanov, who called in Brazul and upbraided him
furiously for ruining all the work he had put into the case.

6

During the second preliminary investigation, which began as
soon as the first indictment was dropped, the administration
looked frantically for new material against Beiliss. The last item
it had collected went back to December 20, 1911, when Cheberyak *père* had deposed that a few days before the murder his
son, Zhenya, had come running home with a story that he and
Andryusha had been chased out of the brickyard by Beiliss.
This deposition was made four months after Zhenya's death,
and we have seen what the administration thought of it. The
renewed questioning of Vera Cheberyak yielded nothing at first,
but suddenly, on July 10, 1912, eleven months after Zhenya's
death, she came up with an extraordinary revelation: before
dying, Zhenya had told her that on the morning of the murder
he and Andryusha had gone to the brickyard and that Beiliss
had dragged Andryusha away. All in all she had made five
depositions prior to and since Zhenya's death and had not so
much as hinted at this crucial information. It had taken her
nearly a year to remember!

A not less remarkable feat of the Cheberyak memory was to

follow, performed this time by little Lyudmilla, the sole surviving Cheberyak child. On August 11, 1912, one year and five months after the murder, she was brought in for questioning. At the time of the interrogation—made by Mashkevich, the new investigating magistrate sent from St. Petersburg to replace Fenenko on the case—she was nine years old. She was therefore seven and a half when the incident she reported was supposed to have occurred. She deposed that at about eight o'clock on the morning of that day Andryusha came to the house and invited Zhenya to go riding the clay mixer. Lyudmilla went along, also the younger sister, Valya, and a few other children, including the daughter of the shoemaker Nakonechny—the honest and courageous neighbor who had run of his own accord to the investigating magistrate and compelled the lamplighter to retract his accusation of Beiliss.

The officialese restatement of Lyudmilla's deposition runs: "They [the children] penetrated to the factory grounds through a hole in the fence and began their ride on the clay mixer. Suddenly they saw Beiliss, accompanied by two Jews, running toward them. They jumped down and ran away, but Andryusha and Zhenya were seized by Beiliss. Zhenya managed to free himself and the two Jews started dragging Andryusha toward the kiln. Her sister Valya, who, being the smallest, was the last to run away, also saw this."

The reader is now acquainted with the total evidence collected by the administration against Beiliss when he was brought to trial. The rest of its case, as developed at the trial, consisted of vague hints and background allegations. Beiliss's connection with the distribution of *matzos* during the lifetime of old Zaitsev was worked up as a highly suspicious circumstance. A common saddle-maker's awl, which might have been anyone's property, and was in any case completely unfit for bloodletting, was produced as the murder implement. The prosecution labored for two days trying to involve the hay and straw dealer Shneyerson in the murder, chiefly because he bore the name of an illustrious rabbinic family; it also tried to show that when the Cheberyak children went to buy milk from Beiliss in the spring of 1911 they were frightened away by Jews in outlandish dress, and that this proved something important. The fact that Beiliss had no cow in 1911, having sold it the year before to pay his son's tuition fees, did not upset the prosecution; it had made the point that Jews in outlandish dress frequented the Beiliss home and frightened non-Jewish children, which was to be sure not the same as killing them and consuming their blood; still, it added to the picture.

There was much more stuff of the same kind, increasingly implausible and irrelevant, proving nothing but the desperation —and the uninventiveness—of the prosecution.

◇◇◇◇◇◇◇◇◇◇◇◇◇◇◇◇◇

C H A P T E R 1 2

◇◇◇◇◇◇◇◇◇◇◇◇◇◇◇◇◇

THE INDICTMENT

1

THE FULL EXTENT of official participation in the Beiliss conspiracy, and the extent of Shcheglovitov's corruption of the
courts, cannot be understood without reference to certain judicial procedures* in Russia half a century ago.

A suspect in a crime was brought by the police before an
investigating magistrate. If he was held, and if after further
investigation the magistrate decided that a case existed, the
material was turned over to the state prosecutor, who prepared
an indictment. The indictment was submitted to the "Chamber
of Accusation of the Court of Appeals," which consisted of five
judges. I shall refer to this body as the Committing Authority.
It acted in the capacity of a grand jury, but did not hear witnesses, basing its decision on the documentary material submitted to it.

A feature of the old Russian system that has a special bearing
on our narrative must now be described at some length. If
the crime was such that a victim or his heirs could claim

damages from the criminal, he or they could demand that the state prosecutor be attended or assisted by private attorneys. It was the function of the state prosecutor to obtain a conviction and that of the private attorneys to obtain damages for an injured party. The state prosecutor and the private attorneys worked independently of each other but with the same aim—to obtain a conviction. In the Beiliss case the claim for damages on behalf of Yushchinsky's mother was theoretical; Beiliss was a poor workingman. Nevertheless she was represented, though she had not asked for it, by two important attorneys, who volunteered their services. One we have met—Zamyslovsky, the anti-Semitic Duma deputy and extreme Rightist, Golubov's patron. The other was the Moscow lawyer Shmakov, whose boast it was that he had never taken on a Jewish client, and who had covered the walls of his office with drawings of Jewish noses. Zamyslovsky was rewarded for his "volunteered" services by a gift of 25,000 rubles—ostensibly for writing a book on the case—from a fund at the disposal of Chief of Police Beletsky; Shmakov worked as an idealist. Since the question of damages was in this case theoretical the real purpose of the addition of Zamyslovsky and Shmakov to the prosecution was to strengthen it, and this was so well done that the state prosecutor, Vipper, was put completely in the shade by Zamyslovsky. Because these "private attorneys" took so vigorous a part in the proceedings, to avoid confusing the reader I shall call them private prosecutors, though the term is technically incorrect.

The question put by the court to the jury—it had to be in writing—could be in single or double form. If in single form it would read: "Is the accused guilty of the crime charged to him?" If in double form the first question would read: "Has it been proved that such and such a crime was committed?" and here would follow the description of the crime. . . . If the jury answered this question in the negative, the case was naturally dropped; if the answer was in the affirmative, the second question would be: "Is the accused guilty of the crime described in the first question?" The choice between a single and double question (*voprosny list*) was of great significance in the Beiliss trial.

Although the court in the Beiliss trial was regularly constituted as a board of three judges—the presiding judge was only *primus inter pares* and could be overruled by his colleagues— the other two judges took practically no part in the proceedings; in the courtroom the only spokesman for the court was Presiding Judge Boldyrev, whom Shcheglovitov had appointed president of the Kiev District Court for the specific purpose of the trial. With negligible exceptions it was he who interrogated, advised, and admonished witnesses and made explanations to the jury, and he alone intervened in the frequent and passionate clashes between opposing counsels, himself becoming involved in acrimonious exchanges. I shall therefore be referring to him when I speak of the court or the Judge.

As we have seen, there were two indictments of Beiliss. The first does not interest us, since it was withdrawn in May 1912 when Brazul published his second series of articles on the case, this time accusing Cheberyak and the Troika of the murder. In speaking of "the indictment" I shall mean the second one, drawn up after the prosecution had, as it believed or pretended to believe, strengthened its case by obtaining from Vera Cheberyak her belated deposition as to what her son Zhenya had told her before his death, and the even more belated deposition of nine-year-old Lyudmilla Cheberyak.

2

The indictment is one of the most astonishing documents ever presented to a court.* It rambles along for forty-one large, closely printed columns and it reviews the history of the investigations, suppressing material here and there, or unduly emphasizing it, and presenting the opinions of experts on various aspects of the case. It would have needed some days of close study and memorization on the part of an intelligent, literate, and informed member of the jury to check its contents for inner consistency and against the evidence presented at the trial.

I give here a brief summary of those parts with which the

reader is already familiar, with slightly more extended mention of new material.

It begins with the finding of Yushchinsky's body and a description of its condition. No mention is made of the first autopsy, performed by City Coroner Karpinsky, but there is a slanted summary of the autopsy performed by Professor Obolonsky and Anatomist Tufanov, in which is included their later conclusions, pointing to a ritual murder, as if those had been part of the autopsy. Then follows the expert opinion of Professor Kosorotov (purchased, as already mentioned, for 4,000 rubles) hinting at ritual murder.

The indictment proceeds to a description of the life of Yushchinsky, followed by an account of the various arrests of his relatives and of Cheberyak, remarking of the latter that though she had "constant connections with the criminal world" no serious evidence had been found connecting her with the murder. Then it reports briefly the arrest of "the Jew Mendel Beiliss" because of "new circumstances [that] were considered as sufficient for suspecting him of the murder of Yushchinsky from motives of a religious character." As Beiliss was arrested on July 22, 1911, the "new circumstances" can only refer to the depositions of the lamplighters and the Wolf-Woman, the nature of which we have examined.

A distorted version of Mishchuk's work on the case is given, without mention of his prosecution and conviction. Brazul's private investigations are treated at length and include misleading summaries of the depositions of Makhalin and Karayev. Krasovsky's part in the investigations is described, and here care is taken to discredit him by mentioning that he was dismissed from the case, but there is no mention of the unsuccessful attempt to get him convicted on the charge of embezzling sixteen kopeks or his later dismissal from the service.

The indictment is marked by two extraordinary features. It devotes to the exoneration of Cheberyak, who was not under indictment and against whom "no serious evidence had been found connecting her with the crime," three times as much space as to the accusation of Beiliss; and it introduces a long discussion by experts on ritual murder as a Jewish practice. This discussion occupies 6 columns, of which 4.8 affirm that the practice exists and 1.2 deny its existence. The two experts who affirm its existence are Professor Emeritus of Psychiatry Sikorsky, whose views we have quoted, and Father Pranaitis. The experts who deny the existence of the practice are two of Russia's leading scholars—non-Jews—in the field of Jewish religion.

The following excerpt from the views of Pranaitis, as set forth in the indictment, will serve as a foretaste of the testimony he was later to offer in the course of the trial.

All the rabbinical schools, notwithstanding their divergences on various questions, are united by their hatred of non-Jews, who according to the Talmud are not considered human beings but only "animals in human form." The hatred and the spite which the Jews, from the point of view of their religious law, feel toward people of a different nationality and religion, are especially strong toward Christians. Because of this feeling, the Talmud allows and even commands the killing of non-Jews. . . . The extermination of non-Jews is commanded as a religious act . . . [that] hastens the coming of the Messiah.

Father Pranaitis further asserts that the Zohar (the outstanding Jewish mystical work of the Middle Ages) "contains descriptions of such a killing." He finds in the wounds inflicted on Yushchinsky's body indications that the murder was carried out in strict accordance with Jewish religious prescription.

This strange indictment encountered rough going with the board of judges, or Committing Authority. The president and the recorder, its two most important and no doubt its most attentive members, were for turning it back. After long debate the other three judges overruled them, for the curious reason that to preserve the dignity of the law a man who had been in prison for such a long time had to be indicted. The president and the recorder resigned from the board rather than sign the indictment, a courageous act in the days of "Shcheglovitov justice."

CHAPTER 13

ANTI-SEMITE IN A PROPHETIC RAGE

ONE OF THE MOST CURIOUS FIGURES prominently associated with the Beiliss case was a certain V. V. Shulgin, editor of the *Kievlyanin* (*Kievan*), the Kiev semi-official reactionary and monarchist daily, strongly anti-Semitic, and rival of the liberal *Kievskaya mysl*. The role he played in the case points up the paradox of his character: lover of justice and anti-Semite.

He describes himself in his memoirs as "a born Kievan, hence an authentic Black Hundred." He certainly did not mean actual membership in one of those hooligan groups but, with a touch of facetiousness, some kind of spiritual affinity. He was in fact opposed to "hot pogroms," favoring the "cold," unobtrusive variety, the quiet, sustained, legal asphyxiation of the Jewish people, and in this he was at one with the majority of Russian anti-Semites. But we must not make too much of Shulgin's distaste for "hot pogroms," for it was essentially a form of hypocrisy. It did not spring from humane considerations but from his high ideal of the law.

He had high ideals for Russia, too, and propounded them in his newspaper and from the rostrum of the Duma, of which he was a prominent member. He was devoted with all his being to the monarchical principle and to the forcible Russification of the many national minorities in the empire—one of the planks in the platform of the Party of Russian Nationalists, of which he was a leader.

Yet this man was ill at ease about the Emperor whose claim to all-autocracy he was pledged to defend. He saw about him the general decay in the fiber of the ruling class, and he saw how the monarch himself was undermining the monarchical principle. "How terrible it is," he exclaims in his memoirs, "to have an autocracy without an autocrat." He was horrified by the rise of Rasputin to power. "Here is the terrible knot. The Sovereign insults the country by admitting to the palace, where the very best find it difficult to gain admission, an exposed debauchee, and the country insults the Sovereign by its horrible suspicions. Century-old ties which held Russia together are being destroyed by the weakness of one husband for his wife." It was the peculiar destiny of Shulgin to be one of the two men who in February 1917 delivered to the Czar the Duma's demand for his abdication.

"Anti-Semite and man of honor" is the description, slightly perplexing in the post-Hitlerian world, that has been applied to Shulgin, and he does in fact illustrate the problem of anti-Semitism as an ideal. He wanted the Jewish people to be put out of business, to be suppressed, to be caused to cease to exist by means of just and equitable laws. Like his deceased father-in-law, from whom he inherited his newspaper, he had despised the Beiliss case from the beginning, and he had watched it moving steadily into its ultimate absurdities and indecencies. He had held himself more or less in check until the second day of the trial when the indictment was read out in court. Then his loathing of the whole business burst forth in an editorial which, coming from a prominent monarchist and anti-Semite, resounded like a thunderclap throughout Russia, its echoes rolling across

the Western world, which was watching intently the developments in Kiev.

I find it a relief to quote the editorial. The credulity of the
reader must have been sorely strained by now, and he cannot
but suspect that not only have I been one-sided but that I
have invented whole passages and otherwise falsified the record,
that such stupidities—to speak only of that aspect—simply
cannot have been perpetrated by men in their right senses.
Here is what Shulgin had to say:

> In undertaking a task which in the courts of the whole world has
> failed throughout the ages, the Prosecution of the Kiev Court should
> have realized that it must produce an accusation so perfect and so
> strongly welded as to break the force of the enormous wave it
> would encounter. . . . To engage in such a fight it was necessary to
> set out with a well-whetted weapon. And now that we have that
> "whetted" weapon before us, alas, one need not be a lawyer, but
> merely a person of common sense, to understand that the accusa-
> tion against Beiliss is such claptrap that a moderately competent
> counsel could tear it to pieces. One cannot help feeling ashamed
> for the Department of Prosecution of the Kiev Court and for
> Russian justice as a whole, which has ventured to appear before
> the world with such paltry equipment. . . .

Here follows a review of the Mishchuk and Krasovsky episodes, which had scandalized the country.

> The whole of the police, terrorized by the peculiar conduct of the
> court, realized that whoever let fall an untimely word—that is to
> say, one not in accord with the desire of the authorities—would
> immediately be deprived of his living and sent to prison into the
> bargain. . . . We shall not tire of repeating that this unjust case
> will not yield the desired fruit. . . . However advantageous it may
> appear from the party point of view to prove the existence of
> ritual murders, the Prosecution Department should not, and has
> not the right to undertake to supply the living object required for
> originating a trial of that kind.
> This, however, is precisely what has been done. "What do we
> care about Beiliss? We do not even mind if he is acquitted! The
> important point is to prove the ritual!" That is the way to talk

about the matter. But you dare not speak like that. . . . In arguing thus you who keep talking of ritual are yourselves carrying out a human sacrifice.

Here Shulgin rises to heights of genuine prophecy:

Gentlemen, take care! . . . Perhaps a time will come when instead of State Prosecutor Chaplinsky looking for ritual murders, there will stand at the head of the prosecution a man bent on discovering the pogrom-makers. What will you say then, when the head of the Department of Justice of the day selects one of you for an operation of this kind? And how will you feel when, across the wall of your prison, will reach you such cynical, indifferent explanations as: "What is Zamyslovsky to us? What do we care about Shmakov? We are only concerned with clearing up the way in which Jewish pogroms were organized."

The parallel drawn by Shulgin was faulty. Pogroms were realities, and the Zamyslovskys and Shmakovs were guilty of inciting to them; a just court therefore could not say: "What do we care about the Zamyslovskys and Shmakovs?" But ritual murder was a fantasy, and Beiliss was innocent of any crime at all. Moreover, without a recantation of his life-long anti-Semitism, Shulgin's passion for justice was palpably flawed. There is a hearty folk saying: "He who lies down with dogs gets up with fleas." Yet it was this flaw that gave the protest its pungency. It was the *Kievlyanin* speaking! For the first time since it was founded this true-blue organ of the monarchists was seized and suppressed by the censor. But of course thousands of copies got out to subscribers and were snatched up at prices ranging from three to fifteen rubles by avid readers of all political convictions; and of course thousands of mimeographed copies of the editorial soon appeared in every part of the country.

Shulgin, however, continued to attend the trial and to report on it objectively. He did not affect its course, but his *J'accuse* is worth remembering as a remarkable human and historical document and as a curious psychological case of limited repentance.

On the prophetic side it is remarkable for the rapidity of the fulfillment. Within less than three and a half years the regime was swept away; within four years the Bolsheviks were in power and their liquidation of the Shcheglovitovs and Beletskys, Zamyslovskys and Shmakovs included all who did not manage to flee the country.*

CHAPTER 14

SEWING UP
THE CASE

1

From all the foregoing one might gather that even with Shchglovitov in control of the judiciary and Beletsky in control of the police the outlook for the conviction of Beiliss and the endorsement of a ritual murder was practically hopeless. The administration did not think so, nor did the public at large or the most intelligent observers at the trial. "The overwhelming majority," wrote the Leftist journalist Bonch-Bruyevich, "was certain of the conviction of Beiliss." The correspondent of *The Times*, London, cabled on the last day of the trial: "All Russia is strung up to the highest point of tension in awaiting the verdict, which, in spite of the nature of the evidence against Beiliss, no one attempts to foretell."

As the reader must have surmised, such pessimism or uncertainty can only have been connected with the character of the jury.* That it would be rigged was to be expected. A year

before the trial the newspaper *Zemshchina,* which had led the
hue and cry for the discovery of "the Jewish ritual murderers,"
had reminded Shcheglovitov editorially "that the trial would
depend chiefly on the composition of the jury"—a pretty example
of someone teaching his grandmother to suck eggs. That the jury
had in fact been rigged was grossly and palpably evident, and
this was more than hinted in the press.

V. G. Korolenko, who may be bracketed with Tolstoy and
Vladimir Solovyov and their like as one of the keepers of Russia's
conscience at the beginning of this century, was a correspondent
at the trial. His interest in it had a personal touch. He had at
one time been deeply involved in another ritual murder case
when a group of the Udmuts, a small, half-pagan Ugro-Finnish
tribe in the Ural district of Vyatka, had been the defendants.
They had been accused by the local police of murdering a beggar
as a sacrifice to their gods. Illiterate, helpless, hardly acquainted
with the Russian language, they had been found guilty and sentenced to hard labor in Siberia. At the head of a group of friends
Korolenko forced a retrial; the Votyaks, as the Udmuts were then
called, were found guilty a second time, but Korolenko would not
rest. His articles and his appeals to the Senate led to a third
trial, and the Votyaks were acquitted.

Korolenko, reporting in his liberal journal *Russkoye bogatstvo,*
commented at once on the composition of the Beiliss jury:
". . . seven peasants, three townsmen, two government clerks. . . .
For a university city the choice is certainly extraordinary." He
took the trouble to make comparisons with another trial that was
being conducted in the building. "I was pleasantly (or unpleasantly) surprised. I learned that for a minor crime there were
two or three professors, ten educated men and only two peasants.
This would mean that the type of people for the Beiliss jury was
formulated in one of the earlier stages. How did it happen? How
was it done?"

The answer was given by the Commission four years later.
Among the documents in Shcheglovitov's files there was a copy
of a confidential circular addressed in 1912 to the thirteen judicial

districts of the empire. It directed the prosecutors to keep an
eye on "persons otherwise eligible for jury duty, but belonging
to that element which is most opposed to the Government and the
Government courts." Persons who are "strangers to the high aims
of justice are usually well engraved in the memory of the
Prosecutors . . . and naturally, they ought not to be included in
the lists at all."

These general precautions for the exclusion of citizens un-
sympathetic toward Shcheglovitov's conception of the high aims
of justice were not explicit enough for the Beiliss trial. The
Minister of Justice had therefore himself supervised the selection
of the jury. The incriminating documents had of course to be
pushed under his nose before he admitted anything.

The chairman of the Commission read out a telegram from
Shcheglovitov's agent in Kiev shortly before the opening of the
trial: "The external surveillance of the jury is still maintained.
Great caution is being used."

SHCHEGLOVITOV: I don't remember this at all. Was there such a
   telegram? Well, then, I read it.
CHAIRMAN: If you read it, why did you ignore such things? Why
   did you remain inactive?
SHCHEGLOVITOV: It seems to me the jurors were confined to the
   court throughout the trial. . . . Then what importance could
   there be in such surveillance?
CHAIRMAN: Which means precisely that the telegram refers to the
   period preceding the trial. . . .
SHCHEGLOVITOV: Of course.

Shcheglovitov denied having instructed the Kiev administration
to cooperate in the rigging of the jury, either directly or through
Beletsky, but the chairman produced another telegram from
Beletsky to the Kiev administration, directing it "to keep a close
watch on the panel from which the jury is to be selected." The
surveillance was to be maintained until the opening of the trial on
September 25. "It is desirable," reads the telegram, "to know their
[the jurors'] mutual relations . . . and any data which could be
used by the judicial authorities as an indication of their opinions
or their state of mind." It was all the more desirable, Chaplinsky

agreed in a communication to Shcheglovitov, "as they [the prosecutors] are not sure that there is evidence enough for a ritual murder case." And Shcheglovitov's agent in Kiev informed him, regarding Chaplinsky: "His whole career is at stake."

Twenty-three agents of the secret police were assigned to shadowing the members of the panel, so that the prosecutors might be able to make the right choice. Since the routine spying in the city could not be suspended, men were brought in from other cities. A supplementary surveillance in depth was maintained by a squad of gendarmery specialists. "Its problem," explained Beletsky to the Commission, "was to understand the inner thoughts of any given person. . . . Information could be obtained through acquaintances. The Ukrainians are very sociable, very hospitable. You strike up an acquaintance with them."

"This is horrible!" exclaimed the chairman of the Commission.

But worse followed. "Do you know," the chairman asked Beletsky, "that when the jurors were already doing their duty, secret agents were introduced into the jury room under the guise of court ushers?"

BELETSKY: I didn't know. If there is any information . . .
CHAIRMAN: Don't you remember that two gendarme officers disguised as ushers were serving the jury?
BELETSKY: Yes, yes, I remember. The Presiding Judge knew about it.
CHAIRMAN: That only makes it the more criminal. . . .
BELETSKY: I blush for myself now; I have had so many experiences. I can only blush for what I have done.

These belated blushes, if not figurative, must have created a continuous roseate glow in the hall. His "experiences," as Beletsky called them, ranged far outside the Beiliss case, and of those that fall within it I cite two more.

The bribing of Kosorotov, professor of forensic medicine at the University of St. Petersburg, was entrusted by Shcheglovitov and Minister of the Interior Maklakov to Beletsky, with instructions to proceed with the proper tactfulness. Beletsky told the Commission: "I began my conversation with Kosorotov most carefully. . . . The Professor, however, took it quite calmly and demanded 4,000 rubles. I stated apologetically that I did not have more than 2,000, though I actually had the 4,000 with me in case of emergency." Kosorotov came across handsomely in the indictment and at the trial, collected the outstanding 2,000 rubles, and was foolish enough to give receipts, which were produced before the Commission.

On the origins of the Beiliss case Beletsky was explicit. They led from Golubev to Chaplinsky to Zamyslovsky to Shcheglovitov. "Chaplinsky was always flexible, and followed the trend of the moment. . . . He trusted him [Golubev] implicitly. . . . The idea of a ritual murder began with them [Golubev and Chaplinsky]."

Beletsky was unfortunately not asked how the "ushers"—the police spies introduced into the jury room—operated. Did they report the conversations they overheard only to Judge Boldyrev, who held almost nightly conferences with the prosecutors, or to a sort of seminar? However it was done, these briefings on the debates and perplexities of the jury must have been enormously useful to the prosecutors in determining their lines of interrogation and the substance of their summations. Had the journalists I have quoted above, already depressed by the composition of the jury, known of the briefings they would have considered the odds against Beiliss overwhelming. As it was, Korolenko wrote, five days before the verdict: "Personally I am not giving up hope. I firmly believe that a ray of good sense and the conscience of these people [the jury] will penetrate the fog which at this moment darkens the horizon of Russian justice." He clung to this glum optimism though the administration had—for once —done its work so well that seven of the jurors were members of the Union of the Russian People.* Had he known on top of that of the briefings he would undoubtedly have considered the fog impenetrable.

2

There were two confidential agents of the government at the trial, reporting daily by telegram and letter to Shcheglovitov via Beletsky. One of them, a former investigating magistrate and state prosecutor, was an "inspector" or "supervisor" of the kind regularly employed by Shcheglovitov to keep judges from succumbing to any propensity toward leniency; the other was a background reporter. For convenience I shall henceforth refer to them jointly as "Agent D.," from the initial of the more important one, Dyachenko. The entire dossier is intact and provides among other things an interesting study in the difference between Machiavellianism and, to use Orwell's now indispensable word, double-think.

Machiavellianism is the art of deception; double-think* the art of controlled purposive self-befuddlement. The Machiavellian is quite clear as to what he is doing; the double-thinker is not— at least, not always. On the whole the double-thinker is the more dangerous, for he can when necessary summon up a genuine sincerity which the lucid-minded Machiavellian can only imitate.

Thus Agent D., reporting early in the trial, places great hopes on Father Pranaitis, who he believes will overwhelm the jury with his arguments demonstrating the practice of ritual murder among the Jews. But he adds that he fears for Pranaitis's life "for the Jews will stop at nothing." For Agent D., who had written Shcheglovitov that Cheberyak had probably poisoned her own children, who knew moreover how the jury had been rigged and how it was being spied upon, it was the Jews who would stop at nothing. That he meant it, or meant to mean it, is evident from another passage, in which he rages at the worldwide public protests against the Beiliss trial and the failure of the scientific experts to back Kosorotov: "Now it has become glaringly clear how this all-powerful international Jewry organizes its forces, and how incapable the Russian Government is of a serious struggle with the Jews. . . . All the luminaries of law, literature, medicine and science are on the side of Jewry, which has succeeded in conditioning them. Against them stands the soul of the simple people [the jurors], which has remained untouched by Jewish enlightenment. They will pronounce their incorruptible verdict, and this will be God's judgment on the Jews."

Thus the fateful contest between the Russian empire and omnipotent world Jewry was to be justly decided by the representatives of "the simple people" as selected by Shcheglovitov, Beletsky and the state prosecutor. There were moments when Agent D. nevertheless had his doubts as to the outcome. "It is impossible," he writes in one place, "to predict the outcome." And in another: "The entire course of the trial will depend on the extent to which the jury will be receptive to the arguments of Father Pranaitis, who is convinced of the truth of ritual murder." Then in a more sanguine note he commends State Prosecutor Vipper, who "seems to be an experienced person, since he has succeeded in keeping all intellectuals off the jury, something that caused consternation among the defense. . . . I noticed how the defense attorneys exchanged glances when the composition of the jury became known, all in peasant jackets and blouses with the exception of the government clerk Melnikov and two or three others." But again he relapses into gloom: "It is my deep conviction—though I could wish that it prove mistaken—that Beiliss will be acquitted." And once again he takes heart: "The ignorant nature of the jury will make it impossible for them to resolve the complex question regarding the existence of ritual murder"; and: "In general the evidence against Beiliss is very weak, but the ignorance of the jury may lead to a verdict of guilty, considering the element of ethnic enmity."

In these vicissitudes of expectation between "God's judgment on the Jews," delivered in the "incorruptible verdict" of the simple folk, and an inadequacy of simplicity or ignorance on the part of the jurors, Agent D. comes to rest on an interesting possibility. "The worst outcome for the defense would be for the jury to recognize the ritual character of the murder while concluding that Beiliss's guilt had not been proved." For, he reasoned, with Beiliss acquitted the case would not be appealed, "and the legend of the use of Christian blood will have received official sanction," whereas if Beiliss were to be found guilty the case would be carried to the Senate, and then most certainly Beiliss's acquittal would be accompanied by a repudiation of the ritual character of the murder.

This reflection occurred to many others besides Agent D. It

was widely felt among the conspirators that Beiliss was, in the reverse sense, expendable. Shulgin commented bitingly on this point of view in his denunciatory editorial. But State Prosecutor Vipper either did not see it thus or was determined to get a verdict of guilty whatever its effect on the larger strategy of the conspirators.

◇◇◇◇◇◇◇◇◇◇◇◇◇◇◇◇◇

CHAPTER 15

◇◇◇◇◇◇◇◇◇◇◇◇◇◇◇◇◇

THE ADVOCATES

1

BEILISS HAD BEEN IN PRISON three months before the leaders of Kiev Jewry realized what was afoot, namely a plot in the highest places to give twentieth-century judicial sanction to the legend of the Blood Accusation. To many of them the idea might have seemed harebrained, wildly anachronistic even in Russia, but the danger could not be ignored.

The first man to be called in for consultation was Oscar O. Gruzenberg, the leading Jewish criminal lawyer of his generation. At forty-five he was already famous for his role in a number of trials involving Jews and the Jewish question. He had defended the young Jew Pinchas Dashevsky who had made an attempt on the life of the Bessarabian fomenter of pogroms Krushevan, and he had taken a leading part in the trials following the Kishinev pogrom of 1903 for which Krushevan had been largely responsible. He had defended the Vilna Jew Blondes, accused in 1903 of an attempt to commit ritual murder—the "victim" in this case being a servant girl. Gruzenberg had reason to recall that case with satisfaction. At the first trial Blondes had been found guilty. Gruzenberg had appealed to the Senate, which ordered a retrial in Vilna, where Blondes was acquitted. But that was in 1903— before the days of "Shcheglovitov justice."

Gruzenberg became the head of the five-man defense team at the trial. According to friends and acquaintances of his with whom I have spoken, Gruzenberg was as temperamental as he was gifted; he was imperious, outspoken to the point of reckless- ness, and utterly fearless. He was a master at cross-examination, and even for a layman who reads the minutes of the Beiliss trial it is a lesson in logic to watch him push a reluctant witness step by step into a corner from which there is no escape. It is also pleasant to watch him standing up to Judge Boldyrev until the latter, having no answer, cries: "Don't argue with me." When Boldyrev interrupts one of Gruzenberg's arguments with: "Oppos- ing counsel did not say that, he said thus and thus," Gruzenberg drops the argument with an icy apology: "Of course, I believe you rather than my own ears."

Gruzenberg cannot have been more than the titular head of the team because it was composed of legal stars of the first magnitude. All but Gruzenberg were non-Jews who without hesitation agreed to serve. In fame Karabchevsky outranked Gruzenberg, but he was fifteen years older and had a correspon- dingly longer career behind him. He was "the old lion" of the Russian bar—Russian *émigrés* in America called him the Clarence Darrow of Russia—and his voice and appearance suggested the nickname. He was tall, stately, with thick gray hair combed back mane-fashion. The London *Times* correspondent saw a resemb- lance to Sir Charles Wyndham. His attitude toward Boldyrev was one of frosty condescension. In the encounters between them Boldyrev fell into the habit of announcing: "I consider the question closed," but more often than not it was Karabchevsky who had done the closing.

From the general point of view the outstanding member of the defense was beyond a doubt Vasily A. Maklakov, whose brother Nikolai, Minister of the Interior, reactionary, unprincipled, anti-

Semitic, was working hand in glove with Shcheglovitov. Vasily Maklakov was not only a brilliant jurist and attorney but a man of the widest intellectual attainments in literature and science. (After the February 1917 revolution he was the Provisional Government's ambassador to France.) He played a minor role in the trial until the closing days, but in his summation he outshone all his colleagues, for with his immense intellectual ability he combined an unusual simplicity of style and a deep understanding of the common man. After the trial Korolenko polled some of the jurors as to the impressions made on them by the defense attorneys; they put Maklakov easily in first place.

The most colorful, as well as the youngest, of the defense attorneys was A. S. Zarudny.* He was a man of idealistic, even Quixotic temperament, with a sometimes uncontrollable tongue. In court he made no attempt to conceal his low opinion of Judge Boldyrev, whom he challenged and corrected at every turn, quite undaunted by the sharp rejoinders he elicited: "Now look here, Counsel for the Defense, don't point out order to me," and: "You point out what I am already aware of." Zarudny: "Allow me to explain—" Boldyrev: "I don't want to know," and: "Sit down and be quiet," and: "I reprimand you for your ill-judged declaration." Zarudny: "I am not an usher." Boldyrev: "If you are not an usher, then sit down." Zarudny: "I am defending not only Judaism, but the Russian court system." Boldyrev: "The Russian court system does not need your defense." Zarudny: "Unfortunately one is forced to defend it." Boldyrev: "I will ask you not to employ such an expression, or I will ask you to leave the hall." And so on.

Less active in the case, and less famous than his colleagues of the defense, was Grigorovich-Barsky, one of the most respected members of the Kiev bar. He was by reason of his knowledge of local conditions a valuable consultant, and one speech of his, directed at Boldyrev's slanted charge to the jury, was an excellent piece of legal reasoning.

2

It would be an affectation of fairness to pretend that the prosecuting team could stand comparison with its opponents, for apart from the moral aspect, the utter fatuity of the prosecution's case could not but repel a lawyer with a decent reputation to preserve. The ablest of the prosecutors was Duma Deputy Zamyslovsky, but he was more rabble-rouser than lawyer. He was skilled in the trickery, speciousness, and fluency of the hustings, and considering the wretched material he had to work on he put on what can only be described as quite a good show. But it was clear that he was addressing himself less to the point than to his constituency throughout the country.

The other private prosecutor, Shmakov, the collector of pictures of Jewish noses, had only one value—his furious anti-Semitism. He was an old man and looked like what he was, half senile. He was a ludicrous figure, barrel-shaped, walking with a kind of seaman's roll. Anti-Semitism was a way of life with him and it had unhinged him; he was an avid student of queer anti-Semitic books and pamphlets, and he interlarded his interrogations with long tirades against Jews and Judaism, with lectures on medieval and ancient history, and with quotations, picked from an astonishing array of obscure authors, on the practices and beliefs of the Jews from the theophany at Sinai till A.D. 1913.

State Prosecutor Vipper had been sent by Shcheglovitov from St. Petersburg to represent the government. He was a man of boundless conceit, coarsely offensive toward defense witnesses, and arrogant even toward his colleagues. He was afflicted with, or simulated, all the symptoms of hallucinatory anti-Semitism, and his summation to the jury abounded in passages like the following: "Although the Jews are legally without rights, they do in fact possess the world. In this respect the Biblical prophecy has come to pass right in our midst. Their position is difficult, but at the same time we are under their yoke." His conceit showed itself even in his personal appearance. Slender and youthful looking, he carried himself proudly, dressed with extreme elegance, and outside the court always wore white gloves.

One does not have to know what went on behind the scenes to include Judge Boldyrev in the prosecuting team; a reading of the trial transcript is enough. Grandfatherly in appearance, with a benign Franz Joseph beard, he made some attempt early in the trial to act like a judge, to the chagrin of the prosecution and the surprised—but suspicious—gratification of the defense. As the days passed he abandoned this pose and showed his hand more and more crassly, and at the end, in his instructions to the jury and his formulation of the question, did everything in his power to make an acquittal impossible.

However, with the best will in the world even the venal Boldyrev could not always sit still under the provocations of the prosecuting attorneys. Zamyslovsky, with his national reputation, found it galling to be corrected mildly by this provincial judge and showed it, so that Boldyrev lost his temper and burst out with: "Mr. Zamyslovsky, no gestures, please, while I am talking." When Vipper, in his handling of defense witnesses, overstepped the bounds of common decency, Boldyrev had to rebuke him for shame's sake; and the firmest of judges would have found Shmakov intolerable, if only out of sheer tedium. Again and again Boldyrev had to remind him that he was in court as a private prosecutor, not as an expert on the Jewish question or on ritual murder cases of the last eight hundred years.

Hardest of all to manage was the prosecution's religious expert, Father Pranaitis, who added to his clerical status the advantage of an imposing appearance. "One of the most striking figures in the court," wrote the London *Times* correspondent. "A lean churchman with beetling brows, dressed in a cassock and with a large golden cross with a figure of Christ upon it suspended at the waist with a silver neck-chain." Him there was no stopping however irrelevant he became. Like his mentor Lyutostansky he viewed his religion as a call to expose the satanic character of the Jewish people. The wearied Boldyrev implored and admonished him repeatedly to stick to the evidence on ritual murder, and in the end gave up.

"Relations between the two sides," reports Agent D. soon after the opening of the trial, "have become extremely sharp." Well might they. At issue was not only justice for Beiliss, but also the future of Russia. The London *Times* put it succinctly: "It is daily becoming clearer that under the forms of law a momentous political struggle is being fought out. This is *not* the Beiliss case. It is possibly a final fight for existence on the part of the innermost powers of reaction against all modern forces in Russia."

In such a struggle one could hardly have chosen two more representative teams. The juxtaposition was the more striking in that not a single member of the defense belonged to the extreme Left. They were liberals (Karabchevsky and Maklakov conservatively so) and constitutionalists, to whom their opponents, the Blood Accusation propagandists, were both politically contemptible and personally unclean. It would have been difficult to say what stirred the defense more deeply, the conscienceless persecution of an innocent man or the readiness to drag Russia's name through filth before a watching world. These feelings of abhorrence were heartily reciprocated by the prosecution, which saw or pretended to see the universal Jew thrusting Russia and the world toward the abyss, with the Russian and other intellectuals as dupes and hirelings hypocritically making an issue of the guilt or innocence of the obscure and piffling figure of the Jew Beiliss.

PART FOUR

THE SHOWDOWN

C H A P T E R 1 6

HIGHLIGHTS OF THE TRIAL*

1

A TENSE, EERIE SILENCE hung briefly over the courtroom after the clerk had ended his one-and-one-half-hour reading of the indictment on the morning of the second day. There was an unspoken incredulity in the air. Was this it? Was this, at the end of two and a half years of preparation, the government's case? Those who had followed the rambling, haphazard discourse closely were profoundly shocked, and even those whose attention had wavered during the droning recital were bewildered. For quite apart from the reasons which led V. V. Shulgin to write his flaming attack the next day, there was one feature of the document about which opinions could not be divided: the contrast between the hurried treatment of the charge against Beiliss and the prolonged concentration on the exoneration of Vera Cheberyak. A tacit question filled the silence: who was being tried here, Mendel Beiliss or Vera Cheberyak?

Officially it remained the former; substantively it turned out to be the latter. Nor from the nature of the material could it have been otherwise; and the prosecution, adapting its strategy to this inescapable negative situation, labored mightily to turn it to advantage.

First, the case against Beiliss.

2

It was part of the prosecution's strategy to spend nearly three days on proving in minute and repetitive detail what no one disputed, namely, that Andryusha's family was not implicated in the crime. It was only in the second half of the fourth day that the proceedings against Beiliss really opened.

There were six prime witnesses for the prosecution: the two lamplighters, the Wolf-Woman, the Cheberyak parents, and their sole surviving child, Lyudmilla. The lamplighters had already as good as disqualified themselves by the self- and cross-contradictions in their pretrial depositions; it was beyond the wit of any correspondent why the prosecution subpoenaed them. The other four proceeded to destroy themselves in court. I have already described some of the relevant scenes; I repeat them in brief before rounding out the picture.

Yuliana Shakhovskaya, the lamplighter's wife, had been the first to report the discovery of an eyewitness to the seizing of Andryusha on the morning of the murder. This eyewitness was Anna the Wolf-Woman, the homeless old derelict who slept where she could, summers in the open and winters in a corner of the covered market. When she had been brought before the magistrate, Anna had repeated with much circumstantiality (so the official deposition said) the story she had presumably told Yuliana—that she had seen Beiliss, with Andryusha on his shoulders, making for the kilns. But in court, to the fury and disgust of the prosecution and the audible amusement of the spectators, she went blank. Whining, bobbing up and down, with many "dearies" and "kind sirs," she denied everything in her deposition. "I didn't say a thing. . . . I didn't see a thing. . . . They wrote what they wrote, and when they told me to leave, I left."

"Nauseating," "comical," "unbelievable" were the words used by some of the correspondents about this performance.

She not only repudiated her own deposition as read out to her; it will be recalled that she even denied, in a confrontation with Yuliana, ever having mentioned the murder to her and ever having seen the Zaitsev brickyard.

Again: Yuliana had reported a second eyewitness to the seizing of Andryusha—this time, her husband. But long before the trial he had denied in a deposition ever having told his wife that he had seen Beiliss carrying off Andryusha. And there, in court, the whole story came out as to the manner in which the original depositions had been obtained, how Polishchuk and an aide, Krasovsky's assistants, prompted by the Golubev team, had worked on these three witnesses with promises, threats —and vodka.

> KARABCHEVSKY: Did the detectives advise you to accuse Beiliss?
> SHAKHOVSKY: They gave me vodka. They told me to say this and
>   that.
> KARABCHEVSKY: Did they tell you to accuse Beiliss?
> SHAKHOVSKY: Yes.

Karabchevsky hounded Shakhovsky on the contradictions in his depositions, driving the point home repeatedly for the benefit of the jury.

> KARABCHEVSKY: You were questioned seven times. You also testi-
>   fied that Zhenya told you how he and Andryusha were chased
>   by a black-bearded man. Didn't you later admit that Zhenya
>   never told you such a story and that you had invented it?

Shakhovsky was dumb, and Judge Boldyrev prodded him: "Remember, did you or did you not say so?" Shakhovsky replied: "I don't remember."

Vasily Cheberyak, father of the dead Zhenya, was the fourth prime witness for the prosecution and was called on the seventh and eighth days. To him too Zhenya was supposed to have reported some time before his death that he and Andryusha had been chased by Beiliss one morning round the time of the murder; so Vasily Cheberyak had deposed on December 20, 1911. On the stand the testimony went like this:

> WITNESS: One day, when I was home, my son Zhenya came running in and told me that when he and his sisters were playing near the clay mixer, Mendel and two other Jews ran after them. They grabbed him and Andryusha; Zhenya escaped, and he saw Andryusha being dragged away in the direction of the kilns. The other two Jews looked like rabbis.
> JUDGE: Were Beiliss's boys there, too?
> WITNESS: Yes, Beiliss's family was there.

According to *this* version, the snatching of Andryusha was carried out in the presence not only of Zhenya Cheberyak and his sisters but of the Beiliss family. As one of the observers at the trial commented, if Cheberyak *père* was telling the truth, Beiliss seemed determined to provide as many witnesses as possible to the crime. But while Cheberyak *père* had given his first version to the investigating magistrate in December 1911, four months after Zhenya's death, Vera Cheberyak had said nothing about Zhenya having witnessed the seizing of Andryusha until July 1912, eleven months after Zhenya's death.

> GRUZENBERG: Why didn't you make your wife tell the magistrate that a Christian boy was kidnapped and had disappeared?
> WITNESS: I didn't pay much attention to it (*Ne obratil vnimanya*).

Nothing in the text enables us to make sense of this remark by father Cheberyak, and neither the judge nor any of the counsels took up the riddle. The session for the seventh day ended on this baffling note, and the next morning Cheberyak *père* was put on the stand again. His deposition of December 20, 1911, was read out to him.

> GRUZENBERG: You have just heard your deposition: "Andryusha ran away pursued by Beiliss," but yesterday you said that Beiliss and two rabbis dragged him away. Why the contradiction?
> WITNESS: When I made my deposition I was very much upset and confused.

After this the prosecution did not seem to know what to do with father Cheberyak. It insisted that the scene in the brickyard had indeed taken place much as he had described it, but it conceded that father Cheberyak was not to be trusted: it was not to him that Zhenya had told the story. As Zamyslovsky put it in his summation: "We must grant some basis for not believing father Cheberyak. Vasily is pitiable and browbeaten. Vera Cheberyak is a depraved woman, a liar, a criminal. She is a woman not to be influenced by conscience or duty. . . . She is as shifty and garrulous as Vasily is pitiable and browbeaten." Zamyslovsky admitted in effect that Vasily Cheberyak had told his story at the prompting of his wife.

To this we may add a pathetic aside. Asked on the stand how long he had been married to Vera Cheberyak, Vasily answered: "A long time."

To whom, then, had Zhenya told the story of the seizing of Andryusha? To his mother, Vera Cheberyak, the "depraved liar and criminal"; and when she repeated it and was backed up by her nine-year-old daughter, the prosecution professed to believe her.

I have already referred to the remarkable feat of memory performed by little Lyudmilla in her deposition on August 11, 1912, one year and five months after the murder of Andryusha. At the time of the deposition she was nine years old; she had therefore been seven and a half years old in March 1911. But she recalled —or at least she recited in precise detail—the events on the morning of March 12, 1911, down to the approximate hour when Andryusha had arrived at her home and called up to Zhenya to go and play with him on the clay mixer. Now on the eighth day of the trial, fourteen months after she had made her deposition, she told the same story with only minor variations.

WITNESS: Andryusha called to my brother Zhenya, asking him to go and play. We all went: Zhenya, Dunya [Eudoxia, the shoemaker Nakonechny's daughter], myself, and some boys [the witnesses to the crime become still more numerous!]. We were

playing on the grounds when Mendel and someone else chased
us away. He got Zhenya and Andryusha. Zhenya got away and
ran, and he got Andryusha, and I ran home with my sister. She
shouted: "They got Andryusha," but I didn't see it.

PROSECUTOR VIPPER: Did you tell anyone about this?

WITNESS: No, I was scared, and then I went to stay with my
grandmother.

PROSECUTOR: Were you questioned about it?

WITNESS: Yes, later on; and I told them the same thing [as now].

PROSECUTOR: When the corpse was found, were you afraid to talk
about it? Didn't your mother forbid you to do that?

WITNESS: God forbid! She wanted me to tell the truth.

The court asked for a confrontation between Lyudmilla and
Dunya, the only one of the children besides Zhenya, Valya, and
Andryusha whom Lyudmilla mentioned by name as having gone
to play on the clay mixer that morning. The two little girls stood
facing each other, and Judge Boldyrev addressed Dunya: "Were
you playing with Lyudmilla, and did Beiliss chase you away?"

She answered: "It never happened." Lyudmilla: "We were
chased by Beiliss." Dunya: "Better think back."

At this point the transcript records that Lyudmilla began to
cry and said: "I am afraid." It was the first time she had been
challenged on her almost letter-perfect repetition of her testimony. Prosecutor Vipper at once asked that the incident be
entered in the record: he was building up the principal thesis of
his summation—that all witnesses against Beiliss who faltered or
retracted had been bribed or frightened by the Jews.

As the sixth of the prime witnesses for the prosecution Vera
Cheberyak labored under the handicap of that evil reputation
which the prosecution itself helped to impress upon the court;
but even without it her testimony would have had as little value
as her husband's. While their children Zhenya and Valya had
been alive, neither the father nor mother had cited them as
having witnessed the seizing of Andryusha. Five months elapsed
between that supposed incident and the death of the children in
August 1911. Four months later, in December 1911, as we have

just recalled, the father first came up with the story that Zhenya, before dying, had told him of seeing Beiliss seize Andryusha. Still another seven months passed before the mother first told a similar story to the investigating magistrate, who had interrogated her at least five times since the murder. This was pointed out to her by Judge Boldyrev—it was obvious enough without any pointing out—when she took the stand on the fourteenth day. It was on that day that Shmakov, one of the prosecutors, entered in his secret diary the raging comment: "On April 22, June 24, July 11, July 26, and September 13, 1911, Fenenko interrogated Cheberyak and she said nothing about Zhenya in connection with Andryusha's visits. She has enmeshed herself in her own lies, the lying bitch. And this is the hinge of the whole affair."*

One may not agree that this was the hinge of the whole affair— there were later developments in the trial that might claim that designation; but it did represent the collapse of the state's case against Beiliss. It came on top of a series of retractions and self-contradictions in Cheberyak's testimony that compelled the judge to admonish her: "You had better tell the truth."

She had, for instance, deposed that she had never set eyes on Andryusha after his family had moved away to Slobodka; on the stand she admitted—after other witnesses had established the fact—that she had seen him more than once when he was living in Slobodka. She had denied in particular that Andryusha had been at her house on the morning of the murder; she was forced to admit that on the morning of the murder Andryusha had left his overcoat in her apartment. Until the end she kept on denying —but by this time her credibility had been completely destroyed —that Andryusha had left his books there, too.

The transcript of the trial does not quite bear out the tribute paid by journalists to Cheberyak's personality, ingenuity, and inventiveness. Reading it side by side with the feature articles and personal memoirs one concludes that as a liar she had an impressive delivery but was weak on supporting material. What was good enough in a brawl with neighbors or in handling a policeman was not good enough in a courtroom. Faced by trained lawyers she was out of her element, and it was obvious that she had a grievance. They did not fight fair; they remembered things she had said hours and even days before. She resented being held accountable for depositions she had made a year and even two years earlier. Improvising as she did, she often fell into what earlier has been called "truth-revealing lies."

One glaring instance has to do with her criminal connections. In her depositions and at the trial she was asked for the names of the men who frequented her apartment, and she submitted, if it may be so put, quite a respectable list; but when it came to the Troika, the threesome strongly suspected along with her of the murder, the only member she mentioned was her half-brother, Singayevsky. She apparently felt that to deny the visits of such a close relative would involve her in tiresome explanations, but she did not think far enough ahead about the others. She should have known that her intimacy with the two other members of the Troika, Latyshev and Rudzinsky, was bound to come out—as in fact it did—and that her suppression of their names would create an even more tiresome complication.

A Yiddish journalist pointed up the incident with a folk story. A Jew named Berel was leaving Russia illegally. He had been supplied with a false passport and was told that henceforth his name was Yossel. Preparing for the questioning at the frontier he went about for days repeating: "My name is not Berel, it's Yossel; my name is not Berel, it's Yossel." When at last he faced the frontier gendarme and was asked his name, he went into a panic and spluttered: "Whatever my name is, one thing is sure: it's not Berel."*

If the prosecution found Cheberyak an unhelpful witness, it had partly itself to blame. The role she was called upon to play was in any case not an easy one. The prosecution made it more difficult by the line it took: she was indeed a depraved, orgiastic, and conscienceless creature, the leader of a gang of criminals; by the malignity of fate she had unjustly been made the object of suspicion in a frightful crime. What stance was she to take under the rain of insults pouring down on her from her own defenders, to say nothing of Beiliss's defenders? How was she to talk and act? with oh-everything-but-that contrition? or with righteous far-be-it-from-me indignation?

She was too often resentful when she should have been resigned, pugnacious when she should have been submissive. A minor argument developed round a dress she had been accused of stealing. She had sold it to a girl living with her at the time, and when the girl learned that the dress had probably been stolen, she returned it to Cheberyak and Cheberyak kept it. Dignified and respected counsel Grigorovich-Barsky asked her: "Did you also keep the money?" Cheberyak flared up: "That's my business." Grigorovich-Barsky: "We are interested in knowing whether you sold that dress." Cheberyak: "I don't want to talk about it. It's nobody's affair whether my servant paid me or not. It's my affair. We are dealing with different things here."

This might have been acceptable from an honest but touchy housewife; it did not suit the noisy and quarrelsome woman on whose low character the opposing sides were in such fervid agreement.

It was apparent at several points that Cheberyak was not at all content with the line chosen by the prosecutors—that is, her defenders. They were making too free with her reputation, and they lacked strategic imagination. Thus on the fourth day of the trial, while she was awaiting her main appearance, she decided to take a hand in her own defense and while in the waiting room tried to persuade a witness, Zarutsky, a boy of eleven, to testify that he had been with Zhenya, Andryusha, and the other children on the morning of the murder and had seen Beiliss seize Andryusha and drag him off. The boy refused. A woman witness overheard the conversation and repeated it in court. When Cheberyak and the boy were called to a confrontation, there was a deadlock.

> JUDGE: Witness Cheberyak, the boy says you instructed him to tell us that he was at the clay mixer at that time.
> CHEBERYAK: It never happened.
> JUDGE: Tell us, boy, how it really was.

ZARUTSKY: She was seated some way from us. She told me to come over and said to me: "Don't you remember when you, Zhenya, Valya, and Linda [Lyudmilla] were playing on the clay mixer, and Beiliss grabbed Valya, Zhenya, and Andryusha, and these two managed to get away and he got Andryusha?"

CHEBERYAK: You are lying. It was Lyudmilla who said that.

The incident was dropped.

Now the case against Cheberyak and the Troika.

3

As the evidence against Beiliss sank, the evidence against Cheberyak and the Troika mounted proportionately. In effect the larger part of the trial consisted of a desperate rear-guard action on the part of the prosecution.

The most important piece of material evidence produced in court was the section of pillowslip, blood-clotted and semen-stained, that had been found in the pocket of Andryusha's jacket, side by side with the body. That this object had not been destroyed is a tribute to the watchfulness and pertinacity of those officials within the administration—Fenenko and Brandorf among them—who fought the conspiracy from the inside.

The strange feature about the semen stains was that Andryusha had not been sexually molested, nor was there any suggestion of a sexual element in the murder. But semen stains had been found on the walls of the Cheberyak apartment, and two witnesses identified the section of pillowslip as having belonged to a set in the Cheberyak apartment.

These were the sisters Katherine and Ksenya Diakonova, the two "floozies" who knew too much and had to be put out of the way, of whom Singayevsky had spoken with such hatred to Karayev and Makhalin. They had long been key figures in the investigations of Detective Krasovsky, Colonel Ivanov, and the journalist Brazul. Habitués of the Cheberyak apartment, pickers-up of free meals and little gifts of money, they did their best to spin out to their own advantage their association with the case.

They gave their main testimony on the fifteenth and sixteenth days.

Krasovsky stated in court, and Katherine Diakonova confirmed, that he had taken her out some thirty times. Brazul had not been less assiduous in his attentions, and Colonel Ivanov admitted that he had been in the habit of regularly handing out to Katherine tips, or "carfare money," up to as much as five rubles at a time. Katherine and Ksenya Diakonova were frivolous, silly creatures, but they were not criminal types and not vicious; this must be borne in mind in view of the serious implications of their evidence.

Ksenya, who was a seamstress, testified that some time after the date of the murder Cheberyak had asked her to sew some new slips for the pillows in her living room. It was noticed by both sisters that one of the four pillows was without a slip. In making the new slips Ksenya did not follow the old pattern of embroidery, but she and Katherine remembered the old pattern nonetheless. At the trial, shown the section of pillow case found with Andryusha's body, they affirmed that what was left of the embroidery tallied with the designs they had seen on the old pillowslips.

But on this issue the questioning by the prosecution was so long and so complicated that nothing short of one of the old pillowslips to place side by side with the exhibit could have settled the question. Cheberyak of course denied the identity of the designs. But there was one peculiarly significant detail in the pillowslip episode. When the sisters made their pretrial depositions before Investigating Magistrate Mashkevich and talked about the pillowslips, he did not show them the exhibit to refresh or challenge their recollection. This was a gross breach of the law.

The sisters testified in pretrial depositions and in court that all three members of the Troika were regular visitors at the Cheberyak home. To this Cheberyak finally had to confess; to all the other damaging statements she opposed a consistent negative.

Both in her depositions and at the trial Katherine asserted that at about eleven o'clock on the morning of March 12, 1911, she had paid a visit to Cheberyak and had been struck by the queer behavior of the three men Singayevsky, Latyshev, and Rudzinsky (the Troika), whom she found there. At the trial she said: "Cheberyak herself opened the door, and I saw in the big room the three men, who got flustered and ran into the small room, where they remained in hiding. She didn't let me go into the living room, but took me into the kitchen. The room was in disorder, the rug was thrown under the table." Some time later, she continued, she was told by a certain Adele Ravich,* a shopkeeper who used to handle stolen goods for Cheberyak, that she had seen the body of Andryusha rolled up in the carpet under the table.

Ksenya Diakonova likewise testified that Adele Ravich had made this statement to her separately. The Raviches, husband and wife, were—like a number of other crucial witnesses—not at the trial. They had left for Canada in the fall of 1911, shortly after Cheberyak's arrest. The defense petitioned the court to have the couple traced by Russian consular agents in Canada and the United States so that their depositions might be taken. The court denied the petition.

On the ground floor, immediately under Cheberyak's apartment, was the government liquor store and the living quarters of the woman who attended it, Zinaida Malitzkaya. There was bad blood between the two women. Cheberyak had made some attempts to sell Malitzkaya various articles—jewelry, furs—and Malitzkaya had refused to buy, had also hinted her belief that the articles were stolen. It came to a state of war: Cheberyak slapped Malitzkaya and Malitzkaya threw stones at Cheberyak's window. Which act came first was not clear. Malitzkaya testified as follows on the seventeenth day of the trial:

Early in March 1911, when my husband had left home for an extended period [he worked seasonally on a farm], I heard in Vera Cheberyak's apartment childish footsteps. . . . The steps went from one room to another. From the small room they went into the large room. Then I heard a door slam, and childish footsteps and cries were heard. I heard a noise, then a pause, whispering,

and then some muffled kind of childish noise. Here I had to go back
into the store. . . . Then I returned again. I heard steps, but particularly clearly I heard the steps of adults, and the childish footsteps were no longer to be heard. It sounded like a dancing couple,
as if they were making steps to one side then to another.
A PROSECUTING ATTORNEY: At what time was this?
MALITZKAYA: I can't say exactly. Approximately between ten and
eleven o'clock.
PROSECUTING ATTORNEY: Tell us in more detail what happened.
MALITZKAYA: I can't describe it in more detail because my business
  is such that I constantly have to run into the store. I heard the
  scuffling or whatever it was. I went into the store and then returned into the room [directly under the Cheberyak apartment]
  again. It sounded as though they were carrying some kind of
  burden. I heard squeals and Cheberyak's shrieks. Thereafter the
  steps went into the other room and it sounded as if they had put
  their burden on the floor. . . . I immediately understood that
  they were carrying whoever had been crying out.

It is to be noted that the hour given by Malitzkaya, between
ten and eleven, corresponded with the hour given by Katherine
Diakonova for her visit to the Cheberyak apartment on the
morning of March 12.

We have just seen that Detective Polishchuk, the assistant
assigned to Krasovsky, was one of the men accused by the lamplighters of suborning them to accuse Beiliss. He was accused by
Krasovsky in turn of having placed himself "at the disposal of
student Golubev and others of the Rightist organizations."
Polishchuk had originally done good work in reporting the deathbed scene of Zhenya Cheberyak and the unnatural behavior of
the mother. The priest called in to administer the last rites,
Father Sinkevich, had confirmed Polishchuk's description of the
mother preventing the dying boy from answering the questions
of the detectives. But what Polishchuk had reported freely to
Krasovsky and his superiors in the early days had to be dragged
out of him in court two years later. For he had become a different man, by now up to his neck in the conspiracy. It was he
who had dug up the accusation against Krasovsky of having

embezzled the sum of 16 kopeks in 1903. But Polishchuk's reluctance to repeat the original version of the deathbed scene only enhanced the effect it produced in the courtroom.

Equally impressive was Detective Kirichenko's account given in court of the mother's frantic and furtive interference with the questioning of Zhenya at an earlier stage of the investigations. However none of the episodes thus far related counted as heavily against the Troika—and therefore Cheberyak—as what is best described as "the frustrated confession," which was taken up on the eighteenth day of the trial; though that was eclipsed by the great scene that almost immediately followed on the same day.

Now let us recall that Singayevsky and Rudzinsky, the two surviving members of the Troika, had come before the investigating magistrate and the state prosecutor and had confessed that on the night of March 12, 1911, they had robbed the Adamovich optical goods store on the Kreshchatik, the main business street of Kiev. They did this, as Rudzinsky frankly explained, because they knew themselves to be suspected of Andryusha's murder. Rudzinsky was under the erroneous impression that the police believed the murder to have taken place on the night of March 12 instead of in the morning of that day. The robbery therefore gave them, he reasoned, a perfect alibi; and they preferred three or four years for robbery to twenty years for murder. But then the shocking thing happened: their confession was thrown out of court. Judge Boldyrev explained it carefully to the jury: "You see, gentlemen, this is the law: if the investigating magistrate finds the material insufficient, he writes a decision for the discontinuance of the investigation. This was done in regard to Singayevsky. In regard to Rudzinsky, the state prosecutor decided to discontinue the prosecution. This conclusion was confirmed by the Kiev District Court. . . . Thus the case was discontinued because the investigating magistrate did not collect sufficient evidence."

But State Prosecutor Vipper would not have it. He undertook to prove there and then that the three men were the victims of a serious miscarriage of justice. They *had* committed the robbery and ought to have gone to jail for it; nor was it for lack of honest effort that they had not managed to get themselves sentenced. True, they had made the confession in order to establish an alibi, but that was not the point. The point was, he insisted, that they had committed the robbery. It was true, again, that the murder had been committed on the morning of March 12, and superficially the alibi might now seem to be worthless. But such was by no means the case. For the robbery had been such a daring and difficult piece of work that it simply precluded the possibility of their having committed a murder on the morning of the same day in another part of the city.

Vipper was, indeed, at his best in pleading the guilt of the Troika in the matter of the robbery, and the correspondents were moved to comment that never before in real life had an attorney labored so diligently to prove his clients guilty of a criminal act in the face of a judicial refusal to indict.

To dramatize his case, Vipper extracted from the lumpish Singayevsky a piecemeal re-enactment of the crime, exhibiting in detail how Rudzinsky had forced an entry, how he himself, the crack picklock, had followed, how Latyshev had acted as lookout, how they had gathered up the loot, how they had made their getaway, how everything had gone off according to plan, and how the next morning they had left for Moscow.

Zamyslovsky then stepped in to spell things out for the jury. He addressed Singayevsky: "Before going to the store you had to find out carefully when the owner leaves the place, and so on. Such an undertaking demands a considerable knowledge of the circumstances. It is necessary to find out where the watchman is stationed, whether near the store or by the gate. In general it is necessary to make prolonged reconnaissance—finding out where the things are kept, how the store is locked up, and so on. When people rob a store it isn't just a simple question of climbing in. There has to be careful investigation. . . . So you were occupied for two days doing this. . . ."

Singayevsky kept nodding approval.

Then Rudzinsky was called up, in chains and accompanied

by two guards. Under prompting from Vipper he added corroborative details: how he had broken in with a jemmy and drill, how they had collected the eyeglasses, knives, and binoculars and passed them out to Latyshev. Jury and correspondents listened with great interest to this professional exposition. It was a pity that Latyshev was dead; but even without him the story was quite convincing.

It all reads like some lost fragment of *The Mikado* or an upside-down detective story: two men confess to a crime and with the help of counsel furnish a highly persuasive account of its details; counsel then defies anyone to establish their innocence. Not the least intriguing feature of the performance is the complacency of the judge, who permits the argument to go on and on after he has read out the record of the judicial dismissal of the case against the burglars.

Having thus established to everyone's satisfaction—including that of Beiliss's attorneys, who for that matter had needed no convincing—the guilt of the Troika in the robbery, Vipper made an about-face in a moving dissertation on the essential decency of his clients. He expostulated at the false position in which they had been placed. It was so easy to believe bad things about the Troika—also about Cheberyak, particularly about Cheberyak—who were thus condemned in advance. He pleaded with the jury to strip itself of any prejudices it might have against professional criminals. "Can you say that these three men are guilty of murder? Rudzinsky came here from Siberia, where he is doing hard labor for burglary. Is this some miscreant who would commit such a horrible crime as the killing of Andryusha Yuschinsky? I am very glad that Singayevsky and Rudzinsky were here. They do not make the impression of villains. Would a thief, an ordinary criminal, subject children to such tortures and agonies? . . . I would certainly not be standing here if I were not convinced that they are innocent and that the man in the prisoner's dock is guilty."

It was a courageous appeal to the intuitions of the jury, since from all the accounts Singayevsky looked like what he was, a

subnormal type—Vipper himself had commented on his stupidity—while Rudzinsky, who "came" to the trial, as Vipper
delicately put it, from Siberia, was serving his sentence not for
burglary but, as the jury well knew, for armed robbery. Having
closed this appeal Vipper brought out the contrast between the
unfortunate handicap of the two "innocent criminals," as the
press immediately labeled them, and the unfair advantage en-
joyed by Mendel Beiliss.

What a contrast! Apart from his participation in ritual murders, argued Vipper, Beiliss might very well be an admirable
character, even though not a professional burglar. So many
witnesses had testified in his favor, none in his disfavor. "It is
entirely possible," said Vipper, "that Mendel Beiliss is a fine
family man, a virtuous and industrious worker like any other
Jew living in modest circumstances, and a religious one. But
does that prevent him from committing a crime? Not at all. . . .
I repeat, this may be a fine person in all respects, he may be a
good family man, he may love his father and mother."

It was not enough to depict Beiliss as a fine family man, a
virtuous and industrious workman like other Jews living in
modest circumstances (and presumably resembling him also in
the practice of ritual murder). Carried along by his own elo-
quence Vipper turned from the "may be" to the "certainly is."
He spurned the aspersions cast by the defense on Beiliss's piety,
refused to believe that he was a Sabbath-breaker and had been
working in the factory on that fateful Saturday morning. "I
assume that if old Zaitsev, who regarded the *matzos* as sacred
food, entrusted the baking of them to Beiliss, he chose him
because he was a devout and religious Jew."

Had Beiliss ever baked *matzos* for old Zaitsev, that would
indeed have said something for his piety. He had, however,
only delivered *matzos*. But for the prosecution Beiliss's piety
was as important as his reputation for general decency of character. It might trouble the jury, said Vipper, that a man with
such an excellent reputation should be capable of ritual murder,
but they were not for that reason to suppose that the reputation

was undeserved. On the contrary, the more Beiliss deserved the good opinion of his neighbors, the more likely was it that as a Jew he practiced ritual murder. In other words, the jury was not to let itself be misled by the truth.

The defense, which had never doubted the truthfulness of the Troika's confession to the burglary, took the position that the Troika could very well have been at the Cheberyak apartment on the morning of March 12, as Katherine Diakonova had testified, and still have committed the burglary the same night.

The ludicrous and the intensely dramatic ran together in the confrontation between Singayevsky and the young revolutionary Makhalin.

If Colonel Ivanov of the *okhrana* and Prosecutor Zamyslovsky had had their way, that confrontation would never have taken place. They wanted Makhalin kept away from the trial, like his fellow revolutionary and fellow investigator Karayev and like Detective Polishchuk and the convict spy Kozachenko. Colonel Ivanov was afraid that he would be called as a witness and would have to face Makhalin, who had once been in his employ. Makhalin would certainly not want that sordid episode recalled, but the defense might know about it and force it into the open. The prospect caused Ivanov acute discomfort on general and special grounds: on general grounds because it was always a black eye for a security officer when one of his double agents double-crossed him; on special grounds because he might be asked why he had trusted Makhalin's word as a security spy but distrusted it in the matter of the Beiliss case.

Zamyslovsky wanted Makhalin kept away from the trial because he was afraid that in a confrontation with him the lummox Singayevsky would break down, a very reasonable fear in view of what actually happened. Zamyslovsky felt so strongly about it that he threatened to withdraw from the case if he did not have his way; but the administration felt it had gone as far as it could in keeping inconvenient witnesses from the trial. Ivanov and Zamyslovsky finally gave way.

The moment they dreaded approached as the scene of the frustrated confession drew toward its close. Singayevsky had been on the stand for more than an hour; with the continuous help of the prosecution he had at last managed to inculpate himself irretrievably in the robbery—at least as far as the unofficial opinion of *this* court was concerned. Now Gruzenberg, having accepted the situation, was hammering away at him: "Why do you think that if during the night of the twelfth you were robbing the store, it means that you could not commit the murder? You said: 'I am not afraid, because on the night of the twelfth to the thirteenth I was in the robbery.' I am asking you why you think that this proves you couldn't have committed a murder on the morning of the twelfth?"

They had been over this ground before. Vipper and Zamyslovsky had already done their best to prove that the robbery had been a difficult and complicated job that had demanded the complete attention of the Troika for at least the preceding two days. But the defense was not satisfied and did not believe that the jury was satisfied. Gruzenberg repeated his question. Singayevsky was silent; he had no ideas of his own. Gruzenberg put the question to him for the third time, and now it was Zamyslovsky who came to Singayevsky's rescue.

ZAMYSLOVSKY (to Singayevsky): Didn't you consider that if a murder is committed, it is necessary to hide the body?
WITNESS: Yes, sir.
ZAMYSLOVSKY: If, then, the murder was committed on the morning of the twelfth, it would be impossible to put the body away until the night of the twelfth.
WITNESS: Yes, sir.
ZAMYSLOVSKY: And on the night of the twelfth you were involved in a robbery, and on the thirteenth you left in the morning.
WITNESS: Yes.
ZAMYSLOVSKY: You consider it definitely proved that you couldn't have been able to hide the body away, since you all left?
WITNESS: Yes, sir.

It was the contention of the defense that the body had been removed from the apartment either that night or the night after by other members of the Cheberyak gang. But all this faded away when Makhalin was called in for confrontation with Singayevsky. It was perhaps the intensest moment of the trial. Evening had fallen and the electric lights were on. The small oblong hall, which accommodated between two hundred fifty and three hundred persons was jammed, as it had been from the beginning, with the correspondents of the principal newspapers and news agencies of Russia and the Western world, with spectators, witnesses, counsel, and judges. There was a constant turning of heads, as at a tennis match, from the crimson-covered bench to the witness stand and back again. Agent D. was in the room, sweating it out with the prosecution and the judges. Judge Boldyrev called out: "Makhalin, come here." The foppishly dressed Makhalin took his stand opposite Singayevsky.

Judge (to Singayevsky): "Look at this young man. Do you recognize him or not?" Singayevsky is silent. Judge: "Do you know him or not?" A long pause ensued. Singayevsky was struggling with himself. Whether he had any coherent thoughts, whether he was formulating the problem to himself, cannot be known. Its essence was clear to the audience. That he had met two men who called themselves Makhalin and Karayev he had already admitted; he had confirmed or contradicted various parts of their depositions regarding the meetings and his conversations with them. The question before him now was whether he should deny that this was the man who had called himself Makhalin. If he could carry that off, he would be spared an ordeal; he would not have to fight it out with Makhalin in the presence of so many spectators. He stood there in a stupor.

There were many who expected Singayevsky to break down at this moment and confess to the murder. Defense counsel Maklakov later said in his summation: "This went on for a few agonizing minutes, and I had the notion that this drama would open up and there would be a confession." Defense counsel Karabchevsky too dwelt in his summation on this crucial episode, but his disappointment at its outcome found a different form of expression: "I am pleased that Singayevsky remained true to himself and just stood there, with his dull look and his small brain." Had Singayevsky confessed to the murder, continued Karabchevsky, Prosecutor Vipper would surely have added him to the long list of witnesses he had accused of taking Jewish money or yielding to Jewish threats.

At long last Singayevsky answered: "I know him."

"That was the moment," said Maklakov bitterly in his summation, "that the prosecution moved in." Actually it was Judge Boldyrev who interposed and from that point on, aided by the prosecution, steered Singayevsky through the remainder of the scene.

JUDGE BOLDYREV (to Singayevsky): Where did you meet him?
SINGAYEVSKY: In Karayev's room.
JUDGE: You spoke with him about the Yushchinsky murder?
SINGAYEVSKY: No.
JUDGE: You affirm that when you spoke with Karayev this young man was not present?
SINGAYEVSKY: He was not present.

The moment of extreme danger had passed. Karayev had stated in his deposition that Singayevsky made his confession to him in the presence of Makhalin. Next to denying that he had ever met this Makhalin, Singayevsky's best move was to deny that Makhalin had been present at the conversation untruthfully described by Karayev. If Singayevsky had ever been on the point of confessing, Judge Boldyrev had successfully pushed him past it. All that remained now was for Singayevsky to repeat mechanically that Makhalin had not been present at the conversation and that during the conversation he had not spoken about the murder.

It may be said with almost absolute certainty that faced with his former idol, Karayev, Singayevsky would have broken down. It may be said with equal certainty that the violent-tempered Karayev, contemptuous of all authority, would never have tolerated the interference of the judge and the shamelessly leading questions put by him and the prosecution to Singayevsky. And if he had not been able to prevent the maneuver he would have created such a scandal round it as to destroy whatever value it had.

"We protested," said Maklakov in his summation, "but the silence had been broken . . . the secret remained hidden." Not altogether, or at least not according to Agent D., who wrote that night to Shcheglovitov: "Without confessing to the murder Singayevsky admitted knowing Makhalin, confirming some details of his testimony. . . . The public speaks of the undoubted acquittal of Beiliss."

On the nineteenth day, the last day of interrogations, a climax of humiliation for the prosecution was reached in the performance of Lieutenant Colonel Pavel Ivanov, aide to Colonel Shredel, head of the gendarmery. It should be recalled that it was Ivanov who had succumbed to the pressure of his superiors and undertaken the manufacture of evidence against Beiliss. It was he who had planted the convict spy Kozachenko in Beiliss's cell and had failed to denounce Kozachenko's ludicrous deposition according to which Beiliss had tried to hire him to poison the lamplighter Shakhovsky and the shoemaker Nakonechny. The reader will recall further that Kozachenko, challenged by Ivanov, had gone down on his knees and confessed to having invented the story out of whole cloth.

We can understand the administration's decision to keep the alcoholic and oafish Kozachenko from attending the trial; it is not easy to understand why Ivanov should have told Professor Pikhno, editor-in-chief of the *Kievlyanin,* of Kozachenko's confession. Pikhno, deceased by the time of the trial, had passed the story on to the converted Jew Breitman, another journalist, and there had been conversations between Breitman and Ivanov on the Kozachenko episode. At the trial Karabchevsky questioned Ivanov on these conversations:

> KARABCHEVSKY: You said you spoke with Breitman [about the Beiliss case]. Did you have occasion to speak to him about information disclosed to him by Pikhno?

IVANOV: I don't remember.

KARABCHEVSKY: Didn't you talk with him at any time about Kozachenko?

IVANOV: I cannot remember exactly conversations which took place two years ago.

KARABCHEVSKY: So you didn't mention the fact that Kozachenko confessed to you that he had accused Beiliss falsely?

IVANOV: I don't remember this.

The transcript does not show that the defense ever put the direct question: "Did Kozachenko confess to you that he made up the poisoning story?" Ivanov was asked only whether he had told the story to Pikhno and discussed it with Breitman. We have just seen his answers.

Ivanov was also involved in "the frustrated confession" in a manner that reflected equally upon his competence and his honesty. It was to Ivanov that Rudzinsky had first proposed that he confess to the robbery, and it was Ivanov who directed him to the right quarters. On this issue Gruzenberg did most of the questioning.

GRUZENBERG: Didn't you ask him [Rudzinsky] how confessing to a crime in the evening or on the night of the twelfth to the thirteenth would give him an alibi against a murder committed on the morning of the twelfth?

IVANOV: No, I didn't ask.

GRUZENBERG: But the information about this [the actual time of the murder] was already in the papers.

IVANOV: This was unknown to me.

As noted, there had been conflicting reports in the press about the time of the murder; it is more than likely that misleading statements had been put about by the police as a trap. But that Ivanov should have been misinformed was simply not to be believed; and this lie too helped to reveal the truth. Ivanov had encouraged Rudzinsky to enter the confession because he was willing to have the Troika gamble on a partial alibi. Thus in his testimony he stumbled on from lie to lie. One gets the impression that he was in something of a daze, for when the prosecution tried to help him along, as it had helped Singayevsky, he failed to take his cue.

He was asked whether to his knowledge work had been going on at the brickyard on the day of the murder. He gave two answers: the first was that Investigating Magistrate Fenenko had entered the report that work had in fact been going on. But this was not the answer the prosecution wanted. Asked again, he replied that he had not been able to find out. Despairingly Vipper asked: "Weren't you interested in the question?" "Yes," replied Ivanov, "but I wasn't able to establish the facts."

Vipper abandoned this line and resorted, not for the first or last time, to the presumable role of Jewish money and Jewish coercion in the setting up of the defense. Vipper: "Is it known to you whether Brazul, Makhalin, and Karayev received certain sums from someone?" Ivanov: "I have a report on this. The Kiev gendarmery has a number of corroborated statements that all the parties in the private investigation received remuneration." According to this report, continued Ivanov, Brazul at one time received 3,000 rubles, while Karayev and Makhalin had received a regular stipend of 50 rubles a month.

Here Gruzenberg, who was giving his services without remuneration, became incensed and wanted to know the source of Ivanov's information. He rejected the explanation that on this matter Ivanov could plead "official secrecy." Thereupon Judge Boldyrev interposed: "The witness said that there is definite information in the gendarmery, of the reliability of which he is convinced, but his duty prevents him from speaking about it."

"That is what I am talking about," retorted Gruzenberg. "Why don't you, Your Excellency, explain to him that his official duty here is to tell only the truth and that he has no secrets here? I ask that this be put in the record."

Zamyslovsky thought this the right moment to twit Gruzenberg with the fact that Ivanov had been put on the stand at the insistence of the defense. Gruzenberg shot back: "It does not matter from whom the request came. There are no witnesses for the prosecution or for the defense. There are only honest witnesses and dishonest witnesses." This was in the famous Gruzenberg style, forthright to the point of recklessness. It was not permitted to imply in court that a senior government official was a liar. Judge Boldyrev called a recess to discuss this and other matters with his fellow judges. On their return he addressed Gruzenberg: "I must warn you that if there will be similar utterances on your part, I shall unfortunately have to take extreme measures."

Gruzenberg retreated a step: "My remark did not refer to anyone personally." Trying to exploit his advantage, Boldyrev lost it. "You allowed yourself an impermissible expression. You know that such categorizations do not exist, and the expression was completely out of place. I warn you that if you continue to make such remarks I will be forced to extreme measures."

But Gruzenberg refused to be pushed back any further. "I repeat," he said, "that I do not recognize any division into witnesses for the defense and witnesses for the prosecution. There are only witnesses of the court, who can be honest or dishonest, and I stand by this opinion." To this Boldyrev made no reply. After the trial the Kiev bar was induced to reprimand Gruzenberg for his aspersion on Ivanov, but that did Ivanov little good at the trial itself.

4

Where is Beiliss? In the long battle for the exoneration of Cheberyak and the Troika, he had practically disappeared from sight. There were interminable discussions about the section of pillowslip, about some saddler's spikes that might have been used in the murder, about the condition of the fences round the Zaitsev grounds at the time of the murder, about the thickness of the walls and floors in the apartment building in which Cheberyak and the liquor-store clerk lived, about the gangsters who frequented the Cheberyak home, about what Katherine Diakonova had seen that morning, about what Adele Ravich had told the Diakonova sisters, about Jewish customs, about ritual murder trials of the past. And interest in Beiliss seemed to dwindle from day to day.

Ivanov gave his evidence on the nineteenth day, and on the twentieth the experts were called in. Thereafter, except when it came to the summations, which began on the twenty-ninth day, Beiliss was mentioned even less frequently. He was the forgotten man.

His ever-increasing absence from the trial, except as a wordless and unmentioned physical object, became farcical. The newspapers kept asking: "Where is Beiliss?" At a session midway in the trial Karabchevsky asked that question in court, and Judge Boldyrev called him sharply to order for frivolity and immediately declared a recess of ten minutes. An observer* thus describes the incident: "As the Presiding Judge led his colleagues into his chambers, the crowd saw State Prosecutor Vipper rocking with laughter. One got the impression that the Presiding Judge had called the recess in order that he himself might laugh freely unseen by the public. The audience, too, which could barely restrain itself as Karabchevsky made his remark, began to laugh loudly after the court had left the hall."

CHAPTER 17

DIABOLISM FOR THE
UNDERPRIVILEGED

1

B Y THE twentieth day of the trial, when the medical experts
were called in, the prosecution seemed to be in parlous condition.
Even the conspirators, among whom must be counted Judge
Boldyrev and the prosecuting attorneys, must have begun to
wonder whether they were not asking too much of this jury, however cannily it had been selected. Nor did the four days of expert medical evaluation improve the outlook for the prosecution
—except, perhaps, to the extent that they dulled in the jurors the
unfavorable impression of what had gone before.

Beyond what has already been said in chapter six on the subject of the medical evidence, it suffices to record that of the five
experts only Kosorotov, who had received a bribe of 4,000 rubles,
interpreted the details of the autopsy as fulfilling the conditions
necessary for a ritual murder. Three were of the contrary opinion,

while one was undecided. Sikorsky, who agreed with Kosorotov, was not a medical expert but a psychiatrist and not altogether of sound mind. But the discussions were so prolonged and so smothered in medical terminology that it was impossible for the jurors to follow them or to understand the conclusions.

On the twenty-fifth day of the trial the religious experts were called in, and the hopes of the prosecution took an upward turn. For this was Father Pranaitis's day, and he, as Agent D. wrote to Shcheglovitov, was the pivot of the trial. Not that he was expected to overwhelm the jury with his learning; erudition and historical proofs were not exactly the line for the twelve Ukrainian peasants and *petits bourgeois*. It was Father Pranaitis's passionate sincerity that was to carry them on its tide to an affirmation of the Blood Accusation and perhaps, in the momentum, to a conviction of Beiliss.

Some show of scholarship was, however, necessary for decency's sake, and this Father Pranaitis provided in the opening address, making heavy weather with such terms as *Chassidism, Tsaddik, Kaballah, Zohar, Shulchan Arukh,* and the like. And he did it in a manner that hinted at a sealed-off world of sinister rites performed to the accompaniment of dark and potent mutterings. Now and then he broke the seal to disclose horror upon horror calculated to make the hairs of the listeners stand on end, their eyes start from their spheres, and a *frisson* run down their spines. To the jurors his erudition may indeed have seemed enormous, but the only thing they could follow was his portrayal of a Jewish people that concealed behind an ordinary human exterior the attributes of ghouls, vampires, and fiends generally.

Pranaitis opened his discourse by quoting at some length from a book purportedly written in Rumania at the beginning of the nineteenth century. He had found the book in the library of the St. Petersburg Theological Seminary. Nothing was known about the author, who wrote under the pseudonym "Neophyte" and represented himself as a converted Jew with special access to the secret practices of the Jews. Here is a small part of the information as read forth by Pranaitis in court:

A curse was laid upon the Jewish people by Moses, who said: "God will smite you with the botch of Egypt." We see clearly that this curse has been fulfilled, since all European Jews have eczema of the seat, all Asiatic Jews mange upon their heads, all African Jews boils on their legs, and American Jews a disease of the eyes, as a result of which they are disfigured and stupid. The wicked Rabbis have found a medicinal cure that consists in smearing the afflicted parts with Christian blood.

Their aim in murdering a Christian is threefold: (a) the great hatred they bear the Christians and the assumption that in committing such a murder they are offering a sacrifice to God; (b) the magical actions which they perform with the blood itself; (c) the Rabbis are not certain whether Christ the son of Mary was not the real Messiah, and under the circumstances they think they might be saved if they are sprinkled with the said blood.

The list of uses to which Jews are supposed to put Christian blood seems almost endless. Thus wrote "Neophyte":

> Four times a year there appears from the air a sort of blood on the Jews' food, and if any Jew tastes of this food he dies. . . . The Rabbis smear a fork with the blood of a martyred Christian and put it on top of their food, so that the blood mentioned above does not fall on their food. . . . When Jews marry, the Rabbi gives the bride and bridegroom a boiled egg sprinkled with the ash of a rag that has first been soaked in Christian blood. When the Jews weep over Jerusalem, they smear their heads with the above-mentioned ash. At Passover they bake a special dish in which they include the blood of a martyred Christian. When an infant boy is circumcised, the Rabbi takes a beaker of wine into which he puts a drop of blood from the circumcision. When these are well mixed, the Rabbi puts his finger into the beaker and then into the mouth of the infant.

The London *Times* correspondent was moved to cable home: "If Neophyte is right, it is indeed difficult to see why the huge supply of such a demand has escaped general attention hitherto."

Leaving "Neophyte," Pranaitis took off on his own into the realm of the Blood Accusation. He said he had found a text in the Talmud that sanctified the ritual murder of a Christian on that doubly holy of days, a Day of Atonement falling on the Sabbath. He spoke of the distribution of Christian blood in special bottles and of the cabalistic signs made over the bleeding victim. "I know," he declared further, "that blood is used to smear the palm of a new-born infant so that when he is grown up and a robber attacks him, he has only to show his hands and the robber will flee." He went on in this strain for some eleven hours, during which he touched on every conceivable diabolistic rite that might work on the nerves and superstitions of his auditors. He was often interrupted by the judge, not for the tenor of his observations but for his prolixity.

2

The problem before the defense was how to expose Pranaitis in terms intelligible to simple, unlettered peasants. The defense had its own experts and scholars, who knew that Pranaitis's "quotations" simply did not exist; but merely to say so would have settled nothing. He was, indeed, asked to produce the books and point to the quoted passages; he pleaded that he had not brought the books with him. The defense offered to supply them on the spot; Pranaitis waved them away. He would not be drawn into a squabble over texts; it was for the defense to prove that the passages did not exist. What was to be done?

The problem was solved ingeniously by a scholarly Hebrew writer, Ben-Zion Katz, who was attending the trial as adviser to the Beiliss Defense Committee. After listening to Pranaitis for a few minutes he perceived that the man was a quack with the merest smattering of Hebrew and no knowledge at all of Aramaic, the language of the Zohar and most of the Talmud. Any Jewish boy with a *cheder* (elementary Hebrew school) education would have perceived it, but the jury of course had not even that. How could it be made to understand?

Katz's plan was bold and simple. Since Pranaitis had mentioned with an air of great familiarity several tractates of the Talmud, the non-Jewish counsels ought to ask him, by way of information, what the titles meant; for example, *Hullin* (on animals permissible as food) or *Erubin* (on Sabbath walking limits) or *Yebamot* (on sisters-in-law). At a worried meeting that preceded the opening of the discussion period Gruzenberg, Karabchevsky, Zarudny, and members of the Defense Committee rejected the proposal. Suppose Pranaitis knew the answers, which would not be impossible even in an ignoramus; they would merely be adding to his prestige. But Katz was excitedly insistent. Pranaitis would *not* know the answers; it was obvious from the very way he pronounced the words; he had picked up all his erudition from scurrilous pamphlets with which Katz was familiar. Moreover, went on Katz, the innocent questions were to be followed by a trap, into which Pranaitis would certainly fall and which would somehow be explained later. He was to be asked: "When did *Baba Bathra* live and what was her activity?"

Baba Bathra (The Lower Gate) is one of the best known tractates of the Talmud and deals with various property laws; even semiliterate Yiddish-speaking Jews have at least heard of it. In American terms the equivalent of Katz's question would be something like "Who lived at the Gettysburg Address?" The question was not only disrespectful to the court, it smacked of *provokatsiya*, and if the trick failed the consequences could be serious. It took Katz some time to win the committee round: let the non-Jewish counsels at least ask the innocent questions, or the first of them. Pranaitis was an infallible ignoramus; he would even be misled by the word *Baba*, so like the Russian word for a (peasant) woman. After long discussion Katz got his way.

The next day the incident went off in court as if it had been rehearsed by both sides. Karabchevsky put the first question. "Will the expert kindly tell us the meaning of the word *Hullin*?" Boldyrev at once interposed: "One may not cross-examine the experts." Karabchevsky respectfully explained that this was far from his intention; he was merely seeking information so as to be able to follow the learned father's argument. The question was allowed and the debacle began.

Q.: What is the meaning of the word *Hullin*?
A.: I don't know.

Q.: What is the meaning of the word *Erubin?*
A.: I don't know.
Q.: What is the meaning of the word *Yebamot?*
A.: I don't know.

And thus, with the non-Jewish attorneys dividing the questions between them, till the trap was sprung.

"When did *Baba Bathra* live and what was her activity?"

"I don't know."

Part of the audience was Jewish, and there was a sudden burst of laughter, above which rose an irrepressible yelp of delight from Katz. He was ordered removed from the courtroom. "I didn't mind it a bit," he writes in his memoirs.

These were by no means the only questions Pranaitis answered with *ne znayu,* but these, and especially the last, when it was tactfully explained, were fatal. That night Agent D. telegraphed to St. Petersburg in bitterness of spirit: "Questioning of Pranaitis reduced the convincing power of his testimony, revealing ignorance of texts and insufficient acquaintance with Jewish literature. In view of the superficiality of his knowledge and his helplessness, Pranaitis's testimony has very little significance."

3

Five scholars of standing, of whom only one, Jacob Mazeh, Chief Rabbi of Moscow, was a Jew, presented the Jewish case against the Blood Accusation and other slanders by Pranaitis—more exactly, against the slanders by Pranaitis, Sikorsky, and the prosecuting counsels. For just as Shmakov, Vipper, and Zamyslovsky did not confine themselves to their functions as prosecutors of Beiliss but throughout the trial made long digressions into the depravity and maleficence of the Jewish people, so Sikorsky, called in as psychiatric expert, digressed at even greater length into folklore, race characteristics, demonology, and the history of the Blood Accusation, undertaking to prove that every dismissal of a ritual murder case had been due to Jewish machinations.

The four Christian scholars made their statements calmly and from sound knowledge demonstrated the contradiction between

the ethical principles of Judaism and the allegations of the Blood
Accusation. Rabbi Mazeh, more deeply versed than they in the
religion of his people, felt the handicap of his position, and his
attestation, more scholarly and informed than theirs, was marked
by nervousness and emotional outbursts. What was taking place
here, in effect, was a reversion to the famous medieval debates
forced by prelates and princes on reluctant rabbis, but with certain differences. Here the protagonists on the Jewish side were
mostly Christians, while Pranaitis was not authorized to speak for
his Church and had in fact been disowned by his superior. The
audience to which the debaters addressed themselves consisted
not of churchmen but of unlettered peasants who had been
chosen, as Agent D. pointed out with so much satisfaction, because they were incapable of understanding the issue or following
the arguments and because it was hoped that their national
prejudices would produce the desired verdict. That a Jew should
be compelled to defend his religion and his people under such
circumstances was one of the most offensive features of the whole
offensive affair.

The argument went in circles. Sikorsky spoke of a course he
had been giving in the "traditional Jewish method" of murdering
Christian children. The defense asked: "Can you point to works in
forensic medicine or psychiatry where we might be able to get
hold of the information you gave of a specific Jewish method of
murdering children—one you felt was applied in Yushchinsky's
case?" Sikorsky's answer was: "There is a censorship that will not
permit the publication of such material." He cited the Damascus
ritual murder case of 1840, which had ended with the acquittal
of the accused; there were documents, he said, which proved
conclusively that the accused were guilty. The defense wanted to
know where these documents were; the answer was that they
were being concealed by the French government. "Talmudism,
Jewish capital, and the Jewish press are all armed for the fight
against the detection of these crimes."

The Commission of 1917 was puzzled, as perhaps the reader is, by the administration's choice of Pranaitis as an expert on Judaism. Could it not have sharked up from somewhere an erudite scoundrel, some falsifier of texts and forger of ancient documents—a type occurring frequently enough in the history of scholarship—who knew his way about in the history and literature of Judaism? He would at least have seemed to be holding his own against the experts for the defense, and Agent D. would not have had to send his distressful telegram to St. Petersburg.

Shcheglovitov was under cross-examination. "Did you not ask yourself why an expert had to be brought from Tashkent? I could understand it if it had been Petrograd, or Moscow, or some intellectual center generally. But you wouldn't consider Tashkent an intellectual center."

"This Pranaitis," answered Shcheglovitov, "was an exceptionally good expert."

"Did you not ask yourself," the Commission insisted, "why this 'well of learning' was in Tashkent? Did Pranaitis occupy a post that proved he was a specialist in the Jewish religion? Was there no scholar at the Academy of Science or at the Theological Academy? Did you not know that the defense had its experts, great scholars in Hebraic literature and religion, and found them right here in Petrograd?"

Shcheglovitov answered that the request had come from Chaplinsky, in Kiev. He was reminded sharply that the Minister of Justice could issue orders to the official prosecutors. The simple truth was that the prosecution had not been interested in scholarship; it had wanted a man who could make the right kind of appeal to the right kind of jury, and thought it had found him in Pranaitis.

◇◇◇◇◇◇◇◇◇◇◇◇◇◇◇◇◇◇

C H A P T E R   1 8

◇◇◇◇◇◇◇◇◇◇◇◇◇◇◇◇◇◇

SUMMATIONS AND CHARGE

1

ON OCTOBER 23 with the cold weather setting in and darkness creeping up on the sessions the trial, which the prosecution had hoped to limit to ten days, entered its fifth week. The jurors were visibly exhausted; two of them had needed medical treatment and many of them repeatedly nodded in their chairs. And now there stretched before them the summaries and rebuttals and the judge's charge, all of which could not take much less than a week.

There were seven summations in all, three of which were made by the prosecution. In these the Jewish practice of ritual murder and the generally noxious character of the Jewish people were vehemently asserted to have been proved. On the guilt of Beiliss there was a slight but significant divergence of treatment.

Vipper and Zamyslovsky both developed the thesis of an inescapable Cheberyak-Beiliss impasse. There had been only three suspects, or sets of suspects: Andryusha's family, Cheberyak and the gang, Beiliss and unknown accomplices. The prosecution had spent the better part of three days demonstrating *ad nauseam* that it could not have been the members of Andryusha's family— which everybody already knew. By this insistence it sought to create the impression that the choice inevitably lay between Cheberyak and Beiliss. If it could not be proved that Beiliss was guilty, it would suffice to prove that Cheberyak was innocent.

In logic the Cheberyak-Beiliss impasse was a *non sequitur*; but this *non sequitur* was an indispensable assumption for the prosecution, and it was the basis for Vipper's and Zamyslovsky's summations. In the main Shmakov accepted it too, though he offered, without following up, an alternative. With this common assumption the prosecuting attorneys deployed along different lines.

Vipper had made his specialty the gold and power of the Jews, local, national, and international. Every witness for the defense—Krasovsky, Brazul, Makhalin, Karayev—and those for the prosecution who had collapsed—the lamplighters and even the poor old Wolf-Woman—had either been bribed or intimidated. Even little Lyudmilla had somehow been frightened. Who knew what enormous sums had been expended secretly, apart from the fees received by such leading members of the bar as Karabchevsky, Maklakov, and Zarudny? Certainly if Cheberyak had rated 40,000 rubles, even the lamplighters and the Wolf-Woman must have cost a pretty kopek. Vipper conveyed the impression that the figures reported by Ivanov—3,000 rubles for Brazul and a beggarly 50 rubles a month each for Makhalin and Karayev—concealed transactions of astronomical proportions. The difficulty of finding evidence against Beiliss had for him only one explanation: Jewish gold and power.

The conspiratorial view of history as developed by Vipper is a variant of the satanic rites hashed up with such gusto by Pranaitis, Sikorsky, and Shmakov, but its material is attuned to the secular and political. History is represented as consisting of dark plots hatched by cabals of criminals, among whom the archplotters are the Jews. To be sure, said Vipper, he was not accusing the Jewish people as such of having committed the murder of Andryusha; he was only accusing Beiliss and his accomplices, whoever they were. But why had this gigantic worldwide force arisen to protect the murderer or murderers? Let the jury ponder that.

His task was not simply to prove Beiliss's guilt. "No, it is far more important. I must prove that those who were witnesses here but were suspected of the murder and charged with it (the newspapers shamelessly called them murderers) are innocent." And while calling on the jury to see to it that the death of little Andryusha should not remain unavenged, he proceeded to argue away the evidence that had been presented against Cheberyak and the Troika. He apologized for the impassioned mood into which he sometimes fell; but the thought of that innocent boy, tortured and done to death, and of the monstrous effort being made to protect the murderers was too much for his self-control.

Vipper spoke for five hours. Zamyslovsky, following him, took only four, and his main thesis was the either/or impasse. "Does not the collapse of the Cheberyak version of the murder offer frightfully strong evidence against Beiliss?" He bracketed Cheberyak with Andryusha's family. Mishchuk and Krasovsky had tried to get Andryusha's family indicted and had failed; then they had tried to get Cheberyak indicted and had failed again. From the beginning Mishchuk and Krasovsky had devoted themselves to confusing the issue and diverting attention from Beiliss, the one remaining suspect. As to what the defense considered its strongest point, said Zamyslovsky—namely, that on the morning of the murder work had been going on at the factory and Beiliss had been supervising the shipment of bricks—that was worthless. There was no reason why Beiliss could not have excused himself for a few minutes, gone after Andryusha, and, the job done, returned to his duties.

Shmakov, who made the last summation for the prosecution, deviated tentatively from the either/or thesis. "Why not Beiliss *and* Cheberyak?" he asked, "This is a possibility. I am not asserting anything here, and I cannot accuse Cheberyak, for she has no one to defend her." Strange as this suggestion was, Shmakov's closing words were stranger. There were two questions before the jury, he said: was this a ritual murder, and was Beiliss the murderer? "When you have answered Yes to the first question, you will have to pass on the second. How you decide the second question is a matter for your conscience."

He did not explain why only the second question involved the conscience of the jury or what grounds he had for suggesting a link, nowhere established during the trial, between Beiliss and Cheberyak. We know, however, from his private diary that he was wild with rage against Cheberyak ("the lying bitch") for having, with her stupid cunning, made fools of the prosecution. His colleagues may have been equally angry, but they seem to have had more self-control.

Shmakov outdid even Vipper in his attack on the Jews. His address was spasmodic, disconnected. Sometimes the discontinuities were abrupt, sometimes the train of thought oozed away into a darkness that lifted only to disclose quite another train of thought with a subterranean beginning. The whole was a livid blur of incoherent malice throbbing amid an onset of mental decrepitude.

2

Before reviewing the summations of the defense I must return to a question already raised in this narrative. Why did the defense both in the cross-examinations and in the summations refuse to take the line, so obvious and so cogent, that the manufacturers of a ritual murder case had been caught red-handed? Why did it all but ignore the letters received by Andryusha's mother and City Coroner Karpinsky? Those letters were written before the publication of the autopsy—one, indeed, before the autopsy was made—yet they gave accurately the number of wounds on the body and they described the murder as ritual in character. Why did the defense ignore the significant statement in Singayevsky's confession to Karayev and Makhalin that Rudzinsky "with his ministerial brain" had been responsible for the mutilations perpetrated on Andryusha's body?

Detective Mishchuk, the first man on the case, had stated

bluntly that a ritual murder had been simulated with the aim
of precipitating a pogrom. It was an over-simplification; the
primary motive as shown by Krasovsky (and secretly admitted
by the administration) had been the punishment and silencing
of an informer. But all the evidence pointed to the simulation
of a ritual murder as an immediate secondary motive: the otherwise senseless multiplicity of the wounds, the letters to Andryusha's mother and the city coroner, the season—shortly before
Easter and the Jewish Passover—and finally the conformity to
the folklore of ritual murders, the leaving of the corpse where
it would easily be discovered.

The answer to our question is nowhere to be found in such
memoirs—those of Gruzenberg, Margolin, Mazeh, Ben-Zion
Katz—as I have been able to consult. But it is supplied by
common sense.

If the defense had risked the statement "This is not a ritual
murder, it is only a crude imitation of one," the way would have
been opened for a discussion among the jurors: "So, they admit
it looks like a ritual murder, only it was done so badly that it
could not have been the work of Jews." Thence it would have
followed that certain standards existed, and the medical experts
would have been asked to what degree the manner of the murder
fell short of those standards. Let us imagine the effect if the
defense had asked the medical experts: "Please explain to the
jury how this crude attempt to simulate a ritual murder differs
from what you would consider an authentic ritual murder."
What the experts actually discussed was the "maximum blood"
question. Had Yushchinsky been killed in such a way as to
drain the maximum of blood from him? Or rephrased, had he
been kept alive as long as possible, with no injuries inflicted
except such as were necessary to draw blood from him? For the
defense to have introduced the words "ritual murder" into the
scientific discussion would under the circumstances have been
imprudent in the extreme. And yet the reader of the stenographic report of the trial often feels like crying out across the
half-century: "Do it! Say openly: 'This is how the Blood Accusation is perpetuated. This is a classic example of the method by

which the great lie has been perpetuated, and you, the administration and the prosecution, are the latest of the long line of *provocateurs.*'"

3

Karabchevsky was the only defense counsel to speak of the murder as an intended prelude to a pogrom, but he too avoided the words "ritual murder." "You know," he said in his summation, "that in health resorts the proprietors speak of 'silk seasons' and 'cotton seasons,' the seasons of the distinguished and wealthy vacationers and those of the piddling little visitors. This gang, too, had its 'silk season,' and later it went through its 'cotton season.' There hadn't been any pogroms, and their situation was shaky."

It was a telling reference to the Kiev pogrom of 1905, when, as was revealed at the trial, Cheberyak had had to burn bales of silk brought in from the looting; it was well known that the classic way of precipitating a pogrom was to raise the cry of the Blood Accusation. But this was as far as the defense went, and perhaps even that was too far. Gruzenberg, in his summation, curtly dismissed the suggestion that there had been an attempt to simulate a ritual murder. The other members of the defense ignored the subject. In respect of the murder they concentrated in their summations on the innocence of Beiliss.

There the problem lay in the obviousness of their case. One could only ridicule the picture drawn by the prosecution: a large group of children playing in broad daylight round the clay mixer, the sudden appearance of Beiliss and his accomplices, the seizing and carrying off of Andryusha. "Suppose this had happened!" cried Maklakov. "How would the children not have told their parents? The state prosecutor solemnly declares he does not know why no one spoke about it. I will tell him why: because nothing of the sort took place, because the story is an invention of Cheberyak's. . . . If Andryusha would have been dragged off before the eyes of all those children and his corpse had been found later in Lukyanovka, then Lukyanovka would have risen,

these humble Russians would have risen, both the Zaitsev works
and Beiliss would have been destroyed, and there would have
been no trial."

Maklakov struck another note when he turned to the last
moments of Zhenya Cheberyak and the behavior of his mother.

> The unfortunate Cheberyak had to think not of saving her son or
> of his peace. She was not able to shout to the detectives: "Get out of
> here, this is death, this is God's business!" She was not able to do
> that. At the very last moment she had to make use of her son:
> "Zhenya, tell them I had nothing to do with it." And what did
> Zhenya answer? "Mama, leave me alone, it hurts." He did not say
> what it would have been so easy for him to say: "I saw Beiliss
> drag Andryusha off." When he wished to speak, this unhappy
> mother—as witnesses have testified—kissed him and prevented him
> from speaking. Before his death she gave him the Judas kiss so
> that he would not speak.

At these words a visible shudder went through the courtroom.

Gruzenberg spoke after Maklakov. He was in the same frus-
trating situation as Rabbi Mazeh; as the only Jewish member
of the defense he was a symbol. He felt that he had to justify
himself, present his credentials as a lover of Russia; he had, as
a Jew, to affirm his own repudiation of the Blood Accusation.
"I say clearly—and I know these words will become known to
Jews throughout the world—were Jewish teaching such as has
been described, I could not permit myself to remain a Jew."
The eternal, hopeless apologia. The eternal posture of the Jew
before this unproved but undisprovable accusation, which he
cannot, in spite of everything, ignore.

Gruzenberg was fighting the wind. The more eloquent he
became, the more futile it sounded. "The charges they have
raised from the graveyard drag us back to the grave. . . . From
millennial tombs, long ago fallen and crumbled into dust, they
extract these ancient charges. . . ." All true and moving but, as
always and everywhere, superfluous to those willing to listen and
wasted on those who were not.

It was only in his treatment of the case against Beiliss that

Gruzenberg could employ his talents naturally, and though he lacked Maklakov's simplicity, he was not his inferior in logic and irony. But again, there was no evidence against Beiliss to be demolished; his shafts were directed against the prosecution and Cheberyak. He had several questions. Why, if human blood had been necessary in the dedication of the synagogue, had the authorities not taken action against the Zaitsevs? If Shneyerson had lured Andryusha to his death, why was he not in the dock? What was the meaning of Shmakov's closing words, which left the question of Beiliss's guilt to the conscience of the jury as long as it pronounced the murder to have been ritual in character? "Mr. Shmakov takes the position that if Beiliss is not guilty, the Jews are." He analyzed with deadly closeness the evidence offered by the Cheberyaks. But whatever intellectual pleasure one may get from the perusal of his forensic performance and those of his colleagues, there is always the feeling that on the Blood Accusation theme they were either battering at an open door or running their heads against a stone wall.

Zarudny followed Gruzenberg, and his summation makes a strange impression. He who had been so tempestuous during the cross-examinations, so biting in his comments on the proceedings and the behavior of the judge, was extraordinarily calm and reasoned in his summation. But he had unfortunately undertaken to play the non-Jewish authority on Judaism vis-à-vis Shmakov. He had therefore devoted some months to Jewish studies and the history of Blood Accusation cases, and though he approached them with an open—and very capable—mind, he could hardly be called an expert. He was too learned for the jury and an amateur to the informed. He was better when he abandoned books and applied common sense to the "scholarly" material presented by the prosecution and at his best when he spoke of the functions of a court. "It is in its way a temple. In a temple or church one prays for one's enemies; it is a place where one must be impartial. . . . Gentlemen of the jury, if any one of you has ever had hostile feelings against Jews, you must not allow them to influence your verdict. . . . Rid yourselves of all superfluous, unnecessary feelings that have no relation to this case. Rid yourselves of all those things that the law, our legal customs, and the clear sense of justice do not permit, for those cannot enter a judge's feelings." But he was asking the jurors to negate the very purpose for which they had been so carefully selected by the administration.

In the rebuttals that followed the summations no new arguments were developed. All that remained now was the judge's charge to the jury, and on this the outcome of the trial might very well depend.

4

At 11 a.m. on October 28 the court reconvened to hear the judge's charge and his formulation of the accusation, after which the jurors were to retire to consider the verdict. This was Boldyrev's hour. For this he had been appointed and promised rewards, and his handling of the charge was a double expression of gratitude and expectation. Vladimir Nabokov describes it thus: "In its substance it was an accusatory speech, deliberate and well-planned. It is true that some trivial words were used for the sake of the decorum required by law in the Presiding Judge's résumé. But this made his conduct only the worse; the lip-service to decorum obscured the real meaning of the address; it made the jury believe in the Judge's fairness and impartiality."

The obeisances to impartiality consisted of reminders to the jury that it did not have to accept the judge's conclusions; it was free to disagree with him; it was free to modify the charge. But Boldyrev made no mention of the ample grounds that existed for disagreeing with him. The most important part of his argument had to do with the locale of the murder, which for him could have been only the brickyard; that is to say, he accepted the prosecution's artificial either/or dilemma, either Cheberyak's apartment or the brickyard, and decided for the latter. He did so on the basis of the evidence supplied by the lamplighters and the Cheberyak family, referring particularly to the little girl Lyudmilla, who, he pointed out, was the only surviving eyewitness of the scene that took place round the clay mixer. By way of supplement to the evidence against Beiliss he even cited the convict spy Kozachenko.

In the whole of the two-hour address there was no attempt to counter the devastating attack delivered by Maklakov on the wild improbability of little Lyudmilla's story. It was as if this, the most powerful single point in the defense, had never been made. But contrariwise, Boldyrev did take advantage of the defense's tactical refusal to raise the issue of a simulated ritual murder. He implied that the defense was afraid to do so because it had in fact been a ritual murder.

Having in effect delivered himself as if he were the state prosecutor rather than the judge, Boldyrev explained that there would be two questions before the jury. The first was: had a murder of such and such a character been committed? The second: was Beiliss (and undiscovered accomplices) guilty of the murder?

However in the actual formulation of the question Boldyrev began with a show of objectivity. He was willing to condense the two questions into one and submitted it thus: "Is the accused, Menahem Mendel Tevyev* Beiliss, guilty of having conspired with others, who have not been discovered in the investigations, in a premeditated plan prompted by religious fanaticism, to murder the boy Andrei Yushchinsky, age thirteen, on the twelfth day of March 1911 . . . in the brickworks belonging to the Jewish surgical hospital, which is under the management of the merchant Mark Zaitsev?"

The question was loaded on two points: that the murder had been committed in the brick factory and that it was ritual in character. But it had this advantage for the defense: in order that the loaded points might be carried, Beiliss would have to be declared guilty, and (as it seemed to the defense) there was more hope that Beiliss would be declared innocent than that the jury would pass negatively on a separate question of ritual murder. The defense was therefore ready to accept the single question form while it objected to the formulation as contrary to law.

The prosecution declared the formulation to be acceptable but requested that the court divide the question into two parts. After a brief recess Boldyrev overruled the objections of the defense and acceded to the request of the prosecution. But now something extraordinary occurred. In dividing the question into two parts, Boldyrev, trying always to safeguard the ritual murder feature of the crime, produced a formulation that led, and was perhaps intended to lead, to ambiguous and endlessly debated results.

The first question does not mention ritual murder or religious fanaticism but implies them. It asks: "Has it been proved that on March 12, 1911 . . . in one of the buildings of the Jewish surgical hospital . . . Andrei Yushchinsky was gagged, and wounds inflicted on him . . . [here follows one list of wounds] and that when he had lost five glasses of blood, wounds were inflicted [here follows another list] . . . and that these wounds, totalling forty-seven, caused Yushchinsky agonizing pain and led to almost total loss of blood and to his death?"

The second question runs: "If the event described in the first question has been proved, is the accused . . . guilty of having entered into collusion with others, who have not been discovered in the investigations, in a premeditated plan prompted by religious fanaticism, to murder the boy Andrei Yushchinsky, and did the accused in order to carry out his intentions seize Yushchinsky, who happened to be there, and drag him off to one of the buildings of the brickworks . . . ?" The rest of the question repeats the clinical details of the first question.

The defense objected strenuously to the partition of the question and to the formulations, which were prejudicial. Its objections were overruled. When the jury had been sent into conference, the defense moved to recall it in order to add some clarifying material. On the intervention of the prosecution the motion was denied. After that nothing remained but to wait.

5

Russian liberal opinion of the Beiliss trial even before the exposure of the conspiracy was expressed by Nabokov in 1914.

Beiliss was tried by jury, and the first impression of everyone was unanimous: people were astonished and perplexed by the choice of jurors. . . . The members of the jury which tried Beiliss represented the most obscure places in the Province—it consisted of practically illiterate peasants and commoners. . . .

During the trial the Judge declared more than once: "Nobody here accuses Judaism, we are talking of individual fanatics only." But the statements of Sikorsky and Pranaitis disprove his words. . . . Both of them spoke about Judaism, about the Hebrew faith. . . . And then came the Judge's charge, and all this complicated research into the Bible, the *Talmud*, the *Kaballah*, the *Zohar*, proved to be irrelevant. The only essential question, from the point of view of those who believed in ritual murder, was never broached. Nobody ever asked if it had been proved that Beiliss was a fanatic. No psychiatric observation or examination was carried out. His spiritual world was never studied. . . . This syllogism remains in all its nakedness: Beiliss is a Jew, consequently Beiliss could have taken part in this bloody sacrifice. . . .

One can point, with absolute confidence, to a series of obvious, unchallengeable legal violations condoned with only one purpose— to instil into the jury belief in the existence of ritual murder among the Jews. . . . Years will go by, the memory of the Beiliss trial will gradually fade away, the impressions will lose their poignancy, but the record, dry and impartial, the stenographic record, will remain. And no matter how many years will go by, the future historian of Russian justice will open the record and will read there the testimonies of the "experts," which the Presiding Judge let pass without hindrance. The historian will read these ravings, these affirmations obtained from anti-Semitic literature of the lowest kind, presented under the guise of the scientific authority of a professor of psychiatry, and he will ask, in amazement: "How did it come about that the Presiding Judge did not stop this expert?" It is true that the Presiding Judge asked Sikorsky several times to come back to the Yushchinsky murder, but the expert paid no attention to his admonitions and continued his harangue in the same vein. . . .

Lack of space makes it impossible to describe in more detail the violations of law which occurred in the Beiliss case. . . . They are closely connected with the very spirit of the trial, and we can say with complete assurance that ten or fifteen years ago such a trial would have been impossible.

CHAPTER 19

WORLD AND
DOMESTIC REACTION

1

I T IS heartening to recall the protests of the Western world against the Beiliss case. They were one of its last flickers of sanity before its engulfment in the horror and stupidity of World War I, and they compare very favorably with the spotty expressions of disapproval that greeted the far more vicious and criminal anti-Semitism of the Nazis in the late 1930's and early 1940's.

The reaction was delayed, not out of indifference but out of incredulity. Even as late as the trial there were some who could not believe that the Russian government meant to push the loathsome farce to its extreme. *The New York Times* commentator wrote: "This case reminds one of the farmer who saw a camel and said: 'There ain't no such animal.'" As we have seen, the London *Times* correspondent could not understand how the government could permit the trial to go on after its eighth day.

First, a description of the manifestoes of notables and then of the public protests and the opinions voiced by the press.

It was not until the spring of 1912 that the first foreign manifesto appeared, in Germany. It was signed by 206 leaders of German thought, among them Thomas Mann, Gerhart Hauptmann, Hermann Sudermann, and Werner Sombart. The British protest which followed was even weightier, both in the number of its signatories (240) and their standing. They included the Archbishops of Canterbury and York, the Primate of Ireland, and Francis Cardinal Bourne; the Speaker of the House of Commons and prominent members of both houses of Parliament, among them A. J. Balfour, Austin Chamberlain, and Ramsay MacDonald; the heads of the principal colleges of Oxford and Cambridge and various provincial universities; James G. Frazer, Thomas Hardy, H. G. Wells, C. P. Scott, John Masefield, Karl Pearson, Oliver Lodge, and E. G. Pointer, President of the Royal Academy. The French protest, with 150 signatures, had large representations from the Academy, the Institute, the Ecole Normale Supérieure, and the Ecole des Hautes Etudes. Among the names were those of Anatole France, Henri de Régnier, Georges Duruy, and Octave Mirbeau. The American protest of notables came late, coinciding with the month of the trial. It was signed by seventy-four leaders of the various Christian denominations.

We need not pause long over the wording of the manifestoes. "Unscrupulous fiction . . . not a shadow of proof" (German). "The question is one of civilization, humanity and truth. The blood accusation is a relic of the days of witchcraft and Black Magic . . . an insult to Western culture and a dishonor to the Churches . . . endangering many innocent lives in the crowded Jewries of Eastern Europe" (British). "Absurd accusation . . . in all ages and all countries religious minorities have been victims of this same calumny. . . ." (French).

The American manifesto was unfortunately couched as an appeal to Nicholas. Its conciliatory tone—a waste of insincerity —did not improve its chances of ever being read by him. It asked Nicholas to have the charge of ritual murder withdrawn "because of the untold evils . . . which may follow its further prosecution," and it closed in the "full confidence that this appeal will be favorably received by Your Imperial Majesty."

A popular world protest accompanied the trial like a universal obbligato. It took the form of mass meetings in England, Germany, France, the United States, Canada, and Austria-Hungary, to name the leading countries. Jaurès addressed an audience of five thousand at the Salle Wagram in Paris, and other speakers addressed the overflow. Count Kuhen-Hedervary in the name of the Government party and Count Karoly in the name of the Independent party spoke before a similar protest meeting in Budapest. Demonstrations took place at Albert Memorial Hall and in Trafalgar Square in London, and there were scores of mass meetings in the United States and Canada.

2

The reactions of the world press may be divided into three groups: (a) condemning the conspiracy—the vast majority, (b) approving or condoning it—a small minority, and (c) neutrals— a somewhat larger minority. If we think of (a) as liberal and (b) as reactionary, we must label (c) as superreactionary, for there are certain cases, of which this is one, in which the pose of neutrality is the most effective moral support of reaction.

(a) *The Manchester Guardian* reproduced almost in full Shulgin's blast at the indictment, adding: "The administration of the country is in a hopeless and chaotic condition, without any guiding principle but a blind dread of revolution. . . . The straits to which it is reduced are indicated by the Beiliss case."

The *Frankfurter Zeitung*: ". . . a comedy, scarcely overshadowed by the genuine tragedy . . . a lunatic asylum . . ."

The *Neue Freie Presse* of Vienna (with *The Manchester Guardian* and the *Frankfurter Zeitung* it represented European liberal journalism at its best): "The trial recalls the most miserable examples of classical Russian trials. . . . Anyone who has read the full text of the indictment will agree that a similar document cannot be found in the annals of the Russian courts. . . ."

Frequent embarrassment at trying to make the indisputable facts of this narrative believable seems to have haunted the correspondent of the London *Times*: "This surely remains, judicially, politically and psychologically, the most baffling of all great modern trials. . . . I have suppressed a score of absurdities from a desire to record [the trial] fairly and without the spirit of *J'accuse*. . . . Who would have supposed that in the twentieth century, when the world is a whispering gallery and the doings of one country are the gossip of its neighbors, we should see a court solemnly discussing Black Magic, Moloch, what Dio Cassius said, what Julian the Apostate did, and whether Jews drink Christian blood out of the hatred of Christians or to counter a divine curse on their anatomy, or to safeguard themselves against the off-chance that Christ was the Messiah."

The columnist of *The New York Times* was equally baffled. "Apparently the only possible result of the trial is to free even the most fanatic and the most ignorant of the Russians of a belief which no others have entertained. To think that this is the purpose of the prosecution is next to impossible, but it is equally difficult to think that any of the government officials expected a trial thus conducted to have any other than this seemingly inevitable consequence. . . . Russian representatives abroad have made no protest that the reports are incomplete or colored."*

The Nation (New York), leaning on the widespread rumor that the Kiev police had arranged the assassination of Stolypin, commented: "The disappointment of the leaders of the Black Hundreds with the showing made by the judicial and police authorities at Kiev must be all the more poignant because in that city, if anywhere, the police might be expected to prove itself efficient. . . . After the removal of a Prime Minister, the manufacture of a ritual murder ought to have been a simple task."

The most powerful American utterance came from *The Independent* (New York) in the form of an open letter to Nicholas. It attracted international attention and is worth quoting at some length, for it summarized the general feeling about Nicholas's personal share of responsibility in the Beiliss case and in Russia's miserable condition generally:

SIRE—When you ascended the throne of the Russian Empire the expectations of your people ran high. They looked forward to a more humane reign than that which had just ended. They were yearning for reforms, for a sympathetic bond between the palace and the huts of the hungry and the homes of the oppressed. . . . Little by little the vision of a better day faded. . . . Your supposed idealism failed to manifest itself. . . . The evil genius of Pobedonostsev, of the Holy Synod, reigned supreme while he lived, and still rules Russia from the grave. . . .

The condition of the long-suffering nationalities of your Empire, instead of ameliorating, has become more tragic. . . . You have gone much further than your father in your anti-Jewish policies. . . . To divert attention from their own incompetence [your officials] are pointing to the Jews as the cause of all the troubles that exist in Russia.

You are now drifting to your ruin and plunging Russia into anarchy. You have become known as the "pardoning Czar," but you have limited your pardons to those who have participated in the massacre of the Jews of Russia. . . . And now, to add to the crown of your infamy, your Minister of Justice has staged a "ritual murder" case. . . .

How can you, the man who suggested the establishment of universal peace at the Hague tolerate, in the land in which you hold universal sway, such refinement of barbarity and brutality, and yet venture to face the rulers of the civilized world as an equal? How can you expect to face your Maker with such a burden on your soul?

The writer might have reflected that if Nicholas, with his well-known streak of religious pessimism, was not looking forward with entire complacency to that meeting, he hoped it would be made less uncomfortable for him precisely by his treatment of the Jews.

(b) Strangely enough, it was in France that voices were lifted most shrilly to approve the Blood Accusation and declare Beiliss guilty, though even there the response they evoked was limited and obscure. I have not come across manifestoes of notables or reports of public meetings supporting the Russian government, and the anti-Beiliss and anti-Jewish declarations were confined to publications associated with the lost royalist cause, the anti-Dreyfus agitation, and all the antimodern malignity of the hankerers after the *ancien régime*. The old figures emerged, slightly decrepit and dishevelled: Edouard Drumont of *La France juive*; his disciple Albert Monniot; Leon Daudet; and—not so old—Charles Maurras,* who lived long enough to be a collaborationist in World War II and to be tried for it in 1945.

French support of the Blood Accusation therefore had its own peculiar setting; it also went in heavily for what I have called diabolism for the underprivileged. Albert Monniot had taken over the editorship of *La Libre Parole* from its founder Drumont. He followed the case closely from its beginning and embellished the reports with a running embroidery of medieval legends; at the end of the year he collected his articles in *Le Crime rituel chez les Juifs*, a book of 374 pages equally divided between the Beiliss case and descriptions of the ritual murders charged to the Jews between 1154 and 1913—a tiny fraction, he declares, of those actually committed during those seven and a half centuries.

One half of the book reads like a yellow-press rewrite of Huysmans or the Marquis de Sade; the blasphemies and disembowelments, the crucifixions and floggings and other tortures go on monotonously, until one doubts whether the addicts of this sort of literature responded with anything but a bored nodding of the head.* The largest part of the material was medieval, and its antiquity was adduced as the proof of its reliability. As Drumont wrote in his preface to the book: "These facts are guaranteed by testimony which had not yet come under the influence of the modern press, the testimony of witnesses who believed nothing but what they had seen with their own eyes, people living closely pressed together in the cities of former days. These facts have been set down by contemporaneous chroniclers, attested by commemorative monuments which still exist. . . ." A strange stance for Drumont and his fellow romantics to take; for suddenly it is modern man who, hypnotized by the press, is ready to believe anything, while medieval man was the hard-nosed skeptic who believed nothing but what he saw with his own eyes.

Those articles in *La Libre Parole*, *L'Action française* and *La Croix* which dealt with the trial consisted largely of quotations

from Pranaitis, Sikorsky, and Shmakov. Only Charles Maurras
so much as pretended—he felt he owed it to his reputation as an
intellectual—to achieve a kind of objectivity. "We are neither for
nor against the theory of ritual murder," he wrote. "We don't
know what it is; but we do know the Jewish defense, we have
seen it at work in behalf of the traitor Dreyfus; we are on our
guard against it."*

(c) The most interesting and most instructive of the press comments were the neutrals, the in-betweens, who counseled restraint
and reflection, with "yes but" and "on the other hand" and "there
must be two sides to it"—all the cautionary exhortations we have
learned to expect from a certain type of spectator while a murder
is being committed.

The London correspondent of *The Yorkshire Post* wrote: "The
Kiev trial is causing considerable uneasiness in political circles in
London. It is really beginning to put difficulties in the way of
our official friendship with Russia, a friendship which has never
been agreeable to advanced Liberals." One gets the impression
that the correspondent is blaming the British Liberals for the
Beiliss case—it fell in so pat with their prejudice against Russia.

The Referee, an influential weekly of those times, was a useful
study in ambiguity: "If there is anything in the British protest
of meddling with the methods by which a foreign government
conducts its internal affairs, it was the duty of the moderate
British press to discourage such interference. . . . [But] the
danger which lurks behind the ritual murder case in Kiev gives
reasonable cause for an appeal. . . . There is little doubt that
the intelligent classes in Russia are deeply annoyed that authorities of any kind should have it in their power to exhibit their
country in so unfavorable a light to the civilized world." This
may be fairly reworded as: "We dislike the Beiliss case and ought
not to say so, and anyone who agrees with us is meddling in the
affairs of another country where intelligent people are ashamed
of what is happening."

To one sector of public opinion the whole Beiliss business was
just a confounded nuisance, coming as it did when high political

considerations called for closer ties between England and Russia. The crudeness of the Beiliss case was, of course, rather obvious; it wasn't, one might say, cricket. All the same, one had in fairness to think of the other fellow. As *The Bystander* put it: "If the wretched Jew of Kiev is condemned . . . the powerful Jews of London, Berlin and Paris will make the Russians feel that if the Jews do not commit 'ritual murder,' they are still adepts at financial murder."

The Bystander's faith in the proficiency of certain Jews at financial murder was wide of the mark. In 1905 Witte floated a tremendous foreign loan in the very midst of a wave of anti-Jewish pogroms. There were indeed some Jewish banking houses that would not do business with the Russian government; such were Kuhn, Loeb and Co. of New York (Jacob Schiff) and the Rothschilds. But there were other Jewish bankers, such as Noetzlin of Belgium and Mendelssohn of Berlin, who were not sensitive on the subjects of ritual murder accusations and pogroms. The latter, a descendant of the distinguished thinker Moses Mendelssohn, even implored Witte to remember that his firm had "served the Russian emperors faithfully for a century."*

At the time of the Beiliss case, opinion in England (and France) was divided between those who saw Russia as a great social stabilizing factor and those to whom Russia was an obstacle in the path of human progress. The same division was to reappear thirty years later in the attitude toward Nazi Germany. In both periods the refusal of the Jews to keep quiet about the persecutions to which their kin were subjected was denounced as warmongering. W. T. Stead, an important figure of the earlier period, wrote in *The Review of Reviews*: "No one has ever accused me of anti-Semitism. I owe too much to the authors of the Old and New Testaments. . . . I am all the more bound to warn my Jewish friends that they may give a dangerous impetus to anti-Semitism if they persist in subordinating the interests of general peace to pursuit of their vendetta with Russia." One cannot say of Stead that he was a reactionary; he fought on the right side in many causes. But one cannot help wondering how he saw a vendetta of the Jews against the Russian government rather than the reverse, or why he thought that if no one protested against Russia's treatment of the Jews, her behavior would take a turn for the better.

Ostensibly remote from practical considerations and based exclusively on academic principles and intellectual scrupulousness, the comments of *The Oxford and Cambridge Review,* which during its brief existence represented itself as the mouthpiece of high-church England, constitute a brilliant period piece. They are in a donnish, Bishop-Blougramish, to-you-and-over-the-wine vein; one can almost hear the Oxford-on-the-epiglottis dialect: ". . . it is absolutely certain that Orthodox Judaism—nay, Judaism as a whole—stands free from even the slightest suspicion of blood-guiltiness; but to say that is not to say that no Jewish sect exists which practices ritual murder. . . . We do not know where the truth lies, and we are sure that widely-signed popular protests are not a good way of eliciting the truth."

It is of course impossible to disprove the existence of a Jewish sect that practices ritual murder; it is also impossible to disprove that ritual murder has never been practiced secretly by the Kiwanians or the Daughters of the American Revolution. And it is true that popular protests are not the best way of eliciting the truth about anything, including the intellectual trickery of *The Oxford and Cambridge Review.* However, if the truth about ritual murder was still unknown, it was surely not improper to protest publicly against the claim of Russian officialdom to have discovered it—and this is to say nothing about the uses to which the "discovery" was being put. On these matters *The Oxford and Cambridge Review* had nothing to say.

3

Whatever complaint Shcheglovitov may have had against insubordinate officials of the Departments of Justice and Police, he can have had nothing but praise for Russia's foreign emissaries. Theirs was an embarrassing assignment. For the most part men of considerable culture, they had somehow to justify the Beiliss case without making themselves ridiculous. To pretend that they or other educated Russians believed in the medieval legend of the Blood Accusation would not have been good propaganda. They fell back on two theses: first, that the Jewish people or religion as such was not in question, that only somewhere a small secret sect of Jewish blood ritualists still carried on and the Jews would not acknowledge their existence; second, that anyhow the Jews were everywhere a noxious element. And while Russian diplomatic and consular agents indignantly deprecated efforts by foreigners to influence public opinion in Russia ("unwarranted interference," etc.), they did what they could to influence public opinion in the countries to which they were accredited and to infect them with anti-Semitism.

Baron Heiking, consul-general in London, wrote in the *Fortnightly Review*: "They [the Jews] feel themselves to be foreigners among the population of the land in which they dwell and strangers to its national aims, and they have but one leading idea, to thrive for their own narrow tribal purposes while at the same time benefitting by the existence of the State and social order which have been built up by the labor and blood of other races."

This was aimed at Jews everywhere. But whatever the readers of the *Fortnightly Review* may have thought about English Jews, they must surely have asked themselves why the Russian Jews should be expected to respond with enthusiasm to a national policy aimed at their elimination—a question still unresolved in the very different Russia of our own time. The baron also referred to the ugly sensationalism to which critics of Russian conditions resorted. "These people indulge the morbid taste of certain classes of the British public for sensational accounts of crimes . . . and all sorts of horrors in Russia." There is a certain artlessness in this statement when we remember the kind of taste the Pranaitises and Sikorskys were indulging.

Commenting on the great British manifesto, the baron wrote in the London *Times*: "The accusation of the ritual murder of the boy Yushchinsky is not at all leveled against 'Judaism and the

Jewish people,' but only the accused, who is believed to belong to a small sect carrying the Talmudic teaching to the extreme of ritual murder." As innuendo this is ingenious: if ritual murder is Talmudic teaching carried to the extreme, Talmudic teaching as a whole must—at least in the baron's informed view—have a peculiar ethical slant. The baron found it most reprehensible in the Jews that they should defend themselves. To his superiors in St. Petersburg he wrote: "With regret we must take cognizance of the new encroachment on our domestic affairs on the part of the English people instigated by the Jews."

Benkendorff, the Russian ambassador at London, was less perturbed. He reassured St. Petersburg that the manifesto "was a sentimental demonstration, which failed entirely to take into account the kind of impression it might produce in a foreign country." The opposite was the truth. The manifesto was written to hearten the liberals of Russia, and it did.

Bakhmetev, the Russian ambassador at Washington, cabled home during the trial that "the American Yids have not failed to take advantage of an opportunity, and have used the Kiev case to foment a new agitation against Russia. . . . Congressman [Adolph J.] Sabath, a Yid, has presented a resolution demanding that the Secretary of State convey to His Majesty, through the Embassy at St. Petersburg, the expression of the feelings of indignation of the American people. . . . Senator [Hamilton J.] Lewis has done the same in the Senate. . . . Bryan [William J., then Secretary of State] with whom, in a private conversation, I discussed the falsity of the newspaper articles . . . was astonished by my explanation."

Our old friend Beletsky, the chief of police, was outraged by the widespread attacks on the person of the Czar. In a survey of the foreign press he wrote to his superior, the Minister of the Interior: "Not limiting itself to insinuations against the Russian government and Russian justice, Jewish hatred has made it its task . . . to inoculate the various strata with the idea that the cause of the initiation of the trial is to be found in the personal anti-Semitic feelings of the Supreme Power" (i.e., Nicholas).

Since Beletsky was supplying the material from which the reports on the Beiliss case were regularly reported to the Czar, his indignation is understandable.

Among the Russian emissaries it was Nelidov, the ambassador at the Vatican, who carried off the palm for service to the government in the Beiliss case.

The defense had learned that Pranaitis intended to denounce as forgeries all copies of papal bulls repudiating the Blood Accusation. It had therefore asked Lord Rothschild of London to send its copies to Cardinal Merry del Val, papal secretary of state, for authentication. The Cardinal had the copies compared with the originals in the papal archives, and confirmed their accuracy over his signature. The certified documents were reproduced in the London *Times* and in all the leading European newspapers, including those of Russia. But Nelidov held up his official confirmation of the cardinal's signature till it was too late to produce the documents in court. The jury, cut off from contact with the outside world, was never told that Pranaitis had been given the lie by the Vatican. It probably made no difference; but Foreign Minister Sazonov thought well enough of Nelidov's resourcefulness to bring it to the attention of Nicholas.

4

It was in Russia that the wide bearings of the Beiliss case were most clearly perceived, and the Russian manifesto, issued as early as December 1911, had as much to say about the danger to Russia as about the threat to the Jews. "The eternal struggle of humanity for liberty, legal equality, and fraternity and against slavery, hate, and social discord," it began, "has been with us from ancient times. And in our times, as always, the same persons who uphold the rightless condition of their own people are the most persistent in exciting among them the spirit of religious and racial enmity. . . . The false story of the use of Christian blood by Jews has been broadcast once more among the people. This is a familiar device of ancient fanaticism. . . ."

The manifesto was signed by 150 leaders in the arts, science, and politics; among them were Korolenko, Gorky, Count Ilya

Tolstoy (President of the Academy of Science), six members of the Imperial Council and sixty-four members of the Duma.

Resentment at the Beiliss case was so general and so vocal that Purishkevich, one of the Rightist leaders, was compelled to declare in the Duma: "I cannot permit that through the Beiliss trial Russia should become another France, that Russia should share the fate of France during the Dreyfus period . . . when the entire country discontinued its usual occupations, all ordinary tasks . . . and turned to the trial of that Jew and waited for its conclusion. . . . I must warn the Imperial Duma . . . that by treading this path . . . we lead the Duma to its dissolution. . . . If we convert the tribune of the Duma into a continuous meeting, if we excite the passions at a time when, owing to the activity of other organizations, the lower strata have already begun to shake . . . then the Imperial Duma cannot and must not exist."

But Purishkevich and the reactionaries were promoting the conditions which they denounced, and their purpose was clear enough: an end to the Duma. The Beiliss case was in some respects what Purishkevich had called it, a Russian replica of the Dreyfus case. "Never," wrote Korolenko, "has there been a case in Russia which attracted to so great a degree the attention of the broad masses. . . . The Beiliss case has pushed aside all other internal and all foreign affairs. . . . The eyes of everyone unfolding a newspaper seek not the items about the latest demands or the new note of Austria, not the latest news of a railroad catastrophe, but first of all news about the Beiliss case. . . . Evidently Russian citizens finally understand that the Jewish question is not only a Jewish but also a general Russian question; that the untruth and corruption uncovered at the Beiliss trial is an all-Russian untruth and corruption. . . ."

It was not only "the lower strata" which had begun to shake, as Purishkevich put it. All the strata were shaking. Lawyers, doctors, students, workers, peasants in every part of the country held protest meetings and called strikes. The trolley-car workers in Kiev made a collection for the Beiliss family. Among the Old Believers—a large dissident section of the Orthodox Church— Bishop Mikhail denounced the Blood Accusation, and the Catholic Metropolitan Kuchinsky strongly censured the priests (Pranaitis was not mentioned by name) who spoke against the Jews. The Holy Synod, from which the conspirators had expected much encouragement, held aloof and brought down upon itself the reproaches of the extreme Rightist *Russkoye znamya* (*The Russian Banner*): "Why is our clergy silent? Why do they not make a pronouncement on the brutal ritual murder of Yushchinsky by the Jews?"* There were, of course, individual priests who sided publicly with the government.

In 1913 the Beiliss case occasioned more governmental action against newspapers than any other public issue. There were six arrests of editors, eight indictments, three cases of complete repression, thirty-six cases of confiscation of entire editions, and forty-three fines. As usual, censorship was erratic in the extreme. Some of the most violent attacks—Nabokov's, for instance—went off without an incident; but sometimes a mere hint of criticism was a signal for repression. At a banquet held in Moscow to celebrate the fiftieth anniversary of *Russkiye vedomosti* (*Russian News*), the brilliant organ of the Liberals, speeches were made attacking the government; nothing happened until a telegram was read declaring that "if there were more organs like *Russkiye vedomosti*, there could not have been a Beiliss trial." At that point the police officer charged with "maintaining order" broke up the banquet and dispersed the guests.

While the Beiliss trial was on, the general assembly of the St. Petersburg bar sent a telegram to the defense counsel in Kiev protesting against "the distortions of the foundations of justice evident in the staging of the trial; against the slander of the Jewish people . . . and against the charging of the court with the task of propagating racial and national animosity." Twenty-five members of the St. Petersburg bar, among them Alexander Kerensky, a member of the Duma and later Minister of Justice and Prime Minister, were tried for this action and sentenced to various terms of imprisonment.*

Shulgin, the "honorable anti-Semite," whose furious denunciation of the indictment was such a shock to the administration,

continued to plead for "a sane Russian anti-Semitism" while repeatedly calling the trial a gross, blind blunder. He declared that
if Beiliss were condemned, those who did not believe in his
guilt would turn from anti-Semitism in horror, a possibility that
filled him with profound dismay. He continued to look for an
effective method of getting rid of the Jews without passing laws
against them and without infringements of the law. He even
wanted, or seemed to want, existing disabilities revoked, stating
in one address to the Duma: "All Jewish restrictions and expulsions are evils that we can only tolerate with difficulty. In reality
they are offensive to us and we strongly desire to get rid of them.
They are full of nonsense and contradictions as well as the most
terrible matter, for, as you all know, the Police of the Pale [of
Jewish Settlement] live on Jewish bribery on account of Jewish
restrictions."* Yet Shulgin remained an anti-Semite even after
the Commission uncovered the mire in which the Beiliss case was
born. And during the Rightist pogroms that followed hard on the
Bolshevik revolution in 1918, he declared that it served the Jews
right—they were only expiating their sins.*

The extreme Rightists drove on relentlessly. That some of them
wanted to reach a critical point which would lead to the suppression of the Duma and the establishment of a dictatorship was
hinted by Purishkevich in the Duma and more than hinted by
Minister of the Interior Maklakov in a memorandum to Nicholas:

> The Duma is in fact entering upon a struggle against all au-
> thority and is paving the way to the attainment of the last freedom—
> the freedom of revolution. . . . If the tempest rises and a militant
> spirit spreads far and wide, the administration in the capital and
> in the provinces will be able to crush all the disturbances and to
> master the revolt by swift and decisive action. But two measures
> will be necessary for this achievement: the dissolution of the Duma
> and an immediate proclamation placing the capital in a state of
> Reinforced Protection.*

From his resort in the Crimea, Nicholas replied at once: "This
is exactly what I should have heard from my government long
ago."*

C H A P T E R   2 0

WHOSE VICTORY?

1

Let us return to the courtroom in Kiev, which the jury has just left to consider its verdict.

The defense and its partisans have been stunned by Judge Boldyrev's brazenly tendentious charge, and they wait in a mood of hope against hope as evening descends on the city and the electric lights shut out the gray October skies. From the outside reports filter in that traffic has been stopped in the vicinity of the court and the streets are patrolled by regular and mounted police. A requiem for the soul of Andryusha is to be held, after the announcement of the verdict, in St. Sophia Cathedral, round which in the late afternoon half-darkness a vast crowd, illumined here and there by torches, has assembled.

Anticipating the verdict is pure guesswork. Had the jury been empaneled at random, the outlook would be excellent; for though the Ukrainian peasant might be poorly educated, he has a merited reputation for shrewdness. He is, in the popular view, the Missourian of Russia; he has to be shown—and he especially resents being put upon. But this jury has not been empaneled at random, and what everyone is really waiting to find out is how well the packing has been done.

If the foreman of the jury, the government clerk Melnikov, is a clue to the answer, the worst can be expected. (Such at least was Korolenko's impression.) At the opening of every session, when the judges are seated and the audience is still standing, the jury is led in by Melnikov. Korolenko tells us:

> . . . a slightly built man wearing a black frock coat and a light vest. He walks fast, as if fearful that someone might get there before him and thus detract from his dignity. When he reaches the jury benches, he makes a half turn and stops, his elbow leaning on the table, his body inclined with a certain gracefulness, his legs slightly crossed. Somewhere there is a statue of a great man in the same pose. In his right hand he has a pencil which, in this setting, is reminiscent of the baton of a marshal or an admiral's telescope. . . .
>
> He remains motionless. If a sculptor or a photographer would like to immortalize him, he is ready for it. He maintains this majestic pose while the jurors file past him like soldiers.

The man is servile. "He does his best to display his attitude toward the case—a strained attentiveness to the prosecution, a haughty inattentiveness to the witnesses and the declarations of the defense."

The reporter of Shulgin's anti-Semitic *Kievlyanin* was equally distrustful. He found Melnikov lacking in the dignity appropriate to his function. Temporarily elevated to a position of world importance, he still made the impression of a small functionary trying to please the authorities, and "since the wish of the authorities, if not expressed aloud, is nevertheless clear, some in the courtroom look at him apprehensively, some hopefully—the latter especially when they see that he uses his pencil to record remarks made by the prosecution."

Beiliss is not in his usual place, guarded by soldiers with drawn swords, opposite the jury box. He is back in the cell that he has been occupying for the last thirty-three nights. He is thinking—so he frankly recorded—of himself and his family, of the alternatives now being weighed by the jurors, disaster or the beginning of a new life, the Siberian mines or freedom. He hears the church bells of Kiev calling to the evening Angelus and takes it for a bad omen. "They have never brought us good tidings."

At last, at long last, they come for him and lead him back to the courtroom. It seems to him that he has been waiting through ages, but it is only an hour and a half since the jury withdrew. He fixes his eyes on the door to the left of the crimson-covered judges' bench. About him is deathly silence; the air is heavy with anxiety.

At twenty minutes to six the foreman enters with unusual solemnity, holding in his hand the text of the two questions. When the jurors have taken their seats he reads out the first question. "Has it been proved that on March 12, 1911 . . . in one of the buildings of the Jewish surgical hospital . . . Andrei Yushchinsky was gagged, and wounds inflicted on him . . . and that when he had lost five glasses of blood [other] wounds were inflicted on him . . . and that these wounds, totalling forty-seven, caused Yushchinsky agonizing pain and led to almost total loss of blood and to his death?"

The verdict: "Yes, it has been proved."

Everything about Beiliss turns black, his heart hammers. "If they place the murder in the brickworks, how can they avoid naming me as one of the murderers?" He was the one who, according to little Lyudmilla, had grabbed Andryusha; she said she had seen it with her own eyes. And according to Cheberyak, her son Zhenya had seen it, too, and had told her so before he died. The lamplighter had reported hearing the same story from Zhenya; he had retracted later, but his was the statement that had led to Beiliss's arrest. He was done for.

As from a distance he hears the second question. "Is the accused . . . guilty of having entered into collusion with others who have not been discovered in the investigations, in a premeditated plan prompted by religious fanaticism, to murder the boy Andrei Yushchinsky, and did the accused, in order to carry out his intentions, seize Yushchinsky, who happened to be there, and drag him off to one of the buildings of the brickworks . . . ?"

The verdict: "No, not guilty."

There was a startled pause, and then an electric shock seemed to pass through the hall, followed by an immense agitation in which were mingled cheers, waving of handkerchiefs, and the sound of weeping. Beiliss himself breaks into a hysteria of tears. The officer of the guard brings him a glass of water. Zarudny runs forward, snatches the glass away from him, and proffers it to Beiliss. "Beiliss is not yours any more. He belongs to us."

When the hubbub has subsided, Boldyrev turns to Beiliss with the formula of acquittal. "You are free. You may take your place with the public."

A crowd has formed round the half-hysterical man. A Russian merchant, unable to get near him, shouts: "I left three factories in St. Petersburg to run on their own while I sat here for a month. I couldn't go home! I couldn't have slept! Now, God be thanked, I can go home, a happy man. I would be happy to shake your hand, but as you see, they won't let me." When Korolenko made his way into the street, he was mobbed by cheering students; he begged them to go home and provoke no disturbance. Within a few hours hundreds of telegrams poured in on Beiliss and the defense, and Beiliss himself, though a free man, had to be spirited back to his cell for fear of the demonstrations his public appearance might set off. He did not get home till late that night.

For the moment the disappointed minority seemed to be overwhelmed. The crowds about the St. Sophia Cathedral dispersed without any urging, the heart taken out of them. The prophecy that there would be a pogrom in Kiev even if Beiliss was acquitted was falsified; nor were attempts reported from any other part of the country.

Contemporaries of the trial living at the time in Russia and old enough to be caught up in the excitement have told how, on the evening of the verdict, telephone girls in Kiev, Moscow, and St. Petersburg spontaneously turned themselves into a news agency. They were so delighted by the verdict that before they asked for the number, they uttered the word: "Acquitted!" It must have happened in other cities, too. A wave of rejoicing passed over the country, as at the announcement of a great military victory. Strangers embraced on the streets with shining faces and streaming eyes; Jews and gentiles congratulated each other, proud of their country and its "simple citizens," gloating over the happy ending and the humiliation of the administration.

2

The festive mood did not last long. The morning after the verdict the *Novoye vremya* (*New Times*), semi-official Rightist and poisonously anti-Semitic, reported that on the question of Beiliss's guilt the jury had been evenly divided, six to six, an acquittal under Russian law. How did the *Novoye vremya* know? Jurors were forbidden by law to disclose the vote, and the *Novoye vremya* would, of course, reduce the moral value of the acquittal to its absolute minimum. But the report was widely repeated and has never been contradicted; it is still generally accepted.

Certainly the acquittal was an immense relief, but what was there to kiss about in the streets? One could, of course, taunt the administration that with all its exertions it had been unable to assemble in the mighty city of Kiev seven bad men and false who would countenance an open perversion of justice. On the other hand, it had fallen short by only one vote—surely not the resounding slap in the face it deserved. Six-to-six was a technical acquittal, a merciful provision for doubt, the equivalent of the noncommittal Scottish "Not proven," neither guilty nor innocent. People could believe what they liked.

On the issue of the Blood Accusation the situation was hopelessly complicated. However the vote had gone on question one, it could properly be asked whether there had been a vote on the issue of ritual murder as such; for question one, on which the jury had voted Yes (the division, if any, was never reported), said nothing direct about the murder being motivated by religious fanaticism. It merely asked whether the crime had been committed in one of the buildings of the Jewish surgical hospital in the Zaitsev grounds; it asked whether it was true that Yushchinsky had been murdered in such a way that he had lost five glasses of blood (an ingenious way of putting it, with its suggestion of drinking) and that he had died from loss of blood. Motive was not mentioned, though the (unproved) circumstances were rehearsed in such a way as to suggest a ritual murder.

It was only in the second question, which asked whether Beiliss was guilty, that the motive of religious fanaticism was mentioned. And on this question the answer was No; Beiliss was not guilty. What was one to make of the strange jumble?

In Manchester, the first elation dissipated, people pondered bleakly the comment of the home paper, *The Guardian*: "The humble jury had the courage at least to acquit the Jew whom so many powerful influences had conspired to destroy. Unfortunately their courage did not carry them further and they added to their verdict 'the murder was committed in the Zaitsev works.'" "Added to" should have read "left in," but the meaning was not affected.

Other important organs expressed themselves in the same or in a darker vein. The London *Times*: "It is to be regretted that the issue put to the jury admitted of a reply which seems to countenance the most shocking part of the Crown case, and which will most certainly be used by Russian reactionaries to perpetuate a horrible and mendacious legend." *The Westminster Gazette*, too, must have been read by Russian reactionaries with a sour kind of complacency: "While it is satisfactory that Beiliss should have been acquitted, the verdict as a whole is as unsatisfactory as it well could be. We cannot blame the jury. The questions which it was asked were framed in such a way as to make their reply a sanction that a ritual murder had been committed."

"The Londoner," writing in *The Daily News* of his city, mingled disapproval with ironic disenchantment: "The Kiev affair has destroyed my interest in the great cosmopolitan financial and political power of Judaism. What has this international force achieved? . . . A verdict which still maintains the wicked old Blood Accusation."

It is hardly necessary to mention that publications like *L'Action française*, *La Libre Parole*, and *La Croix* exulted in the verdict as a sweeping victory. Others with the same coloration were somewhat restrained, admitting that if there had not been victory on one point, it was by far the less important one. As the *Reichspost*, organ of Viennese clergy and the Christian Socialists put it, the verdict "proves nothing against the theory of ritual murder."

The Times, in a second editorial, found the verdict confusing, as did the *Berliner Tageblatt*; and well they might. This much at least, and it was not little, Boldyrev had managed to salvage from the affair, that great numbers of people in Russia and abroad were unable to make out what the verdict amounted to in respect to the Blood Accusation.

One could easily say that the opinion of such jurors on such a question amounted to nothing and influenced nobody. But this had been accepted as a test case, a sort of miniature plebiscite. How did the Russian masses feel about the Blood Accusation? Did they believe that at certain times and in certain places Jews assembled to practice on Christian children cannibalistic rites prescribed by the Jewish religion? They did, proclaimed one side loudly; and the other side could say that the verdict proved nothing except that a confusing questionnaire was presented to twelve confused and exhausted men, eliciting no clue to their real convictions, let alone the convictions of the millions they were supposed to represent.

One thing, however, was statistically clear: among the vast majority it was the consensus that the gamble of the administration had ended in a fiasco, in which lack of scruples had been canceled out by lack of competence. *The Daily News* of London wrote: "The acquittal of Beiliss was the most crushing blow to Russia since the Russo-Japanese War." Morally speaking this was certainly true for the Russian administration, but one asks whether it was not the fact of the trial rather than the acquittal of Beiliss that was the blow. This was the considered view of the Anglo-Jewish historian Lucien Wolf. "I am afraid," he wrote, "that we cannot congratulate ourselves very enthusiastically on the result of the Kiev trial. There can be little doubt that the verdict was engineered by the authorities with the idea of throwing dust in the eyes of foreigners while at the same time preserving the Blood Accusation and even giving it a measure of countenance. Personally I never expected much from the verdict. All that was necessary for us was to obtain the utmost publicity for the trial so as to enlighten public opinion outside Russia as to what is going on in that country."

3

The prosecution and the administration naturally proclaimed that they had scored a great triumph. The omission of the words "religious fanaticism" from the first question, argued Zamyslovsky, was "purely formal. We did not even ask to have those words included. The peculiarities of the act, given in detail, leave no doubt about the ritual character of the murder."* As to the acquittal of Beiliss: "Of course I am not satisfied with it." The Blood Accusation was the thing; the condemnation of Beiliss was expendable.

To signalize the triumph the supporters of the administration in St. Petersburg arranged a great "victory banquet" at which Minister of Justice Shcheglovitov and Prosecutor Vipper were the most distinguished guests. Congratulatory telegrams were sent to Chaplinsky, Shmakov, Zamyslovsky, Kosorotov, Sikorsky, and others (Pranaitis does not seem to have been on the list), hailing them as "the heroes of the Beiliss case" and "celebrating the noble courage and the high moral dignity of incorruptible and independent Russian men."*

Some of the congratulations were followed up by more substantial expressions of admiration and gratitude. Zamyslovsky was given 25,000 rubles to write a book on the Beiliss case; Boldyrev was promoted to the position of Chief Justice of the Kiev Appellate Court; he received in addition the special gift of a gold watch from the Czar and an illegal, clandestine increase of salary. The faithful and diligent Chaplinsky fared best of all: he was appointed to the Senate, Russia's supreme court.

The rewards to the initiators and supporters of the conspiracy were of course canceled by the revolution. What ultimately became of them and the men who fought them is told briefly in the incomplete list below.

Shcheglovitov, Beletsky, and N. A. Maklakov (Minister of the Interior and brother of the defender of Beiliss) were shot by the Bolsheviks in 1918. Shmakov died before the outbreak of the revolution, and Sikorsky in 1919. Vipper found employment with the Bolshevik administration in Kaluga, a provincial capital about 110 miles from Moscow. He was discovered there in 1919 and tried by the Revolutionary Tribunal. The state prosecutor asked for the death penalty, but in view of his usefulness to the Kaluga administration he was sentenced to a short term of imprisonment.* He died before its completion. Golubev was killed in action in World War I. Pranaitis died in St. Petersburg (already renamed Petrograd) in January 1917. Zamyslovsky, who just managed to get his book on the Beiliss case published on the eve of the revolution, escaped to Yugoslavia and was reported living there in 1933. Vera Cheberyak and her half-brother Singayevsky were shot by the Bolsheviks in 1918. The only account of Cheberyak's death that could be found is that by the journalist Chaim Shoshkess in the Yiddish daily *The Day-Morning-Journal*, December 1, 1963. Mr. Shoshkess relates that while a prisoner of the Bolsheviks in Kharkov in 1920, he heard the warden, Antezersky, boast to a group of prisoners that he himself had shot Cheberyak in the Cheka Prison in Kiev.

Little happiness awaited the victim and the defenders in the Beiliss case. Mendel Beiliss left Russia in 1914, finding life there impossible. He was helped by friends to settle in Palestine, but he did not prosper there. In 1922 he came to America, where he tried his hand first as printer, then as insurance salesman, with no success as either. In 1925 he published his "as told to" autobiography, which ran first in a Yiddish newspaper. Public interest in him had greatly declined by the time of his death in 1934. Gruzenberg, Karabchevsky, Margolin, and Nabokov went into exile with the establishment of the Bolshevik regime. V. Maklakov was ambassador to France when the Bolshevik revolution broke out; he never returned to Russia. Karabchevsky, Gruzenberg, and Maklakov died in France (in 1925, 1940, and 1959 respectively). Margolin died in America in 1957. Nabokov's death was a kind of footnote to his life. His son describes it thus: ". . . in 1922, at a public lecture in Berlin . . . my father shielded the lecturer (his old friend Miliukov) from the bullets of two Russian Fascists, and while vigorously knocking down one of the assassins, was fatally shot by the other." Zarudny, like Korolenko, elected to remain in Russia. Korolenko died in 1921; Zarudny was still living in 1933. Brazul-Brushkovsky was arrested during the purges of 1937 and was never heard from again. Of the students Karayev and Makhalin nothing further is known.

Perhaps the strangest story is that of V. V. Shulgin. He left Russia at the advent of the Bolshevik regime and was ultimately tempted back. He was last reported (1965) as taking part in a historical film in which he played himself. He was described as a loyal supporter of the Communist regime.

EPILOGUE

EPILOGUE

ECHOES AFTER
FIFTY YEARS

1

THE BLOOD ACCUSATION has been an insignificant factor in the anti-Semitism of the last half-century. It has cropped up here and there in "cockroach" publications but without setting off a major agitation. One might say that it was killed by the Beiliss case, were it not that the real killer—assuming that the death is real—was the spirit of the time. During the last fifty years the diabolism of the underprivileged has sought satisfaction not in pictures of tortured children and human vampires but in hair-raising stories of world conspiracies and universal ruin. The collapse of the Beiliss case was followed by the rise of *The Protocols of the Elders of Zion*, which did so much to soften up the world for the first phases of Hitlerian anti-Semitism, and the successful launching of *The Protocols* was the work of those Russian reactionaries who had made possible the Beiliss case.

They were undiscourageable and they were unteachable. One cannot simply say that their anti-Semitism was their undoing, for their fatal unadaptability had a far wider range; but their anti-Semitism was an organic part of it as symbol and substance. They continued to believe that they had lost out, had been defeated and undone only because by themselves they had been unable to stand up to world Jewry; and there was only one way to retrieve their fortunes: rouse the world against the Jewish menace.

When *The Protocols* first filtered through to the West, they awakened among the large majority of intelligent people the same incredulity and derision as the first reports of the Beiliss case. That this preposterous concoction that was being spread in 1918 by the White armies fighting the Bolsheviks in Russia's civil war would be taken seriously by a large number of people seemed wildly improbable; yet almost from the first day of its appearance the forgery made its influence felt, and the initial attempts to create a Jewish homeland in Palestine ran up against it.

Chaim Weizmann, later first President of the State of Israel, was in Palestine in the spring of 1918 as head of a Zionist commission sent out by the British government to plan the implementation of the Balfour Declaration in favor of the Jewish homeland. He records in his memoirs: "In an early conversation with General Wyndham Deedes . . . I learned of at least one source of our tribulations. Suddenly, and without introduction, he handed me a few sheets of typewritten script, and asked me to read them carefully. I read the first sheet and looked up in some perplexity, asking what could be the meaning of all this rubbish. Deedes replied quietly, and rather sternly: 'You had better read all of it with care; it is going to cause you a great deal of trouble in the future.' This was my first meeting with extracts from *The Protocols of the Elders of Zion*. I asked Deedes how the thing had reached him. He answered, slowly and sadly: 'You will find it in the haversacks of a great many British officers here—and they believe it! It was brought over by the British

Military Mission which has been serving in the Caucasus on the staff of the Grand Duke Nicholas.'"

2

The Protocols had their day. They were read by millions of people in every country. They died down,* but they left a large residue of hate, suspicion, and fear throughout the Western world, or, to change the figure, a susceptibility that the Nazis exploited with mortal success in Germany and not unsuccessfully in other countries. The surviving supporters of the Beiliss case and the promulgators of *The Protocols* had the satisfaction of seeing their crusade for the liberation of the world from Jewish bondage taken up by Hitler.

Russian anti-Semitism has had a checkered career since the revolution. In the Communist creed anti-Semitism is something like the sin against the Holy Ghost, and its espousal by the Nazis enhanced, if that were possible, its depravity and hatefulness. It seemed natural, then, that anti-Semitism should be denounced as a counterrevolutionary crime that would not be tolerated in a Communist society; and it cannot be denied that during the early years—Lenin's years—of the Communist regime anti-Semitism disappeared from view in Russia. But one must say "*seemed* natural" because, on the other hand, it cannot be denied even by Communists that under Stalin anti-Semitism returned in practice while it continued to be denounced in principle.

It was not, of course, the anti-Semitism of the Nazis nor, in a certain sense, that of the Czarist reactionaries. There was never a suggestion that Jews were an inferior species which had to be expelled, repressed, or exterminated for the good of the country. Nor did anyone dare to advocate the exclusion by law of Jews from any type of employment. But if Communist anti-Semitism is absolutely dissimilar from the Nazi variety while only relatively dissimilar from the Czarist variety, it is because of the return of a number of familiar features.

The over-all point of view of present day Russian Communist anti-Semitism may be summarized thus: there is nothing wrong with the individual Jew as such—he is as capable as anyone else of being made into a loyal citizen; but any hankering he may have for the perpetuation of the Jewish cultural tradition (hence of the group identity), whether embodied in religious or secular forms, in Hebrew (more particularly) or in Yiddish, must be studiously discouraged; by steady pressure, by the withholding of educational means, the Jewish cultural component in the all-Russian complex must be gradually eliminated.

The obvious result of such a policy will be the elimination of the Jew, for a Jew is a Jew by nurture; denied cultural nourishment Jewishness must rapidly starve to death and Jews disappear. In spiritual, though not in physical, terms it is the equivalent of the program set forth by the pre-revolutionary anti-Semitic press. "The Yids must be placed under such conditions that they will gradually die out. This is one of the tasks of the government and of the best men in the country." (But it should, in fairness, be noted that Communists never use the offensive word *Zhid* [Yid, Sheeny].)

Other ethnic groups in the U. S. S. R. are encouraged, by subsidies and by the provision of facilities—schools, theaters, printing privileges, supplies of newsprint, etc.—to develop their special cultural possessions. Some of these groups are considerably smaller in number than the Jews, none has a richer spiritual and cultural heritage. At this writing—1966—widespread protests have moved the Russian government to a grant of derisory token facilities for Jewish cultural self-expression; but given another two or three decades of such spiritual semistarvation, these beggarly concessions will have no meaning. There will be no one to take advantage of them.

We may, with perhaps unjustifiable generosity, pass over the more primitive phase of anti-Semitism that flared up under Stalin, calling it an aberration or idiosyncrasy: the "Doctor's Plot" and the liquidation of the greater part of Russia's Jewish-cultural intellectuals. We should certainly be going too far in extending this charitable interpretation to the post-Stalin practice of emphasizing heavily the Jewish names of those who have been shot for "economic crimes." Yet even this is not the most disheartening manifestation of present-day Russian anti-Semitism.

At irregular intervals* there appear in the Russian press or in special publications strange utterances on Jews and Judaism which one cannot by any stretch of the imagination fit in with the standard Communist attitude on religion as such. Nor can they be regarded as a logical extension of the Russian hostility to the idea of the State of Israel. What they are may be gathered from examination of one specimen, a book of 192 pages entitled *Judaism Without Embellishment* by Trophim Korneyevich Kichko.

It was published in the fall of 1963 and did not attract attention abroad until the spring of 1964, when vigorous protests began to be voiced, not the least among them being those of Communists outside of Russia. Contempt for religious doctrine on Marxist and "scientific" grounds is to be expected in a Communist statement on any religion, and Judaism must not ask for favored treatment; but here the accusations of obscurantism and anti-Communism degenerate into a general vilification of all Jews touched with Jewish loyalty. The almost exclusive preoccupation of this book is with what it considers the ethical indecency of Judaism as such, a religion which, it maintains, advocates theft, deception, and hatred of non-Jews. Thus:

The author claims to find in the Mishnah the following interpretation of the commandment "Thou shalt not steal": "You may not steal from or cause any other damage to your *khavers* [neighbors], i.e., Jews. As to how this applies to 'goys,' to those of different religions, the Jews are free to take from them because, as Judaism teaches, 'Jehovah delivered all of the wealth of the non-Jews to the use of the Jews.'" Or again: "The Talmud morally corrupts people, instilling in them the spirit of commerce and extortion. . . . The Talmud is saturated with contempt for work. . . ." "The Jews like to talk a great deal about the commandment that forbids them to bear false witness. However when the welfare of a Jew is in question, false witnessing and even false oaths are permissible. . . . While giving a false oath it is only necessary, the 'Holy Scripture' teaches, to negate the oath in the heart and soul." The charge of thievery as a religious principle is repeated with another attribution: "One of the commandments of Judaism is: 'Do not steal.' However as the *'Khoshen Mishpat'* interprets, it is only from *khavers* (i.e., from your Jewish neighbors) that you must not steal. But you can steal everything from others, because, as it is written in the 'Sacred Scriptures,' Jehovah handed over to the Hebrews all the wealth of non-Jews." To which is added an interesting variant on the theme of universal Jewish power: "If the Jews did not take everything into their own hands, it was because they did not want to lose the labor power of non-Jewish workers." (This view is of course attributed to religious Jews, who are shown as presumably believing that they could "take everything into their own hands" if they felt like it.)

More generally: "The ethics of Judaism do not condemn such disgraceful actions as hypocrisy and bribery. The well-known commentator on the Talmud, Rashi, teaches: 'Based on biblical teachings, the Jew at the very outset must work with bribery in order to tempt his enemy, and in other cases he must resort to a variety of artifices.'" And: "Speculation in *matzos*, pigs, thievery, deception, debauchery—these are the characteristics of many synagogue leaders." Then follows a curious passage which needs some disentangling: "Under modern conditions the Passover holiday harms us in a great number of ways, through engendering disrespect for work and fostering elements of nationalism among the Jewish workers. In celebrating the Passover the Jews do not go to work for several days, thus they hinder production plans and violate work discipline. The celebration of the Passover is especially harmful because the entire Passover legend, all the prayers, orient the believing Jews toward returning to Israel . . . where they—free workers of our country—will become cannon fodder for Ben-Gurion's clique and for his imperialistic masters."

One would think that if holidays engender disrespect for work, the Sunday, even if observed nonreligiously, is not less injurious to the state than the Passover. But the real intent of all the slander and vilification slips out; what the writer cannot tolerate is the thought of a Jewish nationalist identity, which may awaken in some Jews the longing to live in a land of their own. Were he to make a straightforward statement to this effect, it would be objectionable enough on various grounds; but he conceals this intolerance behind a larger viciousness—a reversion to genuine anti-Semitic strategy.

For what we have here, it will undoubtedly have been noted, is so close a revival of Hippolyte Lyutostansky and parts of Father Pranaitis (there is, however, no mention of ritual murder) that at least a familiarity with their work is suggested. There is the same display of recondite words like *Mishnah, Talmud, Rashi, Khoshen Mishpat, Khaver, Abot Rabbi Nathan*, etc., suggesting scholarly depth where to the moderately informed reader there is only the wearisome, familiar old parade of misquotations, quotations out of context, and pure fabrications drawn from the segregated literature of classic anti-Semitism. The scholarly qualifications of the author in the field of Jewish religion and history are not given. There are only commendations of his work. A brief, unsigned foreword states: "The author of the book reveals to the reader the actual essence of the Jewish religion (Judaism)—one of the ancient religions of the world, which has collected within itself and condensed everything that is most reactionary and antihumane in the writings of contemporaneous religions." A second and longer foreword, signed by "Doctor of Historical Sciences Professor A. Vvedensky" and "Writer Grigori Plotkin," assures us that this is "a profound and substantial work which contains a tremendous amount of factual material conscientiously and scientifically analyzed." We are not given, either, the qualifications in the Jewish field of Professor Vvedensky or Writer Plotkin, though it is evident that the second name is Jewish.

The last sentence of the first foreword reads: "This book is intended for a wide circle of readers," i.e., its purpose is not merely to open the eyes of Jews to the viciousness of their ancestral faith but also to inform others of it. The first printing was twelve thousand copies.

The numerous caricatures that accompany the text of this

"scientific" analysis of Judaism vie with the most offensive that ever appeared in Streicher's *Stürmer*: the same repulsive faces, with blubbery, sensual lips and predatory noses, the same obscene bodies and gestures, the same suggestion of cupidity and craftiness. It was the caricatures more than the text that moved Communist organs in England, France, America, Holland, and other countries to protest; for the text, like the disquisitions of Father Pranaitis, simply does not lend itself to intelligible discussion.

Some six months after publication the Russian Government began to show a little uneasiness. Tass (the Soviet news agency) and *Pravda*, one of the two leading Soviet dailies, expressed reservations about the accuracy of some of the statements in *Judaism Without Embellishment*. As Tass put it: "A number of mistaken propositions and illustrations could insult the feelings of believers and might be interpreted in the spirit of anti-Semitism."* Apparently the insulted feelings of unbelievers, strongly expressed among Communists and non-Communists (among the latter were some distinguished non-Jews), did not enter into the account.

Izvestia, the other leading Soviet daily, expressed astonishment at the furor created by the book. The book was well-meant. "The intention of the booklet [192 pages, M.S.], by itself, can evoke no doubts," although it had to be admitted that it "contains errors" and "many of the drawings . . . can only offend the sensibilities of the devout."* The Communist protests in the countries mentioned did not seem to concern *Izvestia*. It is "the bourgeois press" that "has become alarmed by a small book that has lately been issued by one of the Ukrainian publishing houses."

"One of the Ukrainian publishing houses"* is technically accurate but disingenuous. The institution referred to happens to be the Academy of Sciences of the Ukrainian Socialist Soviet Republic, situated in Kiev. A twinge of memory? Of the four scientists who lent themselves to the frame-up of Beiliss, three belonged to the University of Kiev. The coincidence is painful; more so is the fact that no one responsible for *Judaism Without Embellishment*, neither author nor artist nor sponsors, has been put on trial. The book was withdrawn from circulation—though we do not know how many copies had already been sold. Thus the matter stands as of now, spring 1966.

The Russian censorship today is far more repressive and, of course, more vigilant and more efficient than that of the czarist regime. That *Judaism Without Embellishment* should have been on sale for six months or so, that its withdrawal was ordered only under the pressure of Communist (and bourgeois) protest abroad leaves no doubt about the complacency of the government. But this is a naïve understatement of the reality. The wishes of the Russian government are well understood in Russia, better, again, than in czarist days. It would have been next to impossible for Golubev and Chaplinsky to launch the Beiliss conspiracy without the cooperation of Shcheglovitov; and it is quite impossible that a body like the Ukrainian Academy of Sciences should have ventured a publication of this kind without the sanction of Moscow. As it happened, the experiment failed. The better part of wisdom was then to hush it up.

Judaism Without Embellishment is only one of a number of anti-Semitic publications recurring irregularly in Russia, and these publications are themselves only part of the manifestation of a persistent strain of anti-Semitism in official Russian circles. Here the parallel with the evil old days thrusts itself most unpleasantly on the attention. There is no evidence that the Russian masses are disturbed by the Jewish hankering for cultural minority rights or by Jewish observance of the Passover. There is no evidence that equal treatment of the Jews in the granting of schools, the encouragement of Yiddish in literature and the arts would awaken popular resentment. As of old it is from above that the pressure and provocation (*Judaism Without Embellishment,* as addressed to non-Jews, cannot escape the accusation of provocation) are exerted. And that such should be the situation in Russia is peculiarly disturbing.

3

This study closes with some brief comments on part of the introduction to this book.

The relevance of the Beiliss case to our time springs only in part from its anti-Semitic substance. As an episode in the continuing struggle between progress and reaction it has other, more general bearings. It is, for instance, an early illustration of the modern governmental use of the big lie, which must be distinguished from the traditional modes of lying common to governments and individuals. The big lie does not simply misstate facts; rather it aims at the subversion of the intelligence. It does not ask how plausible the lie appears in the eyes of informed people; it makes its assertions with brazen disregard for what is known and seeks, by immense clamor, by vast rhythmic repetition, to make thinking impossible. Technically the Beiliss case was a primitive affair, predating as it did radio and television and the new psychology of mass communications. Moreover its central lie was ill-timed; for it is a mistake to think that any big lie can be successfully established at any time. The big lie too must count on a certain minimum of receptivity. That was why *The Protocols* did so much better than the Blood Accusation in the twentieth century.

The Beiliss case is also instructive as clarifying the design to subvert the moral sense in government, to establish the working rule that those in the service of the state must find their moral satisfaction exclusively in obedience to superiors who stand outside moral evaluation. But the Beiliss case must be studied in detail; one must become familiar with all its grotesqueries and villainies; one must sense the implicit disregard of all scruples and inhibitions. Only then does one perceive that it was a crude preview of the destructive possibilities of the twentieth century, a hint of the depths to which civilized man could sink.

But all of this is quite useless if we divide the world into areas which fall neatly into the categories of good and evil, or if we place ourselves outside the danger zone, or if we believe this or that noxious force to be worsted beyond the possibility of a resurgence in our midst. For this is where we came in fifty years ago.

NOTES

My principal primary sources are:

A. The stenographic report of the trial (STEN), which includes the indictment and a large number of pretrial depositions made by various witnesses.

The proceedings were taken down by relays of stenographers and reproduced verbatim, day by day, in the *Kievskaya mysl.* This was a considerable technical achievement for that time, the more so as the sessions, which ran for thirty-four days (September 25–October 28, 1913) without breaks for Sundays or holidays, began at ten or eleven in the morning and lasted, with intervals for meals and recesses, until eleven or twelve at night and sometimes later. It was also a notable public service, and the only one of its kind, though practically every newspaper in Russia and abroad printed excerpts, often long ones. Such was the interest in Russia that during the trial the circulation of the *Kievskaya mysl* rose from sixty thousand to two hundred thousand and spread to all parts of the empire. In accordance with Russian procedure, the court itself did not keep a verbatim record; only the most important documents and statements were reproduced in full. However, on request from one of the attorneys, a remark would be "entered in the record."

The entire report was later reprinted by the *Kievskaya mysl* from the original matrices and issued in three volumes containing over fourteen hundred large, double-column pages. Were it not for the survival of a few complete copies, one of which is in the Library of Congress, certain passages which I have quoted at some length would read like pure invention. But these passages were reproduced abroad, and, as noted in the narrative, no allegation of inaccurate reporting appeared anywhere in the defensive propaganda of Russian diplomats and consular agents.

B. The stenographic report of the Extraordinary Commission of the Provisional Government (COMMISSION; see p. 123 and Bibliography, *Padeniye Tsarskovo Rezhima*).

C. The *Krasny Arkhiv* (ARCHIVES), the ongoing collection of documents published periodically by the Russian government since 1918, of which Vols. 44, 46, 54, and 55 particularly are quoted here.

D. The confidential reports of the agents Dyachenko and Lyubimov (AGENT) to Shcheglovitov via Beletsky.

E. The autobiographies or memoirs of Mendel Beiliss, V. V. Shulgin, V. G. Korolenko, Oscar Gruzenberg, Ben-Zion Katz, Rabbi Mazeh; the diaries of Nicholas II and his correspondence with his wife, his mother, and Wilhelm II; official documents quoted by Lucien Wolf (see Bibliography).

Secondary Sources:

A. Alexander Tager's *The Decay of Czarism* (TAGER; see Bibliography). The English translation, slightly abridged from the Russian original, covers much material I have obtained from the primary sources. Wherever this coincidence occurs, Tager shows a trustworthiness that I believe justifies his frequent use as secondary source. I have relied on him for: quotations from the Russian press (excepting the *Novoye vremya* and *Rech*, of which the originals were consulted); quotations from publications and secret files of various ministries (listed in Tager); photostats of confidential official documents quoted here on pp. 81, 90–1), the Russian originals of which are reproduced in the English Tager.

B. KUCHEROV's account of the trial in *Courts, Lawyers and Trials under the Last Three Tsars*.

C. MARGOLIN's account in *The Jews of Eastern Europe*.

D. KENNAN's account in *The Outlook*, November 8, 1913.

E. POLANSKY (see Bibliography).

F. Newspapers and other periodicals identified in the narrative or in these notes.

I have had many conversations with contemporaries of the case and trial who were in Kiev or other parts of Russia at the time. Some of them were present at the trial for varying numbers of sessions.

Authors' names printed in small capitals are in the Bibliography. The number at the right of each note refers to the page of the text to which the note applies.

4 *four Popes:* Innocent IV (1247), Gregory X (1272), Martin V
(1422) and Paul III (1457). Cardinal Ganganelli, later Clement
XIV, issued a strong memorandum against the Blood Accusation
in 1758 (ROTH). See also Salo W. Baron, *A Social and Religious
History of the Jews.* 12 Vols. (New York, 1965), Vol. IX.

6 *Dreyfus case:* The best short account of the Dreyfus case is
in HALASZ; the most detailed is the collection of articles by CLEM-
ENCEAU in several volumes. There is a brilliant interpretative essay
in Barbara W. Tuchman, *The Proud Tower* (New York, 1966),
and a more extensive study in E. Nolte, *The Three Faces of
Fascism* (New York, 1966).

6 *hallucinatory anti-Semitism:* For further observations on anti-
Semitism see p. 272.

7 *anti-Dreyfusism:* For the link between anti-Dreyfusism and Pétainism, see Anthony Hartley, "The Extreme Right in French
Politics," *Encounter,* November 1964. Maurras was a Pétainist
and collaborationist. "On being sentenced to national degradation
and life imprisonment in January, 1945, his first reaction was to
recall the events of forty years back: *'C'est la revanche de
Dreyfus!'* "

7 *The Protocols:* For a full account of the evolution of the text of
The Protocols of the Elders of Zion see HERMAN BERNSTEIN.

8 *one full-length book:* TAGER's *The Decay of Czarism,* described
in the introduction to these notes.

10 *We did then; World's knives:* Both quotations are from Francis
Thompson's *An Anthem of Earth.*

11 *commanding a future:* Quoted from Maurice Samuel's *The Great
Hatred* (New York, 1940).

17 *It is time!:* KENNAN.

17 *A child might be missing:* These are actual instances as reported
over and over again in, e.g., *The Jewish Chronicle* of London.

18 *in the country:* TAGER

20 *gendarmery:* The *okhrana* was the forerunner of the Communist
cheka and its various reincarnations.

20 *bear this in mind:* TAGER

21 *Russkoye znamya:* TAGER

22 *to be noted later:* There was another exception, which did not
count at this stage. On March 8—two days before the raid—a
pawnbroker with whom Cheberyak had deposited some goods
later found to have been stolen, caught sight of her on the street
and had her arrested. She was haled into the precinct police
station, and it gives an idea of her self-possession and resourcefulness that after giving a false name and offering various explanations she managed to slip away in the middle of the
questioning. She was not reidentified until she was denounced
more than a year later by her lover, Miffle (STEN).

22 *innocent woman:* TAGER
23 *supporting my opinion:* STEN
26 *wholesome society:* TAGER. This editorial illustrates the change
that had been taking place in anti-Jewish ideology in the second
half of the nineteenth century: the shift from anti-Judaism to
anti-Semitism, from the religious and sociological to the racist
and "scientific." French and German writers led the way, the
latter, as might be expected, with a superior show of erudition.
Russia was following suit. The medieval world had apparently
been willing, even eager, to accept Jewish converts and admit
them to all the privileges accorded born Christians (we do not
know what the reaction would have been if the Jews had offered
to convert *en masse*). The modern world, less religious, more
competitive, was increasingly unreceptive, and conversions were
far more frequent than in the Middle Ages. According to Matthias
Mieses, *Der Ursprung des Judenhasses*, the Russian Synod reported that between 1835 and 1895 sixty thousand Jews converted to the Orthodox Church, in addition to the unrecorded
number who accepted other forms of Christianity. With all civic
disabilities automatically removed, baptized Jews had found every
field, including the academic and governmental, open to their
talents and had risen to positions of influence, so that Russian
anti-Semites were looking sometimes with uneasiness, sometimes
with rage on the law that still offered Jews an avenue of escape
into freedom and self-advancement. For the time being Russian
anti-Semitism was a mixture of the religious and the racist, with
the racist gaining ground. The racist view classified Jews as
unassimilable. In Germany, where Jews were also converting in
large numbers, the logical conclusion had already been drawn at
least as far back as 1901, when Eugen Dühring wrote, in the
fifth edition of his *Die Judenfrage*: "On the threshold of the new
century it is no longer relevant to speak of the usual half-methods
or merely palliative means to be used against the Hebrew evil
among the peoples. As far as I am concerned . . . the only adequate answer to the Jewish question lies in the wiping out of
the whole questionable species." With the proclamation of a
"Hebrew evil among the peoples" and therefore of the unaccepta-
bility of Jews anywhere, under any conditions, the ground was
being prepared for the worldwide application of the "final solution" by the Nazis. (Dühring laid unwarranted claim to the
distinction of having been the first to shift anti-Semitism from
the religious to the racist base. His anti-Semitism, like Drumont's
and like that of *The Protocols of Zion*, was completely hallucinatory, but its pathological aspect is ignored by Engels in his *Anti-
Dühring*, where it is given a banal and exclusively economic
interpretation.)
26 *this boy:* TAGER

28 *the Supreme Power:* TAGER and COMMISSION, both of which show that Nicholas received regular reports on the case from Shcheglovitov and others.

28 *nineteen-year-old Golubev:* COMMISSION.

30 *after Kushnir confessed:* that he confessed is attested by KENNAN and Nabokov.

34 *An agent of the national administration:* "Agent D"; see p. 173 and "primary sources," p. 270.

34 *criminal type:* LAZAR COHEN.

36 *Kiev pogrom of 1905:* The details of the Kiev pogrom of 1905 are contained in the report of Senator (i.e., member of Russia's Supreme Court) Turau as reproduced in FRUMKIN. The report of Senator Kusminsky (also FRUMKIN) on the Odessa pogrom relates that the local commander, arriving on the scene at the height of the turmoil, took off his hat to the plunderers and said: "I thank you, little brothers." To a Jew who was being beaten and turned to him for help he said: "I can do nothing. You wanted freedom—now you've got your Jew-swine freedom." Other pogroms as described by Russian officials are also listed in this essay.

37 *Andryusha was the illegitimate child:* The description of Andryusha Yushchinsky is drawn from STEN, which contains a vast amount of testimony on him. Much of it was that of children, and Andryusha had been dead for two and a half years, but some of it had been taken down in earlier, pretrial interrogations. At no time after his death would the children be inclined to speak badly of him, and this would also be true of nearly all the adults. Discounting this and discounting the testimony of those who had an interest in running him down, we get a wholly plausible picture of the boy. With some modification this is true for most members of his family. No one disputed the saintliness of his aunt, Nataliya.

38 *illustrious rabbinical family:* The fame of the Shneyerson family began with Shneor Zalman (1747–1812), the founder of the "Chabad" branch of Chassidism. The foremost living Chassidic rabbi is Menachem Mendel Schneurson, of Brooklyn (Herbert Weiner, in *Commentary*, March and April 1957).

46 *interested in the case:* HERMAN BERNSTEIN, in his account of the Beiliss case, *American Jewish Yearbook, 1914–15.*

48 *Krasovsky was an abler man:* The character and methods of Krasovsky are amply revealed in his copious testimony at the trial. His observations on the psychology of murderers are subtle and penetrating.

50 *the quarrel with Andryusha:* STEN; as told by Krasovsky.

53 *resisting the conspiracy:* MARGOLIN describes in detail the struggle between Fenenko and Chaplinsky. He speaks in the highest terms of Fenenko's character.

53 *might expose her:* TAGER; this attestation and the two that follow are not in the seven volumes of *Padeniye.* I assume that they are from the official documents listed by TAGER.

53 *no features of a ritual murder:* See above.

54 *ignored the material:* See above.

55 *Mendel Beiliss:* For my picture of Mendel Beiliss I have drawn on his "as told to" autobiography, of value chiefly where the personal touch is clearly recognizable, and on the recollections of people who knew him personally. There is naturally much biographical material in STEN. The newspaper reports on his bearing during the trial are uniformly laudatory.

60 *so many soldiers:* BONCH-BRUYEVICH.

62 *committee of notables:* A partial list of the Beiliss Defense Committee is given by J. M. Makhover, its last surviving member (October 1965), in his essay "Reminiscences personnelles," in *Du Pogrom de Kichinev à l'affaire Beilis* (Paris, 1963). It included, besides himself, the industrialist L. I. Brodsky, Rabbi S. Aronson, Arnold Margolin, Mark Zaitsev (son of Jonah Zaitsev), and Dr. G. B. Bykhovsky, chief physician at the Zaitsev hospital.

63 *before the investigating magistrate:* All depositions are from STEN.

65 *She belongs:* TAGER.

68 *plied him with vodka:* The references to drinking are very frequent throughout the case. Brazul-Brushkovsky (see p. 143) and Krasovsky were always urging drinks on Cheberyak and the Diakonova sisters (see p. 194 ff.); Makhalin and Karayev (see pp. 146 ff.) tried to get Singayevsky drunk to extract a confession from him; Kozachenko (see pp. 77 ff.) was, like the Shakhovskys, a habitual drunkard; and the Wolf-Woman is never represented as sober except, perhaps, in court, where, for that matter, several witnesses appeared "under the influence." But one gets the impression from the classic Russian novels that Russians used to order up champagne or vodka on the slightest provocation.

70 *The questioning was begun:* From Judge Boldyrev's question: "What do you know of this case" (p. 70) to Volkivna's statement "they told me to leave and I left" (p. 72), I am quoting from Rabbi Mazeh's descriptions of the trial in his memoirs. This is my only digression from the stenographic record, which at this point is obviously condensed. Rabbi Mazeh, graduate of a Russian law school, attended the trial as an expert on the Jewish religion (see p. 216).

73 *Father Sinkevich:* Father Sinkevich prepared for Cheberyak a petition to Czar Nicholas and presented it to him on his visit to Kiev in September of that year. In this petition Father Sinkevich emphasized Cheberyak's "irreproachable life of toil" and stated that for some unknown reason she was suspected of the murder of Yushchinsky (TAGER).

75 *kidnapping of Andryusha by Beiliss:* TAGER.
79 *revolt against them:* STEN.
81 *motive in the crime:* Photostat of original letter in TAGER.
81 *inflicted after death:* TAGER.
83 *4000 rubles:* See p. 172.
84 *leading medical experts:* From *Der Fall Justchinski* (see Bibliography). The point made unanimously by the Western scientists was that Obolonsky, Tufanov, Sikorsky, and Kosorotov drew conclusions that were in complete contradiction to the facts as set down in the Obolonsky-Tufanov report and in the earlier Karpinsky report. The countries represented in *Der Fall Justchinski* are: Germany (five opinions); Austria (two opinions, one of them with two signatories); France (one opinion with two signatories); England (one opinion with three signatories); Switzerland (one opinion). — Professor A. Halberda (Vienna): "It is not shown [by the description] that the inner organs were sufficiently bloodless to warrant the assumption of death from loss of blood. In the first autopsy [Coroner Karpinsky's] the muscles are described as red, the spleen as brown-red; the description of the inner organs as given by the second autopsy [Obolonsky-Tufanov] similarly does not lead to the conclusion of death by bleeding. . . . It is my opinion that the description supplied does not prove that the body was completely drained of its blood, though a considerable loss of blood occurred. . . . Whereas the wounds in the head were undoubtedly inflicted while the boy was alive, the wounds in the buttocks were inflicted when the boy was dying or after death had set in. We may definitely conclude, from the large number of wounds, that the victim was tortured. The state of agitation into which the killer was understandably thrown—the blood frenzy [*Blutrausch*]—explains the senseless character of the wounds. . . . If the killing was committed for the purpose of obtaining and collecting the blood of the boy, the infliction of such a large number of scattered, random, and relatively minor wounds was little to the purpose. . . ."—Professor Ernst Ziemke (Kiel): "Drs. Obolonsky and Tufanov give as the primary cause of death anemia [loss of blood] resulting from the wounds. But for this point of view the autopsies do not furnish the slightest proof [*nicht der geringste Beweis*]. None of the larger veins or arteries are shown to have been injured; from this and from the description of the inner organs it follows that a draining of the blood is out of the question [*kann . . . gar keine Rede sein*]. . . . Death from loss of blood is as good as excluded or at least as highly improbable [*so gut wie ausgeschlossen oder mindistens sehr unwahrscheinlich*]. . . . As to the question of the extent of the loss of blood, the answer of Professors Obolonsky and Tufanov is that the loss of blood may be assumed to have been two thirds

of the total quantity of blood in the body. For this statement there is not a shadow of proof [*nicht der Schatten eines Beweises*]; it is far more probable that what we have here is a purely arbitrary estimate [*eine ganz wilkürliche Schätzung*]. . . . For Professor Sikorsky's opinion [that this was a complicated crime, carefully thought out and executed, etc.] there is not the slightest support in the condition of the corpse. . . . When Professor Sikorsky maintains that the wounds were inflicted by a calm and sure hand . . . he very definitely oversteps the limits of an objective attestant [*Gutachter*] and permits himself to be carried by a tide of fantasy rather than by cool and scrupulous reasoning. . . ." — Professors A. Lacassagne (Lyons) and L. Thoinot (Paris): "The comparative bloodlessness of the corpse is far from sufficient for the pronouncement that death resulted from loss of blood. There are numerous arguments against this assumption; most of the wounds were inflicted when the boy was in his death throes or already dead; most of the wounds were superficial; from the description of the first autopsy [Coroner Karpinsky's] we do not find that the inner organs had the extreme bloodlessness which is associated with death from bleeding. . . . As to the crucial question [*question capitale*] whether this was an ordinary murder or a murder with a special motive . . . it would be an odd way [*façon singulière*] of procuring a sufficient quantity of blood from a human body by inflicting a series of wounds, most of them superficial, and not one of which, in any case, established a channel from a large organ [*vaisseau*] to the exterior. The absurdity of the method employed gives the irrefutable answer [*juge sans replique*] to the question before us. . . ." — Drs. Charles A. Pepper, A. Mercier, W. H. Wilcox, all of London University and holding important posts in private and governmental institutions: ". . . It appears to us quite impossible to suppose that the boy was killed for the purpose of collecting his blood. . . . We entirely and emphatically disagree with the conclusions Professor Sikorsky has arrived at. We hold the strongest opinion that there is nothing in the details of the murder to suggest in any way the race or nationality of the murderer and we are entirely and emphatically opposed to the opinion of Professor Sikorsky that the crime was in any way a ritual murder." — The rest of the attestations in *Der Fall Justchinski* are in a similar vein in regard to the *question capitale* of ritual murder. There are disagreements among the experts on other questions which have no bearing on the issue, such as: the order in which the wounds were inflicted, at what point the victim lost consciousness, whether a sexual motive could be established, whether more than one person was involved in the crime, etc. It need hardly be remarked that the above quotations are not intended to convince the reader that no ritual murder had taken place but to indicate the improbability that Obolonsky and Tufanov had made an honest mistake. Sikorsky's mental condition makes the question of honesty irrelevant.

85 *pseudo-scientific arguments:* TAGER.

85 *excite the Jewish masses:* TAGER.

85 *not discontinued:* TAGER.

86 *their early lives:* The "Cantonist" episode in Russian Jewish history has bitten deeply into the folklore. It was known as the *Boholoh* (Confusion, Terror), and the officers who carried out the seizures were called *die Chappers*—the Snatchers.

87 *attention of the Government:* TAGER.

88 *sound statesmanship:* TAGER.

90 *in the crime:* COMMISSION and TAGER.

90 *into his own hands:* Photostats of the letters quoted in this chapter (Col. Shredel, Governor Girs, Minister of the Interior Makarov, Chaplinsky) in TAGER.

98 *and grow turnips:* Quoted in Barbara Tuchman's *The Guns of August.* Unless otherwise noted, quotations in this chapter are from Nicholas's diary (with annotations in it by his wife) and from his correspondence with his wife, his mother, and Wilhelm II.

101 *assassinated him:* In October 1965 the last surviving assassin, Prince Yousoupov, reawakened interest in Rasputin by his suit against an American television company for invasion of his privacy in a telecast about Rasputin.

102 *a holy purpose:* MARIA RASPUTIN, who became a circus performer in France, thus defends her father: "A great and holy man, nothing like the voluptuary described by some. . . . Of course he did love wine and music, and I do not deny that he had mistresses. How could a man of such vigorous spirit, etc."

102 *on which he battened?:* SLIOSBERG, one of the foremost Russian Jews of the time, highly regarded among Russians, relates that Rasputin expressed himself strongly against the Beiliss trial. It obviously had no effect on Nicholas. However after the trial, when the Kiev reactionaries sought a permit to erect a chapel to the memory of Yushchinsky as a martyr, Rasputin, again according to Sliosberg, prevailed on Nicholas to refuse it. Sliosberg does not give sources.

102 *It was suggested:* To V. V. SHULGIN (see his *Dni*) among others.

104 *all a mistake?:* PARES.

105 *ten hysterics a day:* SHULGIN.

105 *merciless at times:* WALSH.

106 *a capital fellow:* WITTE.

106 *oppressed with grief:* WITTE.

107 *concern me:* WITTE.

108 *curiosities of history:* A. Pierre, the French translator of Nicholas's diaries, draws an interesting parallel between Nicholas, last of

the Romanovs, and Louis XVI, last of the Capets. Concerning the latter he quotes the French historian Aulard: "Limited intelligence, feeble will . . . without plan, without any design whatsoever. . . . If he had been a man of vice, he could have been dominated by a mistress. But he was chaste. . . . Huntsman and locksmith . . . religious sentiment." For Alexandra substitute Marie Antoinette.

111 *article in 1905:* Photostat of the confession in *Rech,* July 9, 1911.

112 *died in obscurity:* After the Beiliss trial Lyutostansky sued a number of newspaper publishers for defamatory remarks they had printed on his views and character, but he disappeared in the middle of the trial when the records of the Catholic Consistory were made available to the court (POLANSKY). See also BORISOV and *Evreiskaya Entsiklopediya* (St. Petersburg).

113 *unnatural behavior:* It is doubtful whether Nicholas ever saw the famous letter that Tolstoy addressed to him in 1900 when, at the age of seventy-two, he thought himself to be dying: "I do not wish to die without having told you what I think of your activities up to the present, what, in my view, they have been, how much good your rule might bring to yourself and millions of human beings, and how much evil they will bring if you continue in the direction in which you are going. One third of Russia is in a state of so-called 'Reinforced Protection,' that is to say, a state of complete anarchy. The army of police, secret and public, is steadily growing; the prisons, places of exile, and penitentiaries in Siberia are filled to overflowing, not only with hundreds of thousands of common criminals but also with political prisoners, with whom workers are now included. The censorship forbids everything with an arbitrariness greater than that which prevailed in the 'forties.' Religious persecutions have never been so frequent or so cruel as they are today, and this state of affairs is gradually growing worse. In the towns and great industrial centers troops are massed, who are called out against the people with loaded muskets. In many places there has already been fratricidal bloodshed, and further bloodshed is preparing and will inevitably occur. As a result of this inhuman administration the peasantry, those hundred millions on whom the power of Russia depends, becomes poorer every year, and famine is a regular and even normal phenomenon in our country." Tolstoy wrote as an extremist, with an otherworldly conception of society and human relations, but his indictment is substantially justified; and it must be remembered that this was some years before the revolution of 1905 and the brutalities which followed its suppression.

114 *natural habitat:* For a full account of the "Björkoe Treaty" and the proposed "Triple Alliance," see LUCIEN WOLF, *Notes on the Diplomatic History of the Jewish Question.*

119 *ex-Minister of Justice Shcheglovitov:* I have found no full-length life of Shcheglovitov. He receives some treatment in all the biographies and autobiographies of contemporary Russian politicians. See *Entsiklopedichesky Slovar* (Encyclopedic Dictionary), where he is treated respectfully in the prerevolutionary edition and with contumely in the postrevolutionary edition. Also *Bolshaya Sovietskaya Entsiklopediya.* Other sources mentioned in the text.

120 *this execution:* TAGER.

121 *for these acts:* WITTE.

121 *reforms . . . Alexander II:* The scope of the judicial reforms brought in by Alexander II is succinctly but well described in WALLACE's *Russia,* the standard prerevolutionary work on that country. From "a depth of insufficiency and corruption difficult to describe" the judiciary system rose to a level that could bear comparison with the best to be found in the enlightened West. One of the features of the reform was the introduction of the jury system.

123 *the Extraordinary Commission:* Where not otherwise indicated, the source for this chapter is COMMISSION.

124 *long before us:* Nabokov.

127 *a certain Malinovsky:* FISCHER; SUKHANOV.

129 *Dmitri Bogrov:* The v. BOGROV of the Bibliography was the assassin's brother.

130 *been a pogrom:* BOGROV.

131 *have been told:* By Alexis Goldenweiser.

131 *everything to God:* TAGER.

132 *their blood brothers:* See Leskov, Nikolai, *Evreii v Rossiye.*

133 *Rightists to the Duma:* WALSH.

141 *Head of Rural Police:* STEN.

141 *outstanding pupil:* In the text I have dwelt perhaps *ad nauseam* on the Mad-Hatter or Gilbert-and-Sullivan atmosphere of the case. I have relegated to these notes the bewildering question why the administration, having burned its fingers with Krasovsky, should have confided the job to his outstanding pupil—and his admirer—Kirichenko.

142 *Rozmitalsky:* Described at the trial as unemployed and an undischarged bankrupt. He was an important figure in the local Black Hundred.

142 *motives of revenge:* STEN.

143 *Brazul-Brushkovsky:* The material on BRAZUL-BRUSHKOVSKY is from STEN and from his book (see Bibliography), which must be treated with caution.

145 *junket we do not know:* She had pretended, said Brazul, that she wanted to get in touch with one of the gangsters, Lisunov; but it turned out that Lisunov was not in Kharkov. In any case, no one thought him to be connected with the murder. Much time

was spent on Lisunov at the trial, but he was not cited as a witness and all the talk about him proved to be irrelevant.

152 *only to confess:* See p. 198 ff.

158 *judicial procedures:* The trial of Katya in Tolstoy's *Resurrection* and the investigation and trial of Dmitri Karamazov in Dostoevsky's *The Brothers Karamazov* provide good pictures of judicial procedure in Russia after the law reforms and before the revolution.

160 *presented to a court:* The *Jewish Chronicle* of London credits Assistant State Prosecutor Pashchenko-Razvodovsky with the authorship of the indictment and states that he was rewarded for it by promotion to the post of State Prosecutor of Uman, Boldyrev's former district. — The indictment makes a point of the circumstance that when Andryusha's parents went to the offices of the *Kievskaya mysl* to insert an announcement in the Missing Persons column, the man who took the announcement was a Jew, Barshevsky, who almost immediately reported to the investigating magistrate that the parents had not seemed distressed but were in fact smiling (which they may have been, with embarrassment). *La Libre Parole* of Paris, following several Russian newspapers, hinted darkly that Barshevsky already knew what had happened to Andryusha. The arrest of Andryusha's relatives by Mishchuk was, according to the indictment, the direct result of Barshevsky's deposition, and State Prosecutor Vipper saw in this deposition the beginning of the conspiracy to set the investigations on a false trial. The indictment also devotes much space to another Jewish journalist on the *Kievskaya mysl*, Ordinsky, who, like Barshevsky, came of his own free will to the investigating magistrate regarding the missing boy. He reported the following: at the house of a friend of his he heard the laundry woman say that her sister met Andryusha's maternal uncle on the street soon after the boy's disappearance, and the uncle said, smiling: "Well, we can't find the boy, he's really disappeared." The laundress went on to say, according to Ordinsky, that a day or two after Andryusha's disappearance "a man and and woman were seen in Kiev, on the Dnieper quay, carrying a heavy sack," and it was the opinion of the laundress that the sack contained the body of Andryusha, who had been murdered by his mother. In this, too, the prosecution saw the beginnings of the Jewish conspiracy to throw the investigation off the scent.

167 *flee the country:* Shulgin was later indicted on a charge of slandering officials. At his trial Zamyslovsky was the principal witness for the prosecution, and Shulgin was sentenced to three months of detention, a milder form of imprisonment. He did not serve his sentence, for, what with appeals and other delays, his case ran into the World War and he was amnestied (POLANSKY).

168 *character of the jury:* TAGER.
172 *Union of the Russian People:* KOROLENKO.
173 *double-think:* TAGER makes surprisingly little use of the Dya-
      chenko-Lyubimov dossier, perhaps the most valuable source of
      information on the behind-the-scenes manipulations.
178 *A. S. Zarudny:* Zarudny's father, like Nabokov's, had been,
      though in a more modest capacity, one of the modernizers of the
      law under Alexander II. One would like to think that in both
      instances a touch of filial piety put an extra dash into their
      detestation of Shcheglovitov, the perverter of the law.
185 *Highlights of the Trial:* The transcript of the trial contains ap-
      proximately one and a quarter million words. I have chosen for
      reproduction the scenes that seem to me the most characteristic.
      Even a much more extensive summary would have to omit long
      passages of great interest. Krasovsky, Kirichenko, Brazul-Brush-
      kovsky, and others were on the stand for many hours, but the
      substance of their roles has been incorporated in the narrative.
191 *the whole affair:* TAGER
192 *It's not Berel:* Given to me orally, source not located.
196 *Adele Ravich:* After the trial Krasovsky, accompanied by Pinchas
      Dashevsky (whom Gruzenberg had defended in the shooting of
      the anti-Semitic agitator Krushevan; see p. 176), went to the
      United States in search of the Raviches and found them in a
      small village. "They gave some highly interesting testimony,
      tending to confirm the fact that Vera Cheberyak had taken part
      in the murder, but there was not in this testimony any *new*
      circumstance, which is required by law before an appeal for the
      reopening of a case may be made. . . . I held a special conference
      with Fenenko about these documents. Alas! We had to admit
      that in these affidavits were given only *new proofs* but no *new
      circumstances*" (MARGOLIN). Margolin was extremely active in
      an effort to get Vera Cheberyak indicted. He complains that he
      got little support in this enterprise from the leaders of the Kiev
      Jewish community, whom he accuses, by implication, of timidity.
210 *An observer:* MAZEH.
228 *Tevyev:* The patronymic form of "Tevyeh."
234 *incomplete or colored:* Oddly enough, it was the French anti-
      Beiliss press that challenged the reliability of the reports, pointing
      to what it called Jewish control of the international news agencies.
      But since it accepted a priori the reality of the Blood Accusation
      and Beiliss's guilt, it can only have meant that the reports were
      colored in such a way as to ridicule the reality.
236 *Charles Maurras:* See "anti-Dreyfusism," p. 271.
236 *nodding of the head:* In *The Brothers Karamazov* Dostoevsky,
      both master and master example of the pathological, gives us in
      the conversation between Lise and Alyosha a classic description
      of the type of addict here referred to. "There's a book," tells

Lise, "in which I read about the trial of a Jew, who took a child of four years old and cut off the fingers from both hands, and then crucified him on the wall, and hammered nails into him, and afterwards, when he was tried, he said the child died soon, within four hours. That was 'soon'! He said the child moaned, kept on moaning, and he stood admiring it. That's nice! . . . I sometimes imagine that it was I who crucified him. He would hang there moaning and I would sit opposite him eating pineapple compote. I'm awfully fond of pineapple compote. Do you like it?" The most interesting part of the entire passage, however, has more to do with Dostoevsky than with his characters. For when Lise asks Alyosha: "Is it true that at Easter the Jews steal a child and kill it?" Alyosha answers: "I don't know." Alyosha is beyond a doubt Dostoevsky's most beloved character, his idealization of what he himself would have liked to be; and it is through Alyosha that he expresses his highest moral and intellectual aspirations.

237 *guard against it:* Maurras here calls to mind the lady who was determined to stay on the narrow path between partiality on the one hand and impartiality on the other.

238 *for a century:* WITTE.

244 *by the Jews:* TAGER.

244 *of imprisonment:* KUCHEROV.

245 *Jewish restrictions:* SHULGIN.

245 *expiating their sins:* GOLDENWEISER.

245 *Reinforced Protection:* TAGER.

245 *government long ago:* TAGER.

253 *character of the murder:* Interview with Zamyslovsky in *Novoye vremya.*

253 *independent Russian men:* TAGER.

254 *imprisonment:* KRYLENKO.

261 *they died down:* Not completely. In 1964 a new Spanish translation appeared in Madrid and a Portuguese translation in Brazil.

263 *at irregular intervals:* The material is collected in *Jews in Eastern Europe: A Periodical Survey of Events in the Soviet Bloc,* issued in London.

266 *spirit of anti-Semitism: Jews in Eastern Europe.*

266 *sensibilities of the devout: Jews in Eastern Europe.*

266 *Ukrainian publishing houses: Jews in Eastern Europe.*

BIBLIOGRAPHY

Allen, W. E. D.: *The Ukraine*. Cambridge, 1940.
American Jewish Yearbook, 1914–15. Philadelphia: Jewish Publication Society of America; 1915.
Baring, Maurice: *The Mainsprings of Russia*. London, 1914.
Beiliss, Mendel: *Die Geshichte fun Meine Leiden*. New York, 1925.
Beletsky, S. P.: *Rasputin*. Moscow, 1923.
Beloff, Max: *Lucien Wolf and the Anglo-Russian Entente, 1907–14*. London, 1951.
Bernstein, Herman: *The Truth about the Protocols of Zion*. New York, 1935.
Bing, E. J. *See* Nicholas II.
Bischoff, Erich: *Das Blut im Jüdischem Schrifttum und Brauch*. Leipzig, 1929.
Bogrov, V.: *Dmitri Bogrov i Ubiystvo Stolypina*. Berlin, 1931.
Bonch-Bruyevich, V. D.: *Znamenie Vremini*. St. Petersburg, 1914.
Borisov Fil.: *Ippolit Lyutostansky*. Kiev, 1912.
Brant, Evgeny: *Ritualnoye Ubiystvo u Evreyev*. Belgrade, 1926–9.
Brazul-Brushkovsky, S. I.: *Pravda ob Ubiystve . . . Delo Beilisa*. St. Petersburg, 1913.
Carmichael, Joel. *See* Sukhanov.
Charques, Richard: *The Twilight of Imperial Russia*. Fairlawn, N.J., 1959.

Clemenceau, Georges. Of several volumes of articles on the Dreyfus case the following were available: *L'Iniquité*, 1899; *Contre la Justice*, 1900; *Les Juges*, 1901; *Injustice militaire*, 1902.

Cohen, Lazar: *Die Helden fun Beyliss Protzess*. Lodz, 1913.

Delo Beilisa (stenographic report), 3 vols. Kiev, 1913.

Dillon, Emile J.: *The Eclipse of Russia*. New York, 1918.

Dühring, Eugen: *Die Judenfrage*, 5th ed. Berlin, 1901.

Drumont, Edouard: *La France juive*, 2 vols. Paris, 1885.

Fall Justchinski, Der, Offizielle Dokumente und Private Gutachten, ed. P. N. [Paul Nathan]. Berlin, 1913.

Fischer, Louis: *The Life of Lenin*. New York, 1964.

Fritsch, Theodor: *Beilis-prozess in Kiev*. Leipzig, 1914.

Frumkin, J. G.: article in *Russian Jewry 1860–1917*. New York, 1966.

Fülöp-Miller, René: *Rasputin, The Holy Devil*. New York, 1926.

Gilliard, Pierre: *Treize Années à la Cour de Russie*. Paris, 1922.

Goldenweiser, Alexis: *Legal Status of Jews in Russia*, in *Russian Jewry 1860–1917*. New York, 1966.

Gruzenberg, Oscar O.: *Vchera, Vospominania*. Paris, 1938.

Halasz, Nicholas: *Captain Dreyfus*. New York, 1955.

Katz, Ben-Zion: *Memoirs* (Hebrew). Tel Aviv, 1963.

Kennan, George: *Siberia and the Exile System*, 2 vols. New York, 1891.

———: "The 'Ritual Murder' Case in Kiev," *The Outlook* (November 8, 1913).

Kichko, Trophim Korneyevich: *Yudaism bez Prikras* (Ukrainian). Kiev, 1963.

Kokovtsev, V. N.: *Out of My Past*. London, 1935.

Korolenko, V. G.: *Collected Works*, Vols. X, XI. Moscow, 1955.

Krasny Arkhiv [*Red Archives*], Vols. 44, 46, 54, 55. Moscow, 1951.

Krylenko, N. V.: *Sudebnye Rechi* (containing summation of case against Vipper). Moscow, 1964.

Kucherov, Samuel: *Courts, Lawyers and Trials under the Last Three Czars*. New York, 1953.

Kummer, Rudolf: *Rasputin, ein Werkzeug der Juden*. Nürnberg, 1939.

Lazarevsky, Vladimir: *Archives secrètes de l'Empereur Nicholas II*. Paris, 1928.

Lockhart, Robert H. B.: *British Agent*. New York, 1932.

Loge, Christian (pseud.): *Gibt es Jüdische Ritualmorde?* Leipzig, 1934.

Lyutostansky, J. J.: *Die Juden in Russland*, trans. Julius Baron Rosenberg. Berlin, 1934. [Originally published in Russian. 2nd ed., 1880.]

Margolin, Arnold D.: *The Jews of Eastern Europe*. New York, 1926.

Marsden, Viktor: *see* Protocols.

Mieses, Matthias: *Der Ursprung des Judenhasses*. Berlin-Vienna, 1923.

Monniot, Albert: *Le Crime rituel chez les Juifs*. Paris, 1914.

Nabokov, Vladimir: *Speak, Memory.* New York, 1951.

"Neophyte," unidentifiable, presumed to be author of book (not found) used by Pranaitis.

Nicholas II: *Journal intime [Diaries]*, trans. A. Pierre. Paris, 1925.

———: *The Letters of the Czar to the Czaritsa*, ed. C. E. Vulliamy. New York, 1929.

———: *The Secret Letters of the Last Czar: Being the Confidential Correspondence between Nicholas II and His Mother, Dowager-Empress Maria Feodorovna*, ed. Edward J. Bing. New York, 1938.

———: *The Willy-Nicky Correspondence*, ed. Herman Bernstein. New York, 1918.

Padeniye Tsarskovo Rezhima (stenographic record of the Extraordinary Commission appointed by the Provisional Government), 7 vols. Leningrad, 1924–6.

Pares, Sir Bernard: *The Fall of the Russian Monarchy, a Study of the Evidence.* London, 1939.

Polansky, N.: *"Otgoloski Dela Beilisa,"* in *Novoye Russkoye Slovo* (New York, August–September 1963).

Protocols of the Elders of Zion, trans. and ed. Viktor Marsden. London, 1925.

Pranaitis,[1] I. B.: *The Christians in the Jewish Talmud, or, the Secrets of the Teachings of the Rabbis about the Christians: the Talmud Unmasked*, trans. and ed. "Colonel S. E. Sanctuary." New York, 1939. [Originally published in Russian. Moscow, 1892.]

Rasputin, Maria: *Le Roman de ma Vie.* Paris, 1930.

Rodzianko, M. V.: *The Reign of Rasputin: An Empire's Collapse*, introd. Sir Bernard Pares. London, 1927.

Rosenberg, Alfred: *Unmoral im Talmud.* Bayreuth, 1935. *See also* Lyutostansky.

Roth, Cecil, ed.: *The Ritual Murder Libel and the Jew.* London, 1935.

"Sanctuary, E. N.:" *see* Pranaitis.

Schramm, Helmut: *Der Jüdische Ritualmord* (contains a Nazi account of the Beiliss trial). Berlin, 1943.

Seton-Watson, Hugh: *The Decline of Imperial Russia*, 6th printing. New York, 1961.

Shulz, Otto, F. H.: *Kaiser und Jude: das Ende der Romanovs und der Ausbruch der Bolshevismus.* Leipzig, 1936.

Shulgin, V. V.: *Dni.* Belgrade, 1925.

Szajkowski, Zosa: *The Impact of the Beiliss Case on Central and Western Europe.* American Academy for Jewish Research, vol. XXXI, 1963.

Sliosberg, G. B.: *Dela Minuvshikh Dnei*, 3 vols. Paris, 1933–4.

Steinthal, Walther: *Dreyfus.* London, 1930.

[1] Author's name as it appears in this publication. Pranaitis's actual given name was Justin. Russian original not found.

Sukhanov, N. N.: *The Russian Revolution, 1917, An Eye-Witness Account*, trans. and ed. Joel Carmichael, 2 vols., abridged. New York, 1962.

Tager, Alexander B.: *The Decay of Czarism: the Beiliss Trial* (trans. from the Russian). Philadelphia, 1935.

Vacandard, l'Abbé Elphège: *La Question du Meurtre rituel chez les Juifs*. Paris, 1912.

Vyrubova, Anna: *Journal secret*. Paris, 1928. *Memoiries* (sic) *of the Russian Court*. London, 1923.

Wilhelm II: *The Kaiser's Letters to the Czar*, ed. I. Don Levine. London, 1920.

Wallace, Sir Donald Mackenzie: *Russia*. London and New York, 1912.

Walsh, Warren B., comp. and ed.: *Readings in Russian History*, 3 vols. Syracuse, 1963.

Witte, Sergei: *The Memoirs of Count Witte*. New York, 1921.

Wolf, Lucien: *Notes on the Diplomatic History of the Jewish Question*. London, 1919.

————: *The Jewish Bogey*. London, 1920.

————: *The Myth of the Jewish Menace in World Affairs*. New York, 1921.

————, ed.: *Darkest Russia, A Weekly Record of the Struggle for Freedom*. London, 1912–14.

————, ed.: *The Legal Sufferings of the Jews in Russia*, with Appendix of Laws. London, 1912.

Zenkovsky, A. V.: *Pravda o Stolypinye*. New York, 1965.

INDEX

A NOTE ABOUT THE AUTHOR

MAURICE SAMUEL was born in Rumania in 1895 and was educated in England. He came to the United States in 1914 and served from 1917 to 1919 in the American army in France. After the war he acted as interpreter at the Peace Conference and with the Reparations Commissions in Berlin and Vienna. He returned to America in 1921, and since then he has traveled extensively in this country and abroad, partly as lecturer and partly to acquire information. Mr. Samuel's present residence is in New York.

His major interest for nearly fifty years has been the position of the Jewish people in the Western world; of his twenty books fifteen are concerned with the exposition of Jewish values or examinations of the relations between the Jewish and Christian worlds. He has occupied himself particularly with the problem of anti-Semitism as a feature of Christian civilization and with its effects on Christendom and Jewry. Mr. Samuel has devoted more than three years to researching the source material of the Beiliss case, the subject of *Blood Accusation*.

A NOTE ON THE TYPE

The text of this book is set in Caledonia, a Linotype face designed by W. A. Dwiggins, the man responsible for so much that is good in contemporary book design and typography. Caledonia belongs to the family of printing types called "modern face" by printers—a term used to mark the change in style of type-letters that occurred about 1800. Caledonia borders on the general design of Scotch Modern but is more freely drawn than that letter.

Composed, printed, and bound by

The Haddon Craftsmen, Scranton, Pennsylvania

Typography and binding design by

JAIME DAVIDOVICH